SLOWSPOKE

Praise for *Slowspoke*

"This is just the kind of epic we need right now—humble, sweet, and very deep indeed. As good a travel story—within and without —as you'll read anytime soon!"

—Bill McKibben, author of
New York Times bestseller *Eaarth*

"Sumptuous language and a disarming gentleness propel this profoundly simple, funny, and sincere memoir. Growing up as the child of idealistic homesteaders in Kentucky imbued Schimmoeller with a deep appreciation for nature and off-the-grid living, while leaving him feeling disconnected from the modern world. After graduating from college and finishing an unsatisfying internship at *The Nation*, Schimmoeller embarked on a solo journey across America on a unicycle. The author's story of finding a way to live in the world on his own terms is told simultaneously with that of his attempts to save old-growth forest adjacent to his homestead in Kentucky. 'It doesn't make a difference one way or the other if I take a break,' he tells a stranger who questions the intensely slow pace of his mode of transport—an explanation that speaks to the author's quest to find respite in a troubled world."

—*Publishers Weekly*, starred review

"The book will remind readers of other homesteading narratives, such as Barbara Kingsolver's *Animal, Vegetable, Miracle*. In some ways, it also transcends personal history, like a modern-day *Pilgrim's Progress*: one man, alone on a road, seeking redemption and ultimately finding it. Not just for unicyclists, Schimmoeller's memoir is beautifully written and often funny—a real find."

—*Kirkus Reviews*

"Mark Schimmoeller's *Slowspoke* captures the multifaceted culture and spirit of America in the early twenty-first century the way *Zen and the Art of Motorcycle Maintenance* revealed us to ourselves forty years ago. Schimmoeller has a gentle, honest, insightful voice, a Thoreauvian vision, and a gift for bringing to life the dozens of individualists he meets along his way, both on and off the grid. *Slowspoke* offers us a unique and hopeful look at who we really are and who we still have the potential to become. This is an important book: moving, deeply personal, and all kinds of fun to read."

—Howard Frank Mosher, author
of *The Great Northern Express*

"In the quest for growth, we have come to undermine the very meaning of life. Someone needs to point a new way. People like Mark Schimmoeller do that for us. *Slowspoke: A Unicyclist's Guide to America* is as wise as it is entertaining."

—Colin Beavan, author of *No Impact Man*

"This is a beautiful book, lushly written and elegantly rendered. In these pages, lines, and gorgeous human moments, we are transported to what the future must include."

—Nikky Finney, author of 2011 National
Book Award winner *Head Off & Split*

SLOWSPOKE

A Unicyclist's Guide to America

Mark Schimmoeller

Foreword by Janisse Ray

Chelsea Green Publishing
White River Junction, Vermont

Editor: Alice Peck
Project Manager: Bill Bokermann
Designer: Duane Stapp

Originally published in 2013
by Synandra Press.

Printed in the United States of America.

First Chelsea Green printing July, 2014.

10 9 8 7 6 5 4 3 2 1   14 15 16 17 18

Chelsea Green Publishing is committed to preserving ancient forests and natural resources. We elected to print this title on 30-percent postconsumer recycled paper, processed chlorine-free. As a result, for this printing, we have saved:

15 Trees (40' tall and 6-8" diameter)
7 Million BTUs of Total Energy
1,238 Pounds of Greenhouse Gases
6,711 Gallons of Wastewater
449 Pounds of Solid Waste

Chelsea Green Publishing made this paper choice because we and our printer, Thomson-Shore, Inc., are members of the Green Press Initiative, a nonprofit program dedicated to supporting authors, publishers, and suppliers in their efforts to reduce their use of fiber obtained from endangered forests. For more information, visit: www.greenpressinitiative.org.

Environmental impact estimates were made using the Environmental Defense Paper Calculator. For more information visit: www.papercalculator.org.

Some names and identifying details have been changed to protect the privacy of individuals.

Our Commitment to Green Publishing
Chelsea Green sees publishing as a tool for cultural change and ecological stewardship. We strive to align our book manufacturing practices with our editorial mission and to reduce the impact of our business enterprise in the environment. We print our books and catalogs on chlorine-free recycled paper, using vegetable-based inks whenever possible. This book may cost slightly more because it was printed on paper that contains recycled fiber, and we hope you'll agree that it's worth it. Chelsea Green is a member of the Green Press Initiative (www.greenpressinitiative.org), a nonprofit coalition of publishers, manufacturers, and authors working to protect the world's endangered forests and conserve natural resources. *Slowspoke* was printed on FSC®-certified paper supplied by Thomson-Shore that contains at least 30% postconsumer recycled fiber.

ISBN: 978-1-60358-590-3

The Library of Congress has catalogued this title under LCC: 2014022397. Complete Library of Congress Cataloging-in-Publication Data available on request.

Chelsea Green Publishing
85 North Main Street, Suite 120
White River Junction, VT 05001
(802) 295-6300
www.chelseagreen.com

FSC
www.fsc.org
MIX
Paper from
responsible sources
FSC® C013483

RAINFOREST ALLIANCE CERTIFIED

For Jennifer

And if we do act, in however small a way, we don't have to wait for some grand utopian future. The future is an infinite succession of presents, and to live now as we think human beings should live, in defiance of all that is bad around us, is itself a marvelous victory.

—HOWARD ZINN, The Optimism of Uncertainty

Foreword

BEFORE I STOPPED FLYING I was once on an airplane landing in Salt Lake City a few minutes behind schedule. My seatmate, wearing a snazzy skirt and black heels, had been immersed in her briefcase of papers for the entire flight and was already standing as we taxied to the terminal.

"We're only five minutes late," I murmured to her by way of comfort.

"You don't understand," she said. "In my life, five minutes is everything." She turned her face away, withdrawing into a daybook with very little room for white space, for rest, for home. In that moment I saw another look cross the woman's face, something close to disdain, which could only be translated to mean that since five minutes were more dear to her than to me, she herself was more valuable.

I've thought about that brief encounter a lot and remembered it again reading Mark Schimmoeller's stunning book. On one hand, *Slowspoke* is a travelogue of a humble unicyclist. But on the other, it offers a love-filled and hard-hitting philosophy that asks us to search our souls for more thoughtful, conscientious, and sustainable ways of living. Five minutes is everything to Schimmoeller, too, for different reasons.

Schimmoeller's narrative—of his slow and deliberate journey across the country, of his homesteading off-the-grid life in rural Kentucky, and of his battle to save old-growth forests from the developer's ax—demonstrates that one's worth is not defined by *how much* can be accomplished in five minutes, days, or even years, but by *what* is done with that time.

Most of us Americans operate under unspoken and pervasive

tenets we don't often question, but which *must* be questioned and *are* questioned by Schimmoeller, making his investigation of the nature of home, travel, landscape, and time absolutely vital. One of these tenets is that filling every minute of our lives with productivity gives us meaning and value. So many of us accept the belief underlying contemporary culture that says to be successful one has to stay busy. One has to run from one thing to the next; otherwise, he or she will not climb the staircase of American enterprise. But what other problems does this rushing create for our health and for the environment?

Another of these tenets is that constant movement in fulfillment of this busyness makes us important. For example, on a Friday afternoon not long ago I received a phone call from a writer acquaintance who was passing through southern Georgia and who wished to stop by my house. She had flown from New England to join a group of friends in Athens. They were scheduled to canoe the Altamaha River and in fact were driving to the put-in. The hour being late, I asked if we might entertain them on their return. "There is no return trip," she said. "I'm traveling on south to Jacksonville to catch a plane." That trip to California would be followed by a week-long residency in Spain.

I'm no enemy of travel. But I'm no longer impressed by a passport filled with customs stamps. I've learned, as did Mark, that the model of constant movement is flawed, and that human needs may best be addressed by dallying, by idling, by settling. Mark does cross thousands of miles, although not as a stunt or for attention or to reach a specific goal, but because there are truths to uncover in life that take time to do so.

Other mostly unspoken tenets shun physical labor, trees, penury, rural life. I'm particularly obsessed by the one that separates us from a relationship to place. No doubt, humans are tribal, communal beings, so much so that over eighty percent of us Americans live in cities. Faced with the need to return to the land and orient ourselves there, how comfortable are we? Can we weigh the minutest decision, asking ourselves, "Which causes the least harm? Can I enjoy myself in my home in the present moment? Do I want a throwaway life or an heirloom life?"

Mark Schimmoeller sinks into the profundities of these questions, and he does so beautifully, artfully, whimsically, gently. He imagines that we might learn to experience ourselves in relation to our inner selves, that we might be seen by elk, wood ducks, and wildflowers, and by the eye of the sun. Our sense of self-worth might derive from our relationships to our beloveds, our places, our communities, our art, and our need to care for creation. He details a certain kind of privacy and humility, living not as if one were being filmed.

I spent many years jetting around the country as an environmental writer, talking about climate change, which began to seem schizophrenic to me in that my solution to the problem caused more of the problem. So I quit. I became intimate with the train, then with a hybrid car, with a bicycle, with my feet. I discovered that rather than having fewer minutes I had so many more.

After the last plane, I never looked back. I can't think of one thing about planes that I miss. I'm a lot like photographer Sally Mann, who told me at dinner one night in her farm that she tries to stay put. Her record is thirty days, if I remember correctly.

"Staying home?" I asked.

"I'll walk as far as the mailbox," she said. "But yes, I don't get in a vehicle."

I really love *Slowspoke*. It has made me happier than any book in a long time, because it's the kind of thinking that humankind needs right now, in that it asks that we claim what we value—what we believe in, what we call precious—and divine how to preserve it.

When I think about the future, the changes in lifestyles and technologies we are being and will be forced to make—the word *simplification* comes to mind, as does the word *local*—I am reminded of an early morning in March in a bed-and-breakfast in Amish country, where I'd gone to give a talk. I awoke to the sound of clopping hooves on the road and I rushed to the window. A sorrel horse, pulling a small carriage, was making its way through a foggy, dewy dawn. Although I was born long after horses quit our roadways, the ringing of their hooves fills me with a nostalgia for something I want to know. What is this something? Perhaps it is a way to move through the world while honoring the world we're moving through: because we can focus, the world doesn't blur by in our haste.

JANISSE RAY
June 2014

Preface

CARRYING A BUCKET OF HOT WATER, I step onto the ice under a shrouded half moon. At once steam rises into the clutch of a frozen mist. I shut the cedar door of our Kentucky house and walk down a slope toward the trees. I also carry a cup, a bar of soap, and a towel. But for rubber clogs, yes, I'm naked. That I'm doing this as a man in my forties pleases me in some way. If I had to wager, I'd wager that a bath of this sort would more likely be a sign of youth than maturity—the same, say, with unicycling. I don't travel on a unicycle anymore, but I take winter baths outside. There's that, anyway.

A recent ice storm has laden everything from trunks to cedar needles with a quarter inch of ice. It has bent or looped or topped most of the cedar and caused some of the stronger hardwood to lean. Even the slightest breeze moves like a marble through the shellacked branches.

Our red hydrant pump is in front of a pignut hickory at the edge of the old woods. Close to mayapples and jewelweed, too—in another season, of course. I placed large, flat limestone rocks around the pump to make a floor. Behind the pump, I set three vertical cedar posts and notched into them a piece of sandstone, making a seat. One of the posts has a branch hook. I drape my towel here. To melt the ice on my seat, I splash hot water over it.

Jennifer is inside by the wood fire.

Before the winter storm, leaf buds had begun forming on branch ends. It's late February. The forecast says the trees will have to wait another day before rising temperatures release them. They'll rebound, then, to spring.

Jennifer and I opposed a city water line intended for our single-lane country road, and we argued against it at Water Board meetings. We catch the rain. If I lift the handle of this hydrant pump, water will flow by means of gravity from a partially submerged tank on the north side of our house and rise above the frost line and out the spigot. In the summer I bathe with this cool water directly.

Maybe it had come to the attention of the Water Board that a situation such as mine could sadly occur. And thus action must be immediate, the infrastructure built, to forestall an unseemly amount of suffering.

Well, so be it. Who knows? It is within the realm of possibility that there are people taking outdoor baths and having a disagreeable experience.

I pour another cup from my bucket on the sandstone ice.

When I dug out the trench for our hydrant pump, I separated the subsoil from the topsoil in order to restore the layers as I had found them on top of the black pipe connecting pump to tank. I couldn't keep myself from doing it. By contrast, the big machines that went up our road disassembled the earth and returned it disorganized.

Yet I'm not out here angry, protesting. I'm out here to feel the cold. That's hard to explain, I realize—and, clearly, I didn't convince the Water Board of the pleasures of what might be seen as deprivation. But I'm out here, too, to feel the heat of the water and more to the point, to feel the heat of the water after being cold.

I'm perhaps not impossibly odd. I want that hot water; I just want to anticipate it more than the average person might.

I strongly suspect that unicycling shaped my thinking on this matter. My parents gave me a unicycle for an Easter present when I was twelve. About the time my classmates began focusing on four wheels, I became obsessed with one. Unicyclists, it occurred to me, experience arrival less often than others. They must become devotees of anticipation. Rushing, I learned under the tutelage of my unicycle—whether down the driveway or toward adulthood—would cause a fall. Instead, after school and on the weekends, my task was to dwell in inefficiency, to wrinkle speed, to arrive somewhere only after much ambling about.

By the time I had become a young man, the rhythms of my unicycle had been so completely inculcated into my thinking that I was, at that point, essentially incompatible with the American workplace. After college, despite the opportunity for career advancement, I quit an internship with a New York City magazine to travel from North Carolina to Arizona on my single wheel.

I questioned it all: how unerringly straight a line America makes from less to more; how breakneck we travel this line; how we abandon the child in us and then later can't return to her.

Of course the problem of slowing down is that America careens past you that much faster. You can feel it even off the main road. We felt it in the bright orange line of surveyor's tape that appeared in the old woods close to my bath, or in the sound of the earth-digging machines.

The sheet of ice on my shower seat slides off like a plate, hits the ground, and breaks. A dozen or so tiny sleds cascade down the hill.

It helps to settle into a happy story (a safe story!), should you be so lucky to find yourself in one—as I do, living with Jennifer on a piece of land we love, with rain, sun, trees, and soil, with this live breath of heat I'm about to slip over tight skin, this lovely reprieve, this membrane of hope.

Chapter One

FEW PEOPLE KNOW OF OUR HOUSE; it is off the road quite a distance. Jennifer and I cannot drive right to it. We park and walk. In the ten minutes it takes for us to leave the car and arrive at what we call the entrance trees, we've fully relaxed into our place. The entrance trees are two shagbark hickories, one straight, one leaning, that stand only a body-length apart, giving us a threshold. On the other side is a small area of mowed grass, an herb garden, terraced beds with flowers, and our board-and-batten house with three solar panels mounted on its metal roof.

Inside, our house smells of the local cedar used in its construction. It faces south, with relatively large windows that allow winter sunlight to flood our interior. In a mansion they would cramp the space, but in our five-hundred-square-foot house they are perfectly sized, and they transport us. We look out to a grove of wild plum, a persimmon, a large redbud, then to a sloping, young field massed with grasses and brambly greenbrier and blackberry. The southwest section of this field includes a one-acre knoll we've fenced off for our garden. In every other direction are woods, with oak, beech, cedar, tulip poplar, hickory, walnut, black haw, white ash, mulberry, sugar maple, persimmon, and sassafras.

The old growth begins on a ridge to the north of our house. In early March, when I discovered the line of surveyor's tape there, the hickory buds were just starting to swell at the ends of branches that looked dead. The tips of the buds gradually turned a light yellow, their bases a deepening brown. As the buds grew, they became disproportionately large on their twigs, so large it seemed they had to either take wing or fall. If I can't remember or notice every plant's progression from dormancy to bloom to decay, then I could at least know these shagbark hickories: the swelling, the leafing, the falling.

We can look out to the east of our house to see a rock cistern, a shed, a young pear tree, a clothesline, and a woods sloping to a cedar and sugar maple cove. Divided into two parts, our shed has a room for tools and a room for a dry composting toilet. A first-time observer of our homestead might be struck by the absence of what has become ubiquitous for a modern American house: a driveway, a telephone line, a water line, a sewer line, electrical lines, gas lines.

That we are untethered from these industrial systems unnerves some of our guests, enchants others. Jennifer and I are among those who are enchanted, solipsistically so, you might say. In spring, with the horizon collaged by new leaves, we believe in a world defined only by how far we can peer through foliage—this foliage that we also are prone to believe filters danger from us.

The other day I picked up a stick at the edge of the woods that extends from our entrance trees to the garden. It was most likely from an oak, hickory, or maple and had fallen into a tuft of grass, one end slanted up, almost touching a cedar sapling. I threw it over the blueberry patch and woodpile in the direction of the garden—and immediately our black lab, Shadow, was on the chase. The stick reached its peak, and I wondered if this was as high as it had ever been, or if it had been blown off from a higher branch. I wondered, too, if it would land in front of our dog, who is, even with graying whiskers, a fast runner, and always at his fastest at this game—the joy of it all propelling him, his feet on the earth, the anticipation of getting in his mouth the stick that only seconds ago had been in my hand. To this joy, I added my own: that Jennifer and I had given him this world and not some other, that he could run like this and not get to the end of what he knew.

SLOWSPOKE

Shortly after discovering the surveyor's tape, I called Mr. Gregory, the owner of the property, and he told me his plans. Though I didn't have the money, I asked him if he would be willing to sell his 150-acre property. I told him that those trees were more valuable to us standing than cut. He said he wasn't interested in selling. When I hung up, my hands were shaking.

Chapter Two

MY UNICYCLE HANGS AMONG THE TOOLS in our shed, the last piece of foam padding I used still strapped to the seat.

I'm occasionally disoriented by its lack of motion, and when people ask me if I'm ever going to travel on it again, I don't have a good answer. "No" sounds like a betrayal of sorts; "yes" seems untrue. It is part of the story of how I arrived here in the northern Kentucky woods with Jennifer, but also part of the continuation of our story.

I remember once sitting in a parked jetliner and looking out its small window to another parked jetliner. We began to move. I felt our motion and saw it, but, in the end, we were stationary; the other jet was moving. Glancing at my unicycle in the shed similarly disorients me for a fraction of a second. Then a hammer or a quick square will settle me to the ground, and I'll be certain once more of my own stillness. I'll be aware of a season passing by, and the awareness of one will bring on the rush of all of them, and I'll sort through again how I happen to be here. My route encompasses three moves: 1) from the southwest, where my father worked as a traveling salesman, to a central Kentucky cow and tobacco farm; 2) from this central Kentucky farm, where my sisters and I grew up, to a cabin in the northern Kentucky woods, where my parents still live; 3) from my parents' cabin to the house that Jennifer and I built and where we now live, about a forty-minute hike away from my parents' place.

No one knew why Daddy bought a travel trailer and took his family to the southwest. He had a well-paying government job in the central Kentucky town of Versailles, and we lived in a normal house in a subdivision. Perhaps what he said was true, that he did it for the adventure. The adventure, however, lasted only a couple of years. Broke and in debt, we returned to Versailles when I was six and my twin sisters four and became the tenants of a run-down farm house a half mile off a country road. For the first few months we had to live in our travel trailer while we hauled truckloads and truckloads of trash out of the house. The house had electricity but no running water or telephone. When we fixed up one room, we moved in and proceeded to work on the others.

One day some people came and took away our trailer because we hadn't been able to make the last payment. If before we hadn't decided whether to stay or not, we now knew that this house was our home. It was on a hundred acres. A short distance down a slope and inside a fold of hills, a huge spring welled from the ground, forming a creek that flowed through part of the property. The water ran clear. We drank from it and hauled buckets and jugs up to the house. On hot days, we would submerge ourselves in its crystal coolness. When cows threatened to wade in it, we put up a makeshift barrier.

Removed from the stress our parents bore, my sisters and I grew up strong and happy. When my grandparents tried to give my parents a television, thinking that my sisters and I were deprived without one, Mama refused. Instead, she took us to the public library once a week, where we checked out armloads of books, and she used the hot running water in the library bathroom sink to wash our clothes. We spent much of the day outside anyway, exploring, sailing homemade boats in the creek, building forts, shooting baskets at a goal Daddy set up by an old barn below the house, and riding horses. We rarely helped weed the garden or do other chores; our parents shielded us from their heavy workload, which included (before we could afford a chainsaw) chopping and splitting all of our firewood with an axe. Freshly out of high school, they had been among the first of Kennedy's Peace Corps volunteers and had met in Ecuador. Later, they were married on the Navajo Nation where Mama was a Vista volunteer. The vigorous physical training they'd undergone to get selected for the Peace Corps had prepared them for this new Kentucky life. As we got older, however, Chris and Trina and I discovered that we wanted to help with the chores; we even competed over who got to carry up bucket and jug water from the spring.

Daddy had a job briefly as a car insurance salesman, and one Easter he brought back a foal for my sisters and me—in the back seat of the insurance company's Buick. He wanted to name the foal "Company Car." My sisters and I thought "Starlight" was better. We agreed to take care of him.

Another Easter we received stilts as a gift. As for what turned Daddy flamboyantly generous on Easter, I wasn't sure. The next year I received a unicycle.

Daddy lost his insurance company job, and we survived six months of poverty by relying on food stamps. When a number of jobs didn't work out or last, he drove away in our old blue Ford pickup to travel with a carnival and operate a game trailer my Uncle Ray owned. We saw him only infrequently during the fair and festival season, but then he had five months off. He put the money he made that year in glass jars in an old root cellar in the back yard. The money would buy us food through the winter. That year my sisters and I would be on the reduced-lunch school plan instead of the free-lunch plan.

With its stunning dissimilarity to home, school shocked me every year, from first grade to the end of high school. I felt like a foreign exchange student, one from a poorer country. Though our house had electricity, my sisters and I grew up thinking that using electricity wasn't an indelible right. Mama taught us never to keep the refrigerator open longer than necessary; before opening the door, we had to think of what we wanted. Hopefully we could find it quickly. Sometimes I'd think of a second choice for a snack for the sole reason of getting the door closed quickly. In the winter Mama unplugged the refrigerator and transferred the food to the unheated staircase that led to the second floor of the house. Though we never had the money to fix the upstairs, Mama used the area for an art studio, where she painted portraits of Native Americans. The food would be placed to the sides of the stairs, leaving a climbing path. We learned, too, that it had to be indisputably dark before we turned on a light. Mama would even allow our guests to almost completely disappear.

At school I discovered I had a lot fewer things than my classmates. The main thing I lacked, the biggest thing in their lives, was a television, which meant I couldn't talk about shows as they would or understand references to these shows. I should have been a diplomat, elucidating to others where I came from, what it was like to live in an old farmhouse and use an outhouse and walk on stilts and ride a unicycle and read armloads of books and dunk in a spring and live practically without electricity and pick blackberries and play hide-and-go-seek in a cornfield. But I was too shy to show them my world.

The clothing I wore wasn't popular, which was why I didn't walk with them in their groups down the hallways. I stayed quiet, longed always for the end of the school day. Though I was happy, sometimes I dreamed of living in a typical suburban house, thinking that then I could make friends.

On Valentine's Day I wanted store-bought cards to pass out to my classmates. But as an artist, Mama was bored with such mass-produced normality. So every year she made valentines for my sisters and me to hand out. Each card had a hole with a marshmallow stuck in it, the marshmallow being part of a drawing and a rhyme she created. Our cards would be put in big paper Kroger bags, because they were bulky, and stored in the empty refrigerator so the mice wouldn't get at them. To have enough time to make them for our three classes, she started the valentines in January, and I secretly reviewed them as she went along. It helped to already be fast with the refrigerator door.

She asked me in sixth grade if Tara was a pretty girl. Although Tara was one of the prettiest girls in the class, my reply was vague. When I saw her rhyme about Tara being as pretty as Farah Fawcett, a popular model, I knew that there was only one option left to me. I dropped it down the outhouse hole. That Valentine's Day every girl in my class got a marshmallow valentine from me except Tara.

On my unicycle after school, I'd go over what happened during the day, what leaned me toward sadness, what lifted me. I'd make the corrections I needed. The words that maybe had failed to come to me would come, and I would perform them alone on our long rock driveway or in a field, alternating between a narrative that could have been and the narrative that was. I explained to Tara again and again why she didn't receive a valentine from me. Then a rock or a ditch would appear, and I would pivot and inch toward what truly happened or what hadn't happened, such as a conversation with a classmate. My unicycle kept me both from being spacey and from being normal.

The years passed, and I found myself at the end of high school without having been on a single date, but with an invitation to deliver a co-valedictorian speech. The first time many of my classmates heard me talk was at our commencement.

I felt, because of that speech, a growing interest in the ability of words—not just to fill in silences, but to make excursions in and out of reality. I majored in English at college and went on to attempt an internship at *The Nation* magazine.

Back at home after quitting the internship, the shock of going from cow fields to skyscrapers too great, I faced the prospect of a quixotic journey. I remember being down at the barn below the house, shooting baskets. Old Starlight was in his stall, eating sweet feed. By then, I liked "Company Car" as a name better than "Starlight." The day was bright and cool, and I was hitting more than usual. My sisters had been star athletes in junior high and high school, but I'd never gone out for a team, always wanting to get home as quickly as possible. I'd learned to shoot, however, and I would play in front of imaginary crowds. After shooting I'd leap after the ball to deflect it from cow patties. That day I had better luck than usual in keeping the ball clean. The idea to travel on a unicycle seemed exquisite, but I decided to keep it a secret for a while. I was afraid of what would happen to it in the open.

My plan, anyway, was eclipsed a few days later when my family received an eviction notice; we had sixty days to leave the farm, which was being sold.

~

On waking at a friend's house in eastern Kentucky on February 28, 1992, three years after graduating from college, I reviewed my course of action: I would put the backpack on, strap the canteen over me, and launch myself on the unicycle. Just three things to remember. Trina would be dropping me off at the side of the road later in the day. In previous months I had gathered addresses of people I thought might be living similarly to the way I would be traveling. "What?" Trina had joked on finding this out. "In houses about to fall?"

I had received an invitation from Mel Resfield, who worked for a bioregional journal, *Katuah*, in Upton, North Carolina. He would be home in nine days, which meant I needed to be dropped off nine days of traveling away from Upton. Trina was driving, and I was looking at a terribly creased road map. Maybe a prelapsarian-sounding community like Eden would be a good place to start. But how far could I get from Eden, pedaling on a unicycle for nine days? Not as far as Upton, Trina thought. Not on just one wheel.

A store at the top of a mountain at the Kentucky-Virginia state line didn't have a map of the immediate area but offered others for free. I took a map of Arizona. If there was ever a time for bravado, it was now. The road widened in Virginia and after a few miles of unsettlingly long views we crossed into North Carolina, where we found a good map of the state at a welcoming station. The small through-roads were marked blue. Gravel roads and other county roads, which I would often seek for refuge, were not marked.

Fields outside the little community of Francisco featured bare, red clay, and narrow log barns were chinked with it.

"Well, I guess the next good place to pull over," I said.

A gravel road appeared just as my words ended, scaring me. We drove past it.

"You mean a place like that?" Trina asked.

"Yes."

When we finally pulled up next to a run-down barn, my heart was pounding. I lifted my stuff out of the trunk. Luckily I had already gone over what to do—backpack, canteen, unicycle. Just three things. I hugged Trina, headed to the road.

I had learned to ride my unicycle with ski poles but eventually could ride without them. With a backpack, however, mounting was more difficult, and I wished again for ski poles, if only to ensure that the inaugural mount of my journey would go smoothly, so Trina could give a promising report to our parents and eventually to Chris, who was in India on a Fulbright scholarship.

Left foot on the left pedal, the seat situated under me, the next action would be to step up and sit on the seat. I hesitated, trembling slightly. My first actual maneuverings past the back porch steps of our central Kentucky farmhouse had been crooked and painstaking, and I had labored a week before I'd had enough balance to toss away the ski poles. Still, I'd moved only slowly, and it took some time after that before I learned to use my body to make turns. The first time I pedaled around the house my sisters ran from window to window to check on my progress, but later, when I was able to circle the house continuously, they had either lost interest or were afraid of becoming dizzy. My record was ten times around the house without falling down.

At the side of a road in the middle of North Carolina, the thought occurred to me that I should have stopped at ten times around the house. Nonetheless, I stepped up, and my right foot quickly found the loose pedal; I wobbled a bit and then moved more surely down the road. I stuck my arm out. Trina beeped the horn. The photograph she took showed my body at an odd angle with the unicycle.

I'd never liked how photographs stole grace from a unicyclist, whose only redemption was movement. Very few could look at such a photo and imagine how a shift of the body could avoid a fall and result in movement, sometimes in the desired direction; how the awkwardness of that captured moment was the genesis of unicycle travel.

Most would look at the photo and be convinced of the rider's doom.

The backpack felt very heavy. I reviewed its contents: the lightweight sleeping bag borrowed from my uncle, who had used it after high school on a hitchhiking expedition to Alaska; a five-pound tent; a candle lantern that weighed practically nothing; a paperback copy of *Small Is Beautiful* by E.F. Schumacher; a one-pound twig-burning camp stove; a water pump for purifying water; a cup, a spoon, and a pot; matches; notebooks for writing; a collapsible plastic water container; peanut butter, bread, cookies, several packages of instant oatmeal, two bananas, one apple, a bag of split peas, instant rice, and some oatmeal squares from Trina. Each item, it now seemed clear, added to the weight of the pack. Daddy had told me I was taking too much.

In my right pocket was $500, money saved while running a basketball game at carnivals and festivals. I would try to keep my expenses under $15 a day.

That my shoulders were sore already was becoming apparent. I shifted the position of my pack. The movement caused my unicycle to turn to the left. So I took a detour, the best of my options. I'd learned to virtually always give in to my unicycle. There were a few more slight corrections—to the right, to the left—before I got myself straightened out, relatively speaking.

In front of me then was a hill. With this hill, I would prove to myself that this journey would be possible physically. I leaned toward the incline.

Each time I pushed one of the pedals down, my unicycle swayed in that direction. I would quickly push the other pedal down to balance myself. A third of the way up the hill, the pedals hardened even more. I moved like a pendulum.

When I was halfway up, a car without a muffler came up behind me, accelerating hard. Without granting me space, it raced past me to the top.

I stepped off my unicycle. My legs were rubber. Going down the hill on the other side, the car backfired. After all, I didn't choose a unicycle for its ability to transport me up a hill, I told myself. I would walk up hills; I needed walking breaks anyway. Sweat streaking my face, I pushed my unicycle to the top.

I walked down the hill too, began to breathe less heavily. At the bottom I encountered a flat section of road with no cars. I mounted again. These are the best conditions possible for a unicyclist. No cars, no hills. I took a small notebook from my shirt pocket, drew out a pen from the metal spiral binding. With my hands thus withdrawn from the air, I wrote a few words. The danger was that I would not be able to use language as precisely as an arm flung out for balance.

"Cross Dan River," I wrote in the notebook, my letters going about the white, lined paper much the same way my wheel was on the road. Still no cars. The number of ants on the road surprised me. I'd never traveled slowly enough to see so many. With a slight shift of my body, I could miss whole columns of them. I set my pen to work again. "I want people to slow down, see a different shape." The sentence was a half-mile long.

Later in the afternoon, the road suddenly had heavy traffic. Vehicles passed me constantly. I'd battle each one in my head to give myself a buffer. The car or truck would pass without hitting me.

As motorists stared, I, too, found myself contemplating a man on a unicycle, a tiny measure of fascination mixed with a larger portion of dread. This man was traveling insecurely, his movement undulating. He was foolish and exposed to the world. He was in pain.

Finally, the exit to Hanging Rock State Park appeared, and I left the main road for a narrow one, which turned steeply uphill. I walked it, pushing the unicycle in front of me, exhausting myself. I took rest breaks, sitting on guardrails.

Closer to the campsite I strapped the unicycle to my backpack. I didn't want to answer questions about my journey. I would pretend that my unicycle didn't exist, that I was only a hiker. That, however, proved hard to do, given that the nonexistent item turned my pack almost unbearably heavy.

I found a site at the end of the campground. Too tired to light a fire for a hot meal, I flopped down and did nothing. A quick look at the map helped me to determine that I had traveled only five miles.

For supper I ate one of the "survival" bars that Trina had baked, one of the few times I'd ever appreciated the weighty oatmeal squares.

Dark came. I lit the candle lantern, took out a postcard. Not enough light to cover the entire card. I wrote home, my sentences ending in obscurity. A park ranger drove over and collected four dollars. She told me there was a phone in the office in case of sickness or, "in your case," she said, "if you need transportation help."

Chapter Three

OUR ENTRANCE TREES STAND TO THE WEST of our house, part of a line of hickory, elm, and oak extending down to the garden. In the summer, we walk in the shade behind these trees. We cross a wooded knoll, then step out into the yellow heat at the garden gate. Because of this path, we've come to know the little woods it traverses, which we've named the "Henbit Forest." The wildflower we initially thought was henbit is actually red deadnettle, but we kept the name. Also here is garlic mustard, an invasive that spreads and that we must pull out; some native wildflowers, like yellow corydalis, early spiderwort, toothwort, and spring beauty; a plant that produces an inch-long narrow seed that clasps on to clothing; a thicket of black raspberry canes; burdock with its boisterous leaves and seeds that also cling to clothing, these in the form of fuzzy balls. Yet from a short distance away we can see only tree leaves.

This spring I've been less inclined to do what a path entices us to do: follow something to its end. I've allowed myself leaves and stillness, and the forays I've made mostly have been backward, toward previous beginnings. I remember touching a hickory leaf bud and being surprised to discover that the brown base was soft and furry, more like an animal than a plant. Our entrance trees had hundreds of such buds, each shaped like a carpenter's plumb and tapering to the thickness of a pencil end, each pointing in a different direction. I would look up at the trees at this time, and I would think that there could be no better visual image (the anarchic desire, the impending movement!) to describe how it feels to be on a unicycle.

I don't mean to depart from the present, only to suspend it.

I guess I've never been in the habit, anyway, of rushing to the end of a path, whatever that end signified—adulthood or acquiring a career or leaving home.

After we had received the eviction notice, I knew I would help my parents find and move into a new place. My sisters and I never thought of leaving them during this time, although we were old enough to do so. In my case, I hadn't established many relationships beyond my family, and I wasn't sure how to leave home. It perplexed me a little that the only thing I could think of was to take off on a unicycle. Once we were settled, I would tell everyone of my unicycle plan. It would have that much more time, I thought, to become inerasable.

After much searching, we found a hundred acres of woods in northern Kentucky that we thought unspoiled and beautiful. By this time Daddy owned his own game trailer and had saved enough jars of cash in the root cellar to make a down payment; for the first time as a family, we had our own place.

The land was hilly and blanketed with cedar and hardwood. The entire property had two small cleared areas, one near the paved county road, one farther away, close to a long, narrow pond, which we could access via an old tractor road that marked one of the boundaries of the property. We would build our cabin at the edge of the pond clearing. The cabin would have no amenities, and we would build it ourselves with a $1,500 budget. We had one month.

The height of the cedar trees on our land—the medium-sized ones, for we passed by the tallest—determined the dimensions of our cabin: eighteen by twenty-two feet. With a new chainsaw, we felled ninety trees. We maneuvered all the logs ourselves, either by hand, or with a come-along, or with a long quarter-inch nylon rope tied to the bumper of our old gray car, to get them close to the tractor road. From there, a friend with a four-wheel-drive truck helped us drag them to the site. The mud from that day is still on some of the logs.

We built four corner platforms out of rock where the logs

would rest. One of our purchases had been a large wheelbarrow. I'd find rocks up a slope from the site, fill the wheelbarrow, and turn it downhill. The wheelbarrow would pull me into a run, and I'd arrive where Daddy was placing the rock. With a flourish of speed and a bit of thunder, I would dump my load onto our rock pile. Daddy and I were the only ones working. Chris and Trina were in their last month of college and Mama was managing our central Kentucky house.

After the foundation, we began stacking the logs, notching the ends of the log being placed and spiking them to the logs underneath. We'd get eight logs placed a day. For the roof structure, we began to inset the logs, creating a pitch. We bought boards for the roof, the floor, and the loft; tin to cover the roof boards; and blocks for a chimney. To put in a window, we'd brace the logs with two vertical two-by-sixes, then saw a hole out of the wall and frame out the rough opening. We'd found the four windows we put in at a yard sale.

Every day we'd take the lunch Mama had packed down the hill from the cabin where water flowed from under the root of a red oak, spilling into a creek bed. We kept two tin cups hanging in a nearby cedar. We would drink spring water and eat under this tree.

"I have a vision of you," Daddy said one day while we were eating our lunch, "becoming a naturalist and writing about this place."

Had my unicycle plan not seemed childish in context, I would have confided in him then. Instead, after a pause, I merely agreed that that seemed like a good plan.

By late afternoon we would drive home, stopping first by my grandparents' house in Frankfort. They lived halfway between our new land and our Versailles farm. We'd take showers and climb into clean clothes we'd washed the day before, put our dirty clothes in Grandma's washing machine, and eat a meal she had prepared. After eating a second supper at home with Mama, we would go to bed exhausted and fulfilled.

We finished the basic structure of the cabin within our budget and time frame. The chinking between the logs, which we would do with a mix of clay, sand, and cement, would happen after we moved.

On our moving day, after our belongings (but for Starlight, already given away to a good home) were packed into two cars and two trucks—one of the trucks my Uncle Ray's—Chris, Trina, and I went down the hill to the spring, our last visit. We splashed our faces and filled gallon jugs. The water would be what we would miss the most. It had given us much pleasure, had been what we took people to see, our house not being much to look at. Reckless, we trusted that it was pure, and it hadn't killed us. We found room for six jugs in the back of our Ford truck along with flowers potted in dark, rich bluegrass soil, another thing we'd miss. We were moving to a land of heavy yellow clay.

Hours earlier we'd attended Chris and Trina's college graduation ceremony. They had each received presidential awards for scholarship and citizenship. The speeches at the orderly outdoor event had not predicted the moving into a primitive log cabin for any of the graduates. They had been abstract and sophisticated, and I'd imagined the words in them crumbled on the ground, smaller, closer to things that were real—a puddle, a clump of grass, a rock.

When we arrived at our new land, a tractor and a wagon waited for us. Because of recent heavy rains, we'd borrowed this equipment from a friend so we could get our belongings down the old lane to the cabin.

Daddy and I had extended the cabin floor joist logs in order to build a porch when we could—but on moving day this project remained unfinished. To get furniture and boxes through the front door, we had to balance on the extended logs, which became slippery with mud. Soon the cabin was impossibly full of boxes, and we spent the rest of the afternoon regaining living space.

We'd built loft areas on either side of the cabin. One side was for me and the other for my sisters. The master bedroom, as we ironically referred to it, was downstairs (down the ladder) in a corner of its own but open to the main living space. My sisters and I discovered that we could stand up in our lofts if we happened to be in the exact middle. I put my bed in a corner; my trek to it would fold me half-size. My loft was more perilous than theirs, in the sense that I had to cross a log to get to the ladder. Chris and Trina could access the ladder from their loft floor.

Late in the afternoon we saw my mother taking a frying pan and cooking supplies outside. Someone stupidly asked why she was going outside to cook. Then it struck us. We helped a little by making a circle of stones for the grill top, just below the cabin in a rocky opening surrounded by cedar, and by breaking up dead cedar branches for firewood. But then she wanted to do the rest herself. We didn't eat until nine o'clock that night, four hours later than usual. Carrying the food into the cabin, Mama slipped in the mud but didn't drop anything. The barbequed chicken was good. We decided we liked the new smoky flavor. We ate, of course, by candlelight, the best kind of light for a small cabin, for it unmoored the walls. Yellowish and insinuating, our candles coaxed the big night inside. A bobcat screamed.

⌒

I pretended to be only a hiker that morning on the first full day of my unicycle journey, choosing a trail through the park rather than leaving by the paved entrance. I'd gotten up early to avoid attention. I didn't want anyone to see me at the risible and somewhat complicated endeavor of strapping a unicycle to a full backpack and then hoisting both to my shoulders and teetering, drunk with the weight, toward the trail head.

If indeed I were in the process of revising something, I wanted to complete the revision in private. I remembered one of my journal entries from the previous year as I debated the merits and potential drawbacks of traveling on one wheel: "I imagine myself on the side of the road on a unicycle, and I am smashed with the thought that I am stupid."

I hadn't envisioned the problem of traveling on a unicycle while attempting to hide it. The revision, of course, would be to get the unicycle off my pack and either wheel it or ride it. But that morning, anyway, I wanted it to be as close as possible to an idea, something that could still be debated and potentially deleted.

With careful, small steps, I walked by pine, oak, mountain laurel, and rhododendron. The ground was spongy with duff, and it absorbed some of the pain of movement. I wanted the trail to last longer, but I came to its end rather quickly and looked out across a farm to a small, paved road that would take me west, and I felt like I'd walked up to a girl with planned words and either needed to say them or walk away. I should, I thought, come up with *A Unicyclist's Guide to America*, something that could help future unicycle travelers (should there be any) with the moments of angst that would come. The guide would encourage riders to completely accept their unicycles. "A unicycle is who you are," it would say. "For whatever reason, you are not any other form of transportation. You are a unicycle. Please love yourself." Or something like that.

I left the park and trespassed across the farm to the road. At the side of the road, I shed the pack. I was surprised that the thing didn't sink into the ground. Or that I didn't float away. I stood there and looked at it. The unicycle could be a getaway vehicle, I thought. Bending over, I unstrapped it from the pack. If it were possible for a unicyclist to feel sophisticated, this would be the moment. A lot more absurd, I decided, would be standing here beside a pair of stilts, which I also owned.

My first attempt at the road—just the thought to start down it—petered out, and I sat down on a rock and ate another one of Trina's survival bars. The inspiration that started me moving on the road that day was to sever my relations with the unicyclist, just as an experiment. I would observe what happened if he did start pedaling down the road; and if I didn't like how the story unfolded—if it seemed, for instance, more tedious than enchanting, more foolish than revolutionary—I could toss that page, start anew.

So the unicyclist headed west on a day that would become unseasonably warm for early March. Traffic was light, allowing him an unfettered focus on the pain in his shoulders. He shifted his pack; he stopped often, squeezed sips out of his lung-shaped canteen.

As the day wore on, the number of things he thought about diminished. Then there was only one thought: arriving at Pilot Mountain State Park. Being the only elevated landmark in a generally flat terrain, Pilot Mountain seemed to be within his reach all day. Yet like a mirage, it would recede. He attempted not to look at it. He avoided even glancing too far up the road, where the blacktop melted in the heat. The road was only solid, for sure, where his wheel was meeting it.

When he arrived at last at the park, he discovered that the campground was closed for the season. Nonetheless, he slipped past the road barrier and made a claim to a spot under a pine tree, where he flopped down. The showers, of course, were closed. Not risking a fire, he ate a cold meal and stretched out with sticky skin against a hillside lacerated at times by headlights.

I looked at what had transpired that day and thought about abandoning the story—but I also discovered I had more than a minor level of interest in this unicyclist. I let him thus continue on. He rumpled the leaves under his sleeping pad in the morning and took a last glance at his camp as he was leaving, satisfied that no one appeared to have slept there. He found himself then pedaling into Ararat and eating biscuits and gravy and eggs at a café. In the gathering heat after breakfast he inched toward West Plains. On the other side of West Plains, he had trouble with camping. Even though he had permission to set up his tent on a Baptist church's property, he by mistake set it up just outside the church property. A man came up to him and told him to move it, said he'd had trouble with intruders destroying things and he would shoot anyone he saw down by his pay lake. The unicyclist moved his tent. The church people brought him hot fried chicken, green beans, and mashed potatoes, along with a group of kids called the Royal Ambassadors. They were supposed to ask questions to possibly contribute to his spiritual awakening, but, to a kid, they remained silent. After this visit, he wrote in his journal, scavenging light from a street lamp close to the church.

On the fourth day, he felt stronger and more confident. Outside Dobson, several school buses passed him, and he transformed them, their windows suddenly opening and kids sticking their heads outside, shouting—an outburst which, to this day, I can still hear and which I attribute to my finally accepting the unicyclist and joining him thoroughly on his journey. A mix of excitement and surprise, their shouting verged on a cheer, like that which is heard at a small-town school basketball game. My own inward surprise at being on a unicycle now seemed to have voices that existed in the real world; for the moment I was Mama saying no to a free television, or Daddy choosing adventure over a middle-class suburban life, their decisions the equivalent of being on one wheel outside Dobson, North Carolina, except that all society would have been halfway out the bus, shouting. I settled into the blue seat, my feet on the pedals, my arms in the air, my body at a slight tilt forward.

When I was erased moments later by a thick fog, I found myself still in the afterglow of their exuberance, my wholeness intact. I remained hidden for two hours. Then I climbed a steep hill and appeared in the community of Mountain Park. I stepped into a pool hall to ask directions. A group of old men stared at me as I told them I wanted the smallest possible roads going toward Austin.

"I could tell you where you're going wrong," one of them said. A big debate ensued. I listened. A man with a crooked back and bright eyes told me he could "carry me there but couldn't give me directions." A half hour may have passed before they agreed on a route I should take, and I left a little wiser.

About five miles from Mountain Park I spent a miserable night in a thorny thicket and the next morning experienced the first rain of my trip. My gear wasn't completely waterproof; as the day went on, I began to get wet.

Wilkesboro loomed up. I kept pedaling, even when I suspected cars gathering behind me. "Let them slow down," I thought brashly. I'd decided to get a motel room, and the prospect of a dry, safe place had emboldened me for the moment.

Then there was a teenage girl alongside the road, motioning to me. I got off my unicycle and walked over to her. She had a big umbrella and placed it so it was over me, too.

"I just wanted to meet the guy who would do such a thing," she said. She was the kind of girl who could try out for cheerleading, the kind of girl who would avoid me in school.

"What made you travel on a unicycle?" she asked.

"I'm not sure," I said, at least not speechless.

"Cool," she said. "Well, good luck."

She smiled brightly and left, and I felt the rain again on my head.

The motel that I found in Wilkesboro was a Days Inn, and it was pure luxury. If a cheerleader stopped me every day on my journey, I thought, I would maybe learn how to talk to one. In my room I stripped off my wet clothes, turned the hotel radio up loud, and danced wildly about the room, even jumping on the bed.

Chapter Four

ABOUT THE TIME THAT LEAVES EMERGED like clasped hands from the hickory buds and slowly opened, the wild plum peaked with white blossoms and rained petals on Jennifer's blue-green jacket spread out on one of the flower terraces. The jacket always accentuated her blue eyes and childlike profile. While I knew she was just away momentarily, getting a wheelbarrow load of mulch, I also knew that in another story her newly petal-decorated jacket would exist only as a memory or a wish or a creation. I considered myself lucky to be where I was, with plum petals in the air and my wife soon to appear.

Now the redbud are leafing out and dropping their blossom petals. On a recent walk in the woods, Jennifer and I chanced upon a pinkish hue on the ground, roughly circular in shape, and we looked up to see a redbud we hadn't noticed when in full bloom, when blossoms had competed with a maze of limbs and shadows and shifting light.

We entered this blossom shade that lightly covered last year's fallen hardwood leaves and newly arisen anemone, toothwort, and spring beauty—disoriented at first, then relieved by how effortless it can be, this passing of time. When I was a kid, my sisters and I would jump rope, two of us swinging the rope and the third attempting to run through without being touched by it. The trick for the runner was to be aware of when the rope was at its low and high points.

It's the same, I think, with spring, judging when to step in. Do we come into this spring as redbud, with blossoms in the tree, in the air, or on the ground? Middle age might suggest that we are that pool of petals on the ground. A loss of color and definition would follow. What seemed easy was that this fading would happen apparently without preparation, just as the blossoms appeared unbidden on the trees. The pink on the ground would be gone, and we'd notice, instead, a nearby sassafras, buckeye, or pawpaw.

I think of resurrections every spring, and every spring I'm surprised by Jennifer. I'd tried for years to create her, but I never thought she would materialize. I'd wished for someone authentically rather than glamorously beautiful. She would be interested in living simply; she would be shy and smart and like to read; she would have straight blond hair and blue eyes like my mother and sisters; she would be healthy and enjoy hiking and gardening.

By candlelight, when I was in my loft in the log cabin, either early in the morning or just before bed, I would be able to see her most clearly, and she would be a presence in many of the poems I began writing in earnest. No one could see her in these poems, which were about living in the forest, about hewing a cedar pole down to its heartwood, about fire and ash, about maple sap, about a frog splashing into the pond under the moonlight, about tree shadows on the leafy forest floor, but I could tell she was there, and I wrote poems to be close to her.

Even after Chris and Trina began to branch out a bit into the world—Trina getting a master's degree and a PhD in English at the University of California at Davis and Chris traveling to India and then becoming the director of a forest preservation organization—I continued to write and to be a forest dweller. I took long hikes and learned to identify wildflowers and trees. I dug out one root cellar and renovated another. I made an onion storage room with shelves fashioned out of weathered oak and tobacco sticks; I made a ladder out of a cedar trunk to replace the board ladder to the cabin loft; I made a solar cooker and a solar food dryer. I began making a cedar rail fence.

Being at home, I didn't need to make much money, and I chose to make only as much as I needed. On many weekends

I would drive to a festival in Kentucky and help Daddy for free in his game trailer, but I would only take my own game, a basketball shoot, to five or six festivals a year.

I wanted, mostly, to be home and to work with the wood, stone, and soil of our place, to make things by day and by the glow of a candle at night or early morning, imbuing my work with longing or wonder or loss. The pull of a rock in my hands during the day would become a love story by night.

It was by candlelight, too, that I told everyone—only a few months after we'd moved into our log cabin, when Chris and Trina were still at home—that I was going to travel on my unicycle. They reacted with shock that I would be leaving and amazement that I had thought of such a thing. Candlelight had seemed the best environment for this idea freshly out of my mind. An incandescent bulb may have killed it. Similarly, daylight.

Either because the pull of home was so great or the prospects for a utopian English major in America so nonexistent, I returned home after my 1992 journey and fell back into my pattern of writing and outdoor work. We'd been lucky enough to buy an adjacent piece of land that had a narrow valley for gardening, an old barn (where I would make the onion room), and a small cleared hillside that included an abandoned homesite and a root cellar.

I began my cedar rail fence around this cleared hillside. We would get a horse one day, maybe. I would go into the woods with a hatchet and a bucksaw, cut posts and rails out of dead or dying or storm-pushed cedar, and haul them by hand to my work site. For whatever reason, though one influenced almost certainly by unicycle travel, I'd decided not to use nails in my fence. Instead, I used a brace and bit for making holes in the posts and a hatchet for hewing the ends of the poles.

I worked for years, off and on, building this fence. It occurred to me that Trina would finish her doctorate in the time it would take me to enclose five acres. I was further struck by the fact that

I was in my late twenties and still at home. I'd been on a unicycle journey and had traveled in Latin America to help people build and use solar cookers, but it seemed that I kept returning home.

In the spring of 1997, when I was twenty-nine, my family and I organized an event called the Cedar Ring Congress, a day of workshops on simple living skills, such as organic gardening and herbal medicine making and building and using a composting toilet. Cedar rail fence making, I decided, would not be on the program. I would, however, lead a workshop on how to build and use solar cookers. One hundred sixty people attended. When I saw her at the registration table and held her gaze briefly, I knew I would look for her again, as I would a reflection in a woodland pond, only briefly lost.

Jennifer. Nerinx, Kentucky. I checked her name on the list, handed her, as I had everyone, a rustic but elegant wooden medallion with her name on it. My parents had produced these "name tags," Daddy cutting and sanding cedar rounds, Mama painting names and designs on them. A soft leather loop was attached to each one through a drilled hole, allowing people to wear them as necklaces. She seemed surprised by hers, glancing at me, I thought, brightly before heading to the main tent.

The eyes, we discovered on that walk over a decade later, adjust to redbud blossoms as they would to any change of light. When we left that pink blossom ground cover, the effect was that of a minor cloud passing over the sun—but soon the less vivid coloring began to seem normal, larkspur and spring beauty bright in their own manner. We climbed a hillside to the southeast section of our land, followed a ridge top distinguished by post oak. We passed a small pond, where sometimes we scared wood ducks, and looped around to our house, approaching it from the direction of the garden. I should mention that even before tree blossoms and before green tip on the hickory, events are happening in the garden. By mid-March, when there's only the anticipation of bud break, when the only wildflower in the woods is harbinger-of-spring, a tiny fleck that appears all white until you get down on your hands and knees and notice maroon pistils, we are planting peas and lettuces and preparing beds for potatoes and onions. This year we also associate harbinger-of-spring with the first spotting of wood ducks. Again, that unexpected streak of maroon up close, then only two flapping bodies, all black, receding from us.

Jennifer wears gloves working in the garden. Her hand feels like silk against mine.

~

Dear Mr. Gregory,

To introduce ourselves, Jennifer and I live
at the back end of the old Wilhoite farm,
our house close to your land. We built our
place with our own hands, much of it with
local materials. We have a large garden, fruit
trees, solar panels for electricity, large
south-facing windows for winter sunlight,
a wood stove for cold, cloudy days. We are very
happy here.

We are writing because your logging and
development plans would take place just steps
from our back door. Jennifer and I are not
the only ones who are concerned; a number of
people in the area believe that your property
has more value as it is: roadless, with the
trees standing. If you would be willing to sell
it to us, we would do everything in our
capacity as a community to buy it.

You probably already know how rare the back
section of your property is. Some of the trees
here are the tallest in the area. I've visited
your woods (forgive me for trespassing) on

many occasions, and though I've hiked all over
these hills, I've not seen a stand of trees
as mature as yours. One of the ash in your woods
rises, I'm sure, eighty feet before branching
out. Yet all the trees are tall, with nice
crowns. The diversity of hardwood here is
similarly distinctive: ash, maple, beech, oak,
hickory, poplar, black gum, basswood, walnut,
cherry. These species just compose the top
story of the forest. The understory of your
woods is also complex: pawpaw, dogwood, black
haw, hornbeam, and serviceberry are what come
to mind. Then the native bushes: spicebush
and maple-leaf viburnum. I can get lost in the
layers. I've come to know a rich diversity
of flora because of your forest and its intact
stories. I would not have discovered blue
cohosh, Dutchman's breeches, goldenseal,
twinleaf, lily-leaved twayblade, trillium,
ginseng, or jack-in-the-pulpit anywhere else.

Your piece of the woods is rare and valuable
as it is, standing, and we want to encourage
you to keep it that way.

Jennifer and I would like to invite you to
our place to talk about this matter. We'll make
a lunch with freshly baked bread.

Respectfully,
Mark and Jennifer

Chapter Five

IF I HAD BEEN IN A CAR, I would not have noticed the possum's expression. Recently hit on a road just west of Wilkesboro, North Carolina, the possum offered up a look of resistance. There seemed to be two extremes: going so fast you couldn't see the dead animals on the road or going so slowly that you adopted their expression.

During breaks, I scribbled diligently in my notebook, wanting to communicate everything I saw. To what result, I wondered. That I didn't know this answer compelled me to record everything, in search. I no longer wrote while unicycling, preferring instead to keep my arms out like oars in the air.

Just past the Kerr Scott Dam and the first hemlock trees I'd noticed in North Carolina, I talked with an old beekeeper sitting on a truck tailgate. He told me about five big tulip poplar that had been recently cut down. He was sitting there, he said, trying to get used to not seeing them.

I could, if I went slowly enough, develop an eye for what was no longer there, such as those tulip poplar. Yet it occurred to me that there were limits, too, to slowness on a unicycle, that the pace should inch just ahead of sorrow. As I headed west, toward a blurred outline of the Appalachians, I wondered if, in fact, there was a correlation between slowing down and increasing awareness. An answer that surfaced—that awareness and velocity weren't directly correlated but that someone going quickly may notice different kinds of things than someone going slowly—startled me. What then would be an optimal pace? If my sole aim were slowness, I could go more slowly walking. As an added bonus, the world would be less wavy. I still couldn't answer the cheerleader's question about why I was on a unicycle. Not that she was waiting to find out.

In a couple of days I found myself inside the Appalachian Mountains, on the way to the home of Mel Resfield, my North Carolina contact. The Roby Martin Road in the Pisgah National Forest had steep ups and downs, slowing considerably the already negligible progress I'd make in a day. Going uphill, I would walk. Downhill, I'd ride. A horseback rider passed me and informed me that I was doing it the hard way.

One night I camped on a flat-surfaced boulder jutting into a river. There, water crashed against rock. If I looked at the river in a particular way, I'd find myself traveling upstream. Kneeling, I leaned over the rock and dipped my plastic water carrier into the river—in an instant it was full. On the other side, multiple rhododendron blocked my vision, keeping it at the bank. A leaning hemlock almost touched the current.

Dusk came. I lit a fire and cooked rice and thought of another principle for *A Unicyclist's Guide to America*: Relax the emphasis on arrival.

Yet was that a valid way to travel, to live?

Questions came and left. I felt that my body was getting stronger.

I'd always been in awe of kids at school who knew exactly what they wanted to be when they grew up. A doctor, a lawyer, an executive, a teacher. The only time I knew this answer for myself was when I was five years old, when I announced my intention of becoming an archeologist. In the years that followed I must have become less decisive.

I dreamed that night I was helping a woman push a car down the road. She was pedaling it like a bicycle, and I was pushing it. When I saw a unicycle lying in the middle of the road, I told her to swerve around it.

I woke up to a cold morning. A heavy dew settled on everything except the rock, which curiously stayed dry. I walked away from that camp, the sound of water on rock disentangling itself from me until I was left by myself, loose on the road.

The road that day turned from a rough-grade gravel to a finer, almost sandy gravel. I pedaled on this finer road into a bottomland forest with several huge walnut trees. The wooded valley ended, and the road swung up sharply to the left. Reaching my left hand behind me to hold the seat, I stepped to the ground and began to push my unicycle up the hill. The road quickly swung back to the right, continuing to climb. I stopped and looked at the map: Globe Mountain. I didn't see any more black walnut, but against the mountain were white and red oak, maple, hickory, dogwood, redbud, ash, and a few beech.

I sat on a log. Downhill from me a beech had a huge hole in its trunk. The sun had illuminated part of the hole. Perhaps at a certain position during the year, at a certain time during the day, the sun would be able to completely pour itself into the beech, filling it.

Back to walking. The road continued to make hairpin curves, though for me they were gradual. At each turn there was a little crest. On making some of the turns, I would notice power lines unhaltingly climbing the mountain. The peak, finally. I took my pack off and climbed on top of a huge boulder where I stood among beer bottles. I stared as the mountain dropped, rolling, to a distant valley. Except for the slash under the power lines, the whole area was forested, with no visible houses. I was breathing hard, but not tired—happy, actually, to have put forth some effort to be where I was.

Although going down the mountain I was tempted to mount my unicycle, the slope was too steep—I didn't trust my legs to hold back the wheel. I saw more beech and maple and less oak. Sometimes the road didn't turn fast enough to stay fully out of the mountain, and I looked up then to see overhanging rocks. These places were cool and drippy like caves; I sensed trees growing above my head. Taking me in and letting me go in this way, the mountain escorted me to the bottom.

That afternoon, after following the Johns River and a gravel road that ended at the foot of a mountain, I arrived at Mel Resfield's house. A bearded young man opened the door of the small A-frame. I'd traveled nine days already.

Mel put me up for two days, during which it rained hard. Rather than hiking as we had planned, he showed me past issues of *Katuah,* a journal of the southern Appalachians that he edited and illustrated. Though thankful for a roof, I became cramped and progressively hungrier as time went on. Our meals of tofu and wintercress did not fill my stomach, even when I secretly supplemented with the last spoonfuls of peanut butter from my jar. With an income of just $2,000 a year, Mel was essentially living off the land. His girlfriend had recently left him. Perhaps she had been starving, I speculated.

Finally, the rain stopped, and I woke up one morning to see big snowflakes dallying in the sky. After two days of not moving, I was anxious to go, regardless of the colder temperatures. Mel gave me a bag of dried apples and a couple of pillowcases to make my unicycle seat softer. I left my split peas with him. I put on a blue sweater, an orange hat, and gloves, and took off, pedaling, the large, cool flakes hitting my face.

~

She chose to attend my solar cooker workshop. When I had people introduce themselves, I found out that she had been to Nicaragua as a volunteer and had built a solar cooker that would not cook food and would not, in fact, even warm water. Afterward, the kids had played funeral with it, using it as a coffin. A situation as improbable as a fairy tale had materialized before me: an attractive woman needing advice about how to cook food with sunlight.

I'd spend quite a bit of time worrying about how someone without a career who had wobbled across much of the country could ever be attractive to anyone, and I'd figured the odds of meeting someone interested in the skills that I had were impossibly slim. The story of Steve McPeak came to mind. In 1965 Steve McPeak was a university student in Wilmore, Kentucky. On campus one day, he saw someone riding a unicycle, which in itself fascinated him. Then the unicyclist stopped to talk to a pretty woman, rocking his wheel back and forth to stay balanced, and McPeak was overcome; he decided then and there that he would not only learn to ride a unicycle but would become the best unicyclist in the world.

The next year he rode a twenty-foot-tall unicycle. In 1968 he unicycled 186 miles without dismounting, this during a larger two-thousand-mile journey from Chicago to Las Vegas. In 1969 he rode a thirty-one-foot-tall unicycle across a tightrope. Then, on April 3 of that year, he carried his bride, Connie Fullerton, while unicycling on a high wire. They made it from one platform to another and were married while a crowd below watched.

I'd read about Steve McPeak after my journey and was startled by how his story resembled some of my daydreams as I unicycled long distances—not because I had a desire for such stunts, but because the mind, to keep itself off of slowly moving ground, sometimes would shed weight like a dandelion going to seed and head in any direction. A balancing technique, a response to a mile marker.

I would become, I thought, the best solar cook in the world. Hopefully, she would be most hungry on bright, sunny days.

My chance to talk with her after the workshop was cut short by someone needing advice on a solar food dryer. I didn't see her again until the end of the day, during the community games. In one of them, the men walked in the smaller of two concentric circles, choosing partners. I was reminded of junior high dance class, when I had attained levels of fear and anxiety previously not experienced in my life.

SLOWSPOKE

But now I would prove that I could gain a measure of bravery, given time.

My hand went out hesitantly to Jennifer of Nerinx, Kentucky. She took it.

Chapter Six

THE WIND CAUGHT MY PACK as if it were a sail. For a moment I was startled, thinking I hadn't attached my sleeping bag. But it was there—my pack, virtually foodless, was just light. The wind did its part to move me, sometimes in the direction I wanted to go. I was tousled and happy and looked up at times to see blushes of red and purple in the woods. Up close to trees, I couldn't see any color, but from a distance it was obvious they were changing. I couldn't gauge my speed with a number, but I felt that I was traveling as fast as spring was arriving. I'd stopped thinking about ending my travels.

The roads were flat for about six miles before they turned uphill. Even after almost two hours of exercise, I had no urge to take off my sweater and hat and gloves. Blowing snow enshrouded the mountaintops. I climbed maybe three or four miles to a community called Gragg: a few houses, a church, a cemetery, and a closed store with an "Open" sign hanging on the door.

After Gragg the climb became steeper and more winding, and the wind batted snowflakes. The sky was curiously blue, somehow unrelated to the tumult of snow. As I climbed, the wind grew stronger and louder. On one side of the road I could see the trunks of trees, and on the other I was face to face with their swaying tips. I continued up. The wind began to hit me with little warning, just an instant after I heard its roar through the trees and saw saplings looped to the ground. I was pushed off balance and had to hold tight to my unicycle, which the wind tried to steal. For the first time I wished my pack were weightier—especially when I followed a long curve in the road, heading up another steep grade, and the wind came from behind, slamming against me. I lurched forward.

I stopped to take a mental check: backpack, sleeping bag, unicycle, canteen. I had everything but nothing seemed secure. The canteen had turned loud, like footsteps against my chest, and I knew ice was forming inside it. I continued on.

At last I saw a wavering stop sign that signaled not so much that I ought to stop (how should I react to a wavering stop sign?) but more importantly that I had reached paved road 221, the top of the mountain.

I attempted to ride my unicycle, but the wind pushed me back to the ground. So I walked, sometimes leaning into the wind. I needed to get my other jacket on, but the cost of stopping and taking my gloves off so I could rummage seemed too great.

In a mile I passed the Blue Ridge Parkway, closed for the season, and shortly afterward the entrance to Grandfather Mountain, also closed. That others arrived here effortlessly and were still awarded nice views struck me as unfair. I headed toward an overlook, but turned around, choosing to focus on arrival. Then my backpack fell to the ground. Had it been blown off? A historical plaque was next to me. I read it like a tourist. Apparently, a French naturalist, André Micheaux, had explored this area in the eighteenth century. I was over six thousand feet.

I sat down and studied my backpack—a screw had come out from a joint in the framing. I was forced then to take off my gloves. I removed a screw from the framing in a place where it wasn't crucial and put it in the loose joint, turning the tap as far as I could with my red fingers.

In a few minutes I began walking down the other side of the mountain. By increments, the severity of the wind lessened. But without it as strongly against me, I felt colder for some reason. Parts of my face burned and parts of it were numb. My canteen with its frozen water occasionally beat against my chest.

In three miles I reached the town of Linville, North Carolina.

Crusted by snow and ice and watery-eyed from the wind, I walked into the warm, still air of a convenience store. A cashier stared at me. "What's the weather?" I asked. My mouth had a hard time formulating the words.

"Just like this," she said.

"When is it going to get warmer?"

She didn't know.

Outside, I glanced at the town, which appeared to have everything I needed: a grocery and a motel. I walked across the street to the motel. I had gone thirteen miles. When the motel clerk handed me a pen, my shocked right hand came so slowly around it that it must have seemed like I had forgotten how to write. I choked back a giggle.

It wasn't until I was in the room and the television told me that the temperature was dropping to a single digit and the wind chill was way below zero that I began to shiver. I moved from sitting on the bed to sitting directly on the heating vent. There, gradually, with heat rising through my body, the anxiety I'd developed during the day loosened its grip. I moved to the bed when I feared my pants were starting to burn and wrapped up in a blanket. I'd never appreciated a motel room as much, its instant warmth, comfort. Yet I found myself becoming sanguine about the blizzard too, how linked it was to the room, to my feeling of thankfulness. This shouldn't happen often, I thought.

Swirling weather patterns on the map bored through the southern Appalachians. There had been gusts up to eighty miles per hour.

My unicycle was currently upright, leaning against the door, dripping. It had been pushed for several miles during a blizzard. I thought of it then as a pet. Why couldn't my mind rest on the thing without thinking of it as something else?

I got tired of the weather channel, turned it off, and resumed the study of my unicycle. I was determined to see it for what it was.

Instead I saw a seahorse. I attempted to focus, then, on my

backpack. It still had the piece of reflective tape across its width—something I hadn't thought of; Daddy, when we had finished packing that night by candlelight, had produced it and placed it across the pack. In the morning he and Mama had accompanied Trina and me out of the cabin and down the wooded lane to our car to see us off.

It could be an eggbeater as well. I was staring at my unicycle again.

Some people looked at my unicycle and—judging from their vocal reactions—clearly saw the absence of a wheel. It would also be possible, you would think, to see the existence of a wheel.

⌒

The surveyor's tape is gone now. Its absence is an immense improvement, like the deletion of an ill-fitting sentence in an otherwise beautiful paragraph. By beautiful I mean something allowed to become fully realized—a hickory leaf, for example, emerging after an uninterrupted process. This hickory had surprised us with a false bud opening. The buds had become puffy with air pockets and had then unfolded, petal by petal, yet these petals were not yet the leaves (patience!), but the protective sleeves that opened like parachutes.

With its color coming out of nowhere, with no connection to what had gone on before or to what would happen in the future, the surveyor's tape had stymied the transformation of the world.

Trina saw the problem immediately when I showed her the tape. Braver than I (though I did remove a couple of the closer ones), she walked down the entire line like an eraser, cleaning the woods of every piece of orange. Now their path (for what, a logging road?) is gone (though still probably marked in their minds), and the only interruption to the shimmering greens and silvers is the occasional white pedestal of the dogwood suspended here and there in midstory. And the dogwood blossoms are more a subtext than an interruption. Unlike the tape, they were being transformed themselves, starting out creamy as tree leaves unfolded from buds and becoming white at the peak of their blossomhood, as leaves were spreading to maturity.

The people who placed that tape hadn't known the way here, at least as I had learned it.

Shortly after moving into our log cabin, I began taking long hikes. For those who would find it suspect that I had not left home at this point, I would argue that, on a miniature scale, I was leaving home, discovering the terrain beyond my immediate home, trying to fit my home into a larger context. I was especially interested in finding big trees.

This entire area north of Frankfort used to be sheep country. Virtually all of it had been logged to create pastures. Now the pastures have grown back, the early successional cedar the dominant species in many areas but hardwood gaining good footing in others. In my family's new land, half the slopes were cedar, half hardwood. I combed our property, finding the tallest trees—one of them a white oak over a hundred inches in circumference at chest height. I suggested that we circumambulate our property every year, measuring these trees. Now every year on New Year's Day we take what we call "The Chosen" hike, a notebook and tape measure on hand. With all of us now married and my sisters with two kids each, the hike has become bigger and represents three generations—yet we still cheer when the circumference number is higher than the previous year and groan a bit on the rare occasion it declines, lamenting our lack of scientific discipline.

After my rough inventory of our land, I headed into the state wildlife management area and explored the draws emptying into Brammell Branch. In one of them I discovered a red oak twice as big as the biggest tree on our property, a true giant— but a lonely one, apparently, given the small girths of the trees around it. It had once stood alone on a hillside pasture. The discovery of this tree marked the second phase of my quest: I wanted to find a community of these trees, a stand of old growth.

I studied the property maps of our area that showed tree cover, and I planned hikes in uninhabited areas that would keep me in the woods. I often would hike on rainy days, for I liked knowing that I was probably the only one in the woods. I had a preference, too, for fog and mist. Even a young cedar stand in these conditions had the feel of a deep, long forest.

Our area was sparsely populated but not wild. Yet if you did as I did and always stayed in the woods or in overgrown fields (those with saplings at least twenty feet tall, my rule) and always changed course to avoid clearings that could potentially open a view of a barn or a house or a road, a wilderness, nonetheless, could be found. With every hike, the woods around our cabin grew in my mind in size, and human encroachments into it became fewer and fewer.

One day I made it to Long Branch and discovered numerous tall standing trees and a downed tree as big as the old growth oak. On my next hike, I crossed Long Branch and explored the other side. Soon I was walking up a slope into a woods that made me feel as if I were on my knees. Surrounding me stood trunks that were branchless for dozens of feet above my head, a canopy even higher above.

I judged these trees to be twice as tall as the average for our area. As sunlight can change depending on the time of day or on other conditions, such as being sprayed out between two black clouds, those tall trees altered space and time, and I walked in awe among them.

Now on my hikes I would always come here. When I sensed one of the wood's edges, I would turn and go back deep inside. Years later, I would be surprised to discover that this patch of forest that grew as I wandered in it was only fifteen acres.

On one hike, however, I stepped over a sagging strand of barbed wire and out of the old forest, into an abandoned field. My heart thumped as if I'd crossed an international boundary. No house or barn. The field had not been mowed for five years or so. Fescue, lespedeza, blackberry, multiflora rose, and greenbrier grew around emerging saplings: cedar, persimmon, plum, locust, Osage orange, redbud, oak, and ash. The young field was surrounded by woods. Next time, I thought, I could skirt this field for the woods at its far end. I'd connect my piece of old growth with another stand, just beyond this field, hopefully. The prospect that I was standing at the exact site where my future wife and I would build a house did not, of course, occur to me.

Now I can see the frightening symmetry of it all: that my hopeful meanderings as a young man would lead me here, at the edge of what we now know to be the oldest stand of woods in a several-county area; that the thud of my heart on crossing that barbed wire, on leaving the forest for the field, is the same thud I feel now in my chest, crossing the other way, into this forest that had been so recently infiltrated by bright orange.

Chapter Seven

"YOU AIN'T GOING NOWHERE," a Tennessee man told me. "I seen you yesterday down by the river where I live."

He had stopped his car and rolled down his window to share this thought with me. Just as abruptly, he then turned his car around and left, heading in the direction he had arrived.

Being the only words spoken to me that day, they, unfortunately, made an impression. I attempted to dislodge them, and if I had not drawn a blank on where I had been in the last few days since the blizzard on Grandfather Mountain and the motel in Linville, I might have been able to forget them immediately. But for the moment I knew nothing, and the man's statement returned unbidden.

Details of my recent travels slowly arrived: a restaurant meal in Elk Park; a visit to an upholstery shop in Roan Mountain, Tennessee, where I bought a thick piece of foam for my unicycle seat, and the proprietor expressed her opinion that I wouldn't survive the week traveling as I was; the discovery that my squeeze-sip canteen was leaking and the purchase of a new one in Erwin, Tennessee.

"You ain't going nowhere."

I'd set up my tent one night in a nice elderly couple's yard, and it snowed an inch during the night; in the morning my movements had to be shrunken, for touching the tent sides would set loose a shower of icy drops. When I had climbed out of the tent, my hosts greeted me, visibly relieved I hadn't perished overnight. They fed me a huge breakfast.

I'd pedaled by Unicoi (Cherokee for "beautiful valley") and along the Nolchucky River, probably where the "you-ain't-going-nowhere" man had seen me first. According to him, I should have been, by now, much farther beyond the Nolchucky. Someone had spoken to me yesterday as well, as I was pedaling on Highway 107. I'd looked up to see an old couple standing motionless by a pickup truck, some snow falling. They had reminded me of Grant Wood's *American Gothic*, and I had the distinct impression, drawing near to them, that I was about to be scolded. However, they only wanted to wish me good luck as I traveled. "We're the Meeks," the husband said. "We like to say that 'the Meeks shall inherit the earth.'" They both smiled.

"The Meeks shall inherit the earth." I would supplant "you ain't going nowhere" with "the Meeks shall inherit the earth." And I knew nothing about the Meeks.

The weather began to warm up in the afternoon, but the traffic turned bad. Just past Chuckey, Tennessee, I came to 11E, an extremely busy road that I needed to cross. For several minutes I stood facing the grain of heavy traffic. Finally there were no cars. With my backpack making me feel like a turtle on the road, I walked across.

∽

We had been alerted to another potential danger. Our local water district announced its intention to put a water line up our road, which is narrow and hilly and passes by only a couple of residents who would want to be hooked up. Fearing that city water would usher in development, we attempted to alter the project. Jennifer and I, along with members of my family and a couple of neighbors, attended the water board meetings once a month, arguing in favor of an alternative: that with a fraction of the allotted money, every house on the road could have a rain water collection and purification system, coupled with modern, water-efficient appliances.

Our proposal was voted down, and pipeline construction was scheduled to begin.

Of course our fear of what a water line would bring has already been realized with Mr. Gregory's logging and subdivision plan.

I wonder now if I could have communicated more clearly the pleasure of harvesting the rain. I could have mentioned our system: that water slides off a metal roof into gutters, through a downspout, and into a roof washer. The first chamber of the roof washer screens out any big debris, such as leaves, before the water enters the larger second chamber. Here, the water must rise to a certain level (thus allowing smaller particles to settle) before passing through a cotton-like filter that removes any foreign matter that might remain. Finally, the water flows in a pipe through the cellar wall and into our stainless steel cellar tank. We use this water for washing and pass it through a ceramic filter for drinking.

If we are in our bed, I might have added, which is close to the cellar door, we can hear first the rain on the roof, then minutes later trickles of clear water into our tank. The feeling is the same, I could have pointed out, as pulling a carrot out of the ground, or having sunlight stream into the house in the winter.

~

Rain splashes specks of soil onto the spring greens that haven't yet been mulched. In other places in our well-drained garden, it leaves less of a trace. The garden sits on a knoll, the surrounding field sloping away from it in every direction. Raised beds are aligned along the contour of the knoll, and, following them, we are ushered into a semicircular space. In the winter we can look southeast from the garden to see wooded ridge tops, miles away. Now tree leaves keep us local. Lettuces, radishes, asparagus, and peas are ready to eat. Also growing is the over-wintered garlic that will be ready for harvest in July, recently planted broccoli and cabbage sets, onions, and potatoes that have newly risen.

SLOWSPOKE

We plant the potatoes around Easter. After they poke out of the ground, we cover them with an inch or so of compost from our garden's compost pile, which produces about four wheelbarrow loads per year. Then we put six inches of straw on top of the compost. The potatoes will emerge again from the compost and straw and begin to grow vigorously—up to our waists in some years—sending out pale purple blooms. When the plants begin to die back in midsummer, we can reach past the straw into bulging soil (still cool!) and find firm, moist potatoes with translucent skins. We store them in our root cellar and eat them well into the winter. Thus we are brought back to the garden by spring.

We take a crate of seed potatoes from the cellar, walking up the steps that months ago we'd stepped down, and then enter the garden. The potatoes are entangled with sprouts, their bodies soft and wrinkled, and we plant them one by one, four inches deep, into warming April soil.

Chapter Eight

A RECENTLY DIVORCED WOMAN WHO had let me camp in her yard invited me into the house for hot potato soup. Her twin sons, Jason and John, were about seven, and they were still expecting their father to return.

Jason and John and I sat on the living room couch. Electric lights burned my eyes that were now accustomed to candlelight. The mother prepared the soup in the kitchen while talking with a classmate on the phone.

Jason turned on a hand-held computer game and repeatedly pressed a red button, and John flipped the pages of a television guide. "Do you want to hear our favorite music?" John asked, then ran upstairs and brought down his boom box. He put on the Oak Ridge Boys, and we listened to his favorite song about kids and heaven. Then Jason got his boom box. "Why don't you two just use the same stereo?" I asked. "'Cause we like different music," Jason responded, turning on Vanilla Ice. His head went up and down with the choppy beat, and both of them tried to sing along but weren't fast enough.

After supper I went outside to my tent, which I'd pitched in their yard, and, blind, felt my way into it. It was ten o'clock. Though tired, I had a Vanilla Ice song lodged in my head, keeping me awake. I'd grown up with classical music, the only music my mother considered to be worth the electricity. One of the first times I was exposed to a big dose of pop music was the last day of fifth grade, when everyone was allowed to bring in their favorite albums. The effect of that music—mostly disco tunes—on my body was similar to that of a sugar high, and I experienced a concomitant feeling of guilt. My heart raced and my skin flushed. This was probably bad for me, I thought. Everyone smiled and talked, but, stubbornly, I remained expressionless. As a kid, I would never have thought of playing such music as Vanilla Ice at home, partly because I wasn't aware of this music. After fifth grade, though, I would, if everyone in my family was gone, waste electricity and sneak a pop song.

⌣

Our house is lit at night by the warm glow of twelve-volt compact fluorescents, powered by sunlight. The sun also gives us a passive solar gain, a majority of our windows facing south. In the winter we receive light and heat from the sun, which angles underneath generous eaves. These eaves keep the higher summer sun out of the house, and our entrance trees block out the mid- and late-afternoon sun.

Now in midspring, when waxy bright leaves have fully opened around us, sunlight only slips into the house a couple of feet. As its arc gets higher in the sky in these days leading to the solstice, the sun gradually withdraws from our house. Soon the heater will be off.

We hadn't intended to live here permanently. Our twelve-by-twenty-four-foot space (we followed plans for a garden shed) was to be temporary while we built a bigger house. Once, however, we entered this relationship with sunlight, we gratefully committed to settling here. We named our house "Snuggery."

Now an addition to Snuggery, an extension to the east and south, is almost complete. It will double our square footage, a surprisingly modest endeavor since we started with only three hundred square feet. With one wall out between the old and the new, our first glimpses into six hundred square feet give us a feeling of indulgence that statistically we're not supposed to feel. We've preserved the same ratio of window to wall space in the addition, and we've designed comparable eaves. The sun's changing position in the sky, from dawn to dusk and from season to season, will continue to be patterned beneficially inside our house.

Another source of heat is our tiny Vermont Castings wood-burning stove. The stove looked like a toy in the Lexington, Kentucky, show room, but in here it is properly scaled and indeed is actually bigger, now with two warming shelves—expensive extras, but their installation has allowed us to keep more pots on the stove for cooking and heating water.

The stove is a top-loading cast-iron with a glass front. A fire in the morning and the evening is sufficient to warm the house, unless it's cold and overcast. Then we keep it burning most of the day. On sunny days, if our timing is right, the last of the wood has collapsed into embers just as the morning sun is rising. We are transported gradually to the larger glow. Red, orange, then yellow light enters our living space; the wood stove goes out.

If we put a folded towel on top of the water pot, we will have hot water all day, enough for supper dishes or for taking a bath.

Soon we won't have fires at all. The sun or a back-up propane stove will cook our food and heat our water, and we will be that much further into a new season.

⟿

If Mr. Gregory agreed to sell his old woods, we would need to mortgage our property to get a loan. A property valuation official would have to come out, which makes us wonder, among other things, how to describe this multifaceted heating and cooling of our house. Would the property valuation official be flexible with the paperwork?

Would there be room on the appropriate form for shade trees, or the rotation of the planet?

Chapter Nine

UNSURE WHERE I WAS, I walked up to a man working on a pickup, the first person I'd seen all day. Half his body had disappeared under the hood. I had been pedaling on a cow manure-splattered road that was narrowing at an alarming rate. I had seen no signs for three hours.

I waited for him to come out, then told him I was lost. He took the map I gave him, turned it around to orient his world. I watched him slowly touch my map with a greasy finger.

"I can't get you any closer to where you are than that," he said.

I thanked him. I had passed the town of Locust Springs without noticing it.

In a few miles I was on a bridge on top of Interstate 81, stunned by the cars and tractor-trailers roaring under my feet. Though not hit, I felt unzipped after getting to the other side. At least I was no longer lost.

I ate a Reese's Peanut Butter Cup in Burns Market in Romeo, Tennessee, asked about roads that could keep me away from traffic. The checkout woman caught me as I was leaving.

"You left fifty cents on the counter, sugar. Where you are going you are going to need it."

Luckily, 70N and 66N had paved shoulders. At 6:05 p.m. I arrived in Rogersville. Thirty-four degrees and snowing. I walked into the Sandman Motel and asked if they had any unfurnished rooms. All I needed was a windbreak. An elderly woman at the reception desk stared at me and my unicycle. An uncomfortable moment passed. Then she said she would give me a room for free on the condition that I buy myself a hot meal someplace.

I thought about her the next morning as I mingled with heavy traffic on 11W. The act of giving, it seemed to me, was the antithesis of cars and trucks consuming landscapes and throwing them out their back windows. I, too, felt tossed backward with each passing vehicle.

I came upon a couple of men selling manufactured crafts outside the little town of Bean Station. They told me that there was a detour up ahead, but they did not know if that applied to me. When they asked how fast I could go, I said I went a little faster than a walk.

"You start going down the mountain to Tazewell, hell, you can go fifty miles per hour," one of the guys said.

I looked at him. "What do you think I do," I asked. "Coast?"

What they didn't know was that you must keep your feet on the pedals, which are directly connected to the wheel. If the wheel moves, the pedals move. You had to stay with the wheel the whole way. If you took your feet off the pedals, it would only be a fraction of a second before you found yourself on the ground. The only brake on a unicycle is the backward pressure placed on the pedals. Fifty miles per hour!

I didn't follow the detour signs and chose instead to slip between a strainer of orange and black barrels that kept the cars out. A road to myself! Nonetheless, I stayed on the shoulder to keep in the habit. After pedaling uphill for maybe a mile, the reason the road was closed became readily apparent: there was a crevasse up ahead the size of a mountain's shadow. As I got closer I made out construction workers on the other side, laughing.

"I can see why the road is closed," I yelled.

"You lost your other wheel," someone responded.

They motioned that I could cross on the side. When I got over I thanked them for not making me turn around. One of them asked why in the world I wasn't at least on a bicycle, and I told him I liked having two free hands. Enjoying the interruption, the workers stared at me as if I were pure fiction. The operator of a gigantic dump truck even got out of his machine to listen.

"What about brakes?" someone asked.

"There are no brakes on these things," I said. "That's why you saw me coming up the hill."

"He's nuts, just plain nuts," I heard one of them say as I left, pedaling up a long, gradual hill. Their stares at my back, I pedaled beyond the point at which I would normally take a walking break, waiting to dismount my unicycle until I imagined I was so small in their eyes that I was about to disappear.

I walked to the top of the hill, which merged with the detour traffic, took a break at a roadside scenic overlook rest stop. No one was there. The view of hills and towns and woods and farmland was dizzying. Where had I started in the morning? The Sandman Motel. Rogersville. I wasn't sure, in that huge vista, which town Rogersville was. And the day before? That was harder. Oh yes, I had stayed in the yard of that recently divorced woman. At a certain point in your travels you would not be able to remember every step of the way. You would look behind you and be surprised.

⌐

Though years have passed, it only seems like a short while ago that I climbed down from my loft in my parents' log cabin on April 20, 1997, the morning after the Cedar Ring Congress and five years after my unicycle journey. I literally climbed down, for recently we'd replaced our board ladder with a trunk from a standing dead cedar we found in the woods. Originally we'd sawed the climbing branches off at a good distance from the trunk, thinking it would be more aesthetically pleasing, more tree-like, but we soon discovered that the branches with their artistic lengths were absurdly impractical in our small cabin, and we had to cut them down again to regain square footage.

I stepped to the cabin floor. Everyone was fixing breakfast. That morning I would write Jennifer. Though the cabin had no interior walls or rooms, we each had our own space near enough to a window to read or write. I would sit at one end of the table my father had made by gluing together small blocks of walnut discarded from a trophy factory.

The table swayed slightly. That would enable it to survive an earthquake, my father would say. Then, as now, leaves had been born from branch ends—and in the attempt to see as far as her reaction to my letter, I would get only to the chinquapin oak and persimmon. Nonetheless, at a table that could withstand an earthquake, I wrote a letter with one sentence stretched like a winter glance through the woods, into an open area I did not know, asking if I could see her again.

⌒

According to the roadside stand fellows, I could pedal fifty miles per hour down this mountain that now unraveled before me. Another principle for *The Unicyclist's Guide to America* would be for unicyclists to not even think about fifty miles per hour. I did, however, imagine myself, as the sun dropped, to be part of much larger revolutions, as long as they did not gather too much speed. Lean back, slow the pedals. At the bottom I looked unsuccessfully for camping spots. Too crowded. The traffic got heavier. Dusk. A car coming toward me slammed on its brakes. I saw it, as it was passing me, make a U-turn on two wheels. Its tires screeched. The maneuver demonstrated both how much quicker it was to turn on two wheels rather than four and how it was possible for a vehicle without a gas cap to pour gas on asphalt. Had I caused this maneuver? I wanted to be invisible. As it passed me again going the other way, I saw three men inside looking ecstatic and terrified. They raised their sloshing beer bottles to me. I couldn't match their salute, but I nodded.

In different circumstances, a transition from four wheels to two wheels would have pleased me, but the way it was done that evening unnerved me.

The sky darkened, and the paved shoulder merged with the main road of whizzing vehicles. I had no other choice but to get off my unicycle and walk by broken bottles at the side of the road, just feet away from getting leveled by the American mainstream. Around the next bend, I saw a motel. Okay, I'd spend more money. My whole body relaxed. I had developed no real intellectual framework for rejecting motels that appeared in front of me like gifts.

I picked up the next morning where I had left off—pushing my unicycle on a gravel shoulder on the side of a heavily traveled road. I willed each car to pass safely. Not to engage in this mental activity, to allow free-ranging thoughts, would seem too dangerous. So I maintained mental discipline: my backpack, my wheel, my footsteps, my mental traffic shield. Seven miles passed. Then the shoulders were small but paved. I rode a little. I learned how to tighten my feet to the pedals when I heard a truck coming, prepare myself for its gust. Mostly I walked. I passed a store named "Get-It-N-Go."

The road cut through a mountain about midday, and finally there was no traffic. Water spurted from one of the cut rock faces, and I walked over to it, continuing to relax. It dawned on me that the road took us through what used to be a whole mountain, where that water, hidden, had been a secret. I caught some in my canteen. That the ending of its privacy hadn't changed it helped me cope with the day. Even now, after being blasted into public view, the water flowed down the rock face, into the road gully, with no greater urgency than before.

I pedaled on. In a Harrogate Shoney's, a waitress asked me if I were in a race. I told her I wasn't, but I liked the assumption that there was another unicyclist out there.

Though uncomfortably full after their all-you-can-eat buffet, I was excited about arriving in Kentucky that afternoon. I asked a couple of construction workers outside the restaurant how far it was to Middlesboro. They pointed to a mountain and laughed. I pedaled in that direction until the road got too steep, then walked to the top, which was steep but not that far. I rested by a historical plaque. In 1750 Dr. Thomas Walker reached the Gap, which he named for the Duke of Cumberland, son of George II.

The road had no shoulder going downhill, but it swung back and forth so abruptly that it slowed the cars enough for me to feel safe riding. The simple act of reducing your velocity, it occurred to me, could eliminate a significant number of sharp turns in the world.

At the bottom the road became wide and straight and cars were able, once again, to rush past me. Soon I was in Middlesboro. Kentucky! It began to rain hard and I didn't care. I let myself get wet. I'd made it to Kentucky from North Carolina. I would get a motel to celebrate.

Chapter Ten

HER LETTER HAD COME QUICKLY in response to mine. Daddy gave it to me at the Duck, one of the few flat, cleared places on the homestead, where the cars were parked. We had named it "The Duck" after a block of wood my sister Chris's fiancé had carved into the shape of a duck. It sat in a small pool of purple irises. Go a half mile in one direction from the Duck and you would arrive at the mailbox and the nearest paved road. A half mile in another direction would take you to the cabin. A mile in yet another direction—down an abandoned county roadbed—would take you to a wildlife management area, where a few unfortunate guests over the last few years had found themselves.

As was my custom with important mail, I didn't read it right away. Had unicycling across the country taught me this restraint? Or was this quality a prerequisite for embarking on a unicycle journey?

"Open it up," Daddy had said. But no, the letter would wait until that night when I was in my loft, a candle lit.

Meanwhile, I would go through the day anticipating her letter. My body would move fluidly; I would get caught by something beautiful, a locust blossom, a branch fallen across a mayapple patch; I would get one and a half or two sections of fence done instead of one. I would remember what I could of her—her straight blond hair, blue eyes, slender figure, lack of make-up. The image of her handwriting on the envelope would stick with me—how small it was, how neat, so different from my own.

Nothing seemed familiar at first when I opened my eyes in a
Middlesboro motel room. I had slept fourteen hours. Gradually
one thing, then another (I am traveling on a unicycle!) came to
me until I realized I had traveled from north-central North Carolina and at the moment was in Middlesboro, Kentucky. I
opened a new map across the motel bed. I had no idea where I
was going. West, I supposed. The Burns Market checkout
woman in Romeo, Tennessee, had told a customer as I was leaving the store that I had come clear from North Carolina and was
going plumb to California on that one wheel. I told myself not
to allow another person's perception of where I was going to
significantly alter the course of my journey.

Impulsively, I took out my money and counted it. I'd gone
through half of the $500 already. If I could find some quiet
roads, I could camp more, save on motel costs. I'd been encoun-
tering too much traffic. It seemed to me I should be able to focus
on something other than keeping myself alive.

It would take a day without traffic. Without cars and trucks
passing me, I could, instead of assimilating drivers' adjectives
for me—slow, wobbly, wild, backward, foolish—let other de-
scriptions come to me, if others were out there. The progress I'd
make in a day would be just fine. And if I decided not to make
any progress, not to be any farther west at the end of the day
than at the beginning, if it seemed right to travel in the manner
of a leaf descending to the ground, then there would be no motorists to make a mockery of my rhythms.

Fresh with this vision of unicycling heaven, I turned to the
map before me. Kentucky and Tennessee were fibrous with
roads. The gray ones were the smallest; the red ones were the
state roads; and the blue highways, wide like varicose veins,
were the interstates. I looked more closely, saw that the only
road going west out of Middlesboro was, luckily, a gray one.

I pedaled out of town on a sidewalk between pruned trees

and storefront windows. The town dwindled away, and I was left on this road that would last a while in Kentucky, then dip into Tennessee. In a few minutes I came to a coal mine. Coal trucks ground past, and black dust thickened the air. A long conveyor came out of a mountain, depositing coal onto a pile; and the pile had acquired the same shape as the mountain it had been ripped out of. I wondered if mining operations affected the grip of trees against a mountainside. Just a single rock could throw me off.

For an instant a goldfinch with its bright yellow body and black stripes on its wings blocked out the entire operation.

And I understood a little better my role as I traveled. I was to do the opposite of what a coal mine did.

A coal truck, for no very necessary reason, blasted its horn as it passed me. Yet how could I put a mountain together?

Shortly past the mine entrance, the road turned steeply up-hill. I walked, pushing my unicycle, truck blasts still in my head though trucks no longer passed me. In a few minutes I gathered enough height for the road to have steep drop-offs at one side. Looking down, I saw trash everywhere. Even appliances—a pale yellow refrigerator, a white electric range—had been tipped over the embankment, ultimately disgracing the tree or boulder that would stop their tumble.

Looking uphill was more satisfying, for there were sixty-foot beech and maple unadorned with junk. I discovered a spring rushing from a crack in a cut rock face. I stopped there, drank, continued on.

I wanted to avoid two extremes as I traveled: either dwelling exclusively on what was ugly or exclusively on what was beautiful. I had to find my way out of both.

I made it to the top, then followed the road down the other side of the mountain into a valley flooded with shadow. I left the blacktop and climbed up a narrow ridge, letting trees gather between me and the road. I stopped by a large beech, rolled out my sleeping bag. The ridge was too narrow for a tent. After eating, I stretched out and stared at the beech tree. In the last light of the day, red spiders moved about the trunk. Farther up, branches tangled in a half moon. Lightning streaked the southwest sky. I pulled a sheet of plastic over my bag, closed my eyes.

I dreamed I was reading in a lot a carnival had recently vacated. Someone had pulled away my game trailer. A teenage girl was next to me, also with a book. She repeated simple sentences aloud, trying to learn grammar. I asked her if she wanted anything else to read. She didn't answer me. I ran down the street to where my bookcase was, but when I saw it on a street corner with only a couple of books in it, I realized I was leaving town. Close to the bookcase were cardboard boxes, some of them packed with stuffed animals. I wondered about the others; I looked for my college grammar text. When I returned to where the girl had been, I found only her mother and a man who said he was a micropsychologist.

Big scattered drops hit my plastic covering during the night. It worked well. Maybe I didn't need a tent. I looked up at the beech. The red spiders were gone.

⌒

The game trailer that Daddy operated for my Uncle Ray was called a Pokerina. We learned what that was that first summer, when Mama drove my sisters and me up to visit him at the Jacktown Fair in Jacktown, Pennsylvania. When we arrived, he was open and hurried us into the trailer. Suddenly, we found ourselves facing a crowd, poker machines in front of us, and prizes behind us—from plaster cats to "I love you" mugs to black plastic pocket combs, which Daddy liked giving out to big men with wild hair.

"If they want to know how to play," Daddy told us, "just tell them they need jacks or better and deuces are wild."

People put dimes in machines and pressed buttons to stop spinning reels of cards. The better the poker hand they had, the more merchandise coupons they received.

SLOWSPOKE

We only visited Daddy once each summer, always at the Jacktown Fair. One summer he drove home after a fair, surprising us. The fair had been busy. He dumped a huge pile of crumpled cash, mostly one-dollar bills, in the middle of what we called the blue-rug room, got us all to count money.

Surely this meant we were now rich. I'd never seen so much money in my life. But I remember both of my parents becoming quiet when I asked if this was enough to pay our debts.

One summer Daddy made a down payment on the Pokerina, buying it from my Uncle Ray. He would now get all the proceeds from the trailer. The same summer, at the Westmoreland County Fair, two federal agents jumped up in his trailer, told him he had a right to remain silent, arresting him for running a gambling operation. They confiscated his newly bought poker machines.

But luckily not the trailer. The next week he opened up with a balloon game. Kids could throw till they popped a balloon. Prizes every time. The first strands of gray appeared in his hair.

He began finding festivals in Kentucky, then got me a trailer, which I took out infrequently, to make money. I never made as much as I could with it because I never called out to people. I relied on people walking up to the game. Every summer I told myself that this would be the last summer. Yet every summer I continued to take my trailer to festivals Daddy booked for me.

Chapter Eleven

THOUGH WE WAIT FOR A RESPONSE from Mr. Gregory, no letter arrives—and we can't know for sure that a day of waiting will inch us closer to a destination. When I journeyed on a unicycle, I learned not to expect arrivals. At the same time I trusted that I always approached something. Similarly, in the simpler world we had before the surveyor's tape, we would be calmed by the repetition of the seasons, the faith of one thing following in the wake of another. Now, for example, small nuts are forming on our entrance trees; apples on the Liberty, Hubbardston Nonesuch, and Winesap. And soon it will be time to plant sweet potato slips, which we have in a jar of water on a windowsill. The time for planting these slips is in mid-May, after the last chance of cold weather.

Mr. Gregory's letter, by contrast, does not have to arrive as a result of a natural sequence, a call and response. The letter Jennifer and I sent him wouldn't be an act of pollination, of course, nor his the resulting fruit, though we sometimes long for a simpler, more rule-abiding world.

These sweet potato slips form root hairs in the water—remarkable given that just a week ago we snipped the slips from seed potatoes being germinated in a bin of damp sand. Their story begins (or does it end?) in the fall before the first frost, when they are harvested—sometimes as late as early November. We snip the vines, drag them to the compost pile. Then we loosen the bed with a garden fork. The sweet potatoes can grow as long as eighteen inches, sometimes curving at the deep end. We have to pull them with care not to snap them. We put them in a wheelbarrow and transport them to Snuggery. Immediately after the harvest they like being in a warm, dry place for two weeks, so we spread them out in a loft area above the kitchen. After two weeks, in a surprising reversal of preference, they want a cool and damp environment. At this point we transfer them to our root cellar, where they keep all winter, actually gaining in flavor and sweetness in the first couple of months of storage. We put aside several of the potatoes for starting slips. In April we retrieve these seed potatoes from the cellar and place them in a plastic bin with two inches of rock and one inch of water. We place clear plastic over the bin and keep it by a sunny south window. After experiencing first warm and dry and then cool and damp, they now want another possible microclimate: warm and damp.

In a couple of weeks the potatoes will sprout. Then we transfer the sprouted potatoes to damp sand, a nutrient rich medium that promotes slip growth. Finally, we snip off the slips and place them in a jar of water.

I imagine explaining this process, too, to a property valuation official. We are due to have an appraisal, which will help us know what kind of offer we can give to Mr. Gregory. Please note, I'll say, that our house is equipped for storing sweet potatoes and producing slips for planting. I'll point out our house's microclimates and hopefully communicate the satisfaction of using them in food production and storage. And were it not for this particular spring, with its threat to the natural order of our place, it would all be true, and we would look again upon these sweet potato slips with undisturbed love.

⤺

In Jennifer's first letter to me, which I read by candlelight in my loft after everyone had gone to sleep, she invited me to the convent where she was doing a retreat and working as an organic gardening intern. It would be a two-hour trip to the Sisters of Loretto Motherhouse in rural Washington County. I began to prepare my family. I had always had a hard time talking to them about girls, but informing them of an impending trip to a convent to see one was doubly difficult, as Catholicism had fallen out of favor in my immediate family. In his youth, my father had been expelled from seminary after he threw a cherry bomb into the priests' sleeping quarters. That Jennifer was simply doing a retreat and gardening internship at the convent was perhaps too fine of a distinction to make.

"Wouldn't you have better luck going to a dance?" someone asked. I took the teasing. Trina, too, had met someone at the Cedar Ring Congress. Chris had been engaged for a few months.

Though two years older than my sisters, I had a harder time with transitions than they did. It was harder for me than for them to relinquish belief in Santa Claus; to adjust to school and classmates whose lifestyle was so different; to accept puberty; to imagine living away from home, dating, marrying. I'd always approached the next stage of life with diffidence and caution.

Then, as now, a light spring green was encircling us. On a slope where I looked for cedar posts, I spotted dozens of ferns unfurling their green selves—some of them complete ladders, some still balled up, some like commas. Taking them all in, I thought I saw certain individuals move. I paused a second more, then moved on.

∽

I touched the ground by my sleeping bag—slightly wet from the rain. Wet beech leaves stuck to my bedding as I rolled it up. Later that morning, I passed a sawmill with giant logs stacked indiscriminately next to each other, oak piled onto pine, pine onto hickory, etc. The beech tree I'd camped under had been the same circumference as these lot logs. Realizing that, I felt places torn from my spirit.

It began to rain, and like a refugee I pedaled on, gradually leaving the sawmill. I didn't want to be involved in any aspect of society that wrecked places and left people like me feeling threatened, vulnerable. I worried about the prizes I gave away from my game trailer, how and where they were made, what impact they had on people and the land. Maybe in the course of my journey, sorting through all that was ugly, all that was beautiful, I'd find some way to go from one to the other, not tilting irrevocably in either direction, just inching forward. Then maybe it would come to me what I wanted to do.

In Eagan, Tennessee, I walked out of the rain into a post office so small I wondered if it was about to close. The sides of my backpack scraped against the doorframe and once I was inside I had to take the pack off just to turn around. I wrote a postcard home, asking them to send money, general delivery, to Scottsville, Kentucky. Was everybody okay, I wondered. Were they starting to plant the garden? My backpack leaned against one of the corners like another person, dripping. This would be the first spring for my family to live in the log cabin Daddy and I had built. We had pulled out most of the cedar logs for the cabin on a rainy day with an old gray car and a quarter-inch nylon rope. The abandoned county road that bordered our new land was only partly graveled, so we parked our car where the gravel started, facing it downhill. We tied one end of the yellow seven-hundred-foot rope to the car, then threaded it through the woods to various places we'd felled cedar trees. I imagined pulling one of those giant sawmill logs with a quarter-inch rope and decided that it couldn't be done. The cedar we used for building the cabin were only medium-sized; we passed by the biggest. Daddy drove the car, and I guided the log on its erratic journey. The rope would stretch, the log would move a few feet and get caught, I would dig a cedar pole under it and pry it up, and it would jump forward again, a few more feet. If I dawdled in prying the log loose, the rope would break. If the rope stretched a good amount and I did manage to free the log, the log would shoot forward. I'd run to keep up with it, my heart pounding. I thought of it as a sport. Eventually we got walkie-talkies, which theoretically enabled me to tell Daddy—seven hundred feet away—to stop pulling the log if it was caught. The problem was, I needed two hands to use my pry pole as I trotted by the log, guiding it and unjamming it. I'd toss the walkie-talkie in front of me as we went along, so it was only occasionally within reach.

"Deuces are wild," I'd think to myself.

"You'd better stop," I'd tell Daddy, sometimes when I only needed a break. I'd sit down on a rock or a downed tree while my breathing returned to normal. During one of these breaks, I spotted the first wildflower, harbinger-of-spring. I came to learn the whole procession of woodland flowers.

I handed the postcard to the clerk, then took myself and my backpack out of the post office. It was no longer raining. I mounted my unicycle, began pedaling down the road.

Chapter Twelve

A PROBLEM ARISES, I KNOW, in the communication of a simpler life. How could we have more artfully defended this life to the Water Board? And how will we talk to a potential property valuator?

I faced a similar problem soon after my unicycle journey, for I had a hard time ushering people into my recent travels. How did other people talk about unicycling? In our public library one day I looked up "unicycling" and discovered that only one person had chosen to write on the subject. I checked out Jack Wiley's *The Unicycle Book*.

It turned out to be more of a book of facts than I'd wanted, less about the feeling one can get riding a unicycle.

Wiley listed ten things unicycling had to offer. Among them, it was a way to amaze and enchant your friends; it was good training for other sports; it was fun exercise. Yet he said nothing about how it could affect the pace of your life, how it could take you to the edge of one world, tilt you toward another. He offered no warnings.

Wiley wrote that in 1892 Sebastian Merrill Neuhausen was riding a penny-farthing and decelerated too quickly. With this miscalculation, the small wheel in back left the ground, leaving Mr. Neuhausen perched on the single, larger wheel. Whether you would regard this as serendipity or an unfortunate accident, the unicycle was discovered.

It appeared that the unicycle would engender no further discoveries, that the attempt to further divide it might only result in its disappearance. In all likelihood, a more inefficient way to travel would not be invented.

Perhaps, then, what was missing in Wiley's book, and in my portrayal of unicycle travel, was this notion of inefficiency, how linked it could be—understood better perhaps by a child about to enter adolescence, or a middle-aged person taking that first step into old age, or anyone on the cusp of one world, entering another—to danger, joy.

⟿

So maybe we could have more ardently praised inefficiency in front of the Water Board. Of course there is more work involved, we could have said, in harvesting your own water supply, but every step of that process, from the guttering to the piping to the filtering, leads not only to the completion of a rainwater catchment system but also to an infrastructure of pleasure. When we hear, we could have said, the tinkling and splashing of rainwater flowing into our metal tank, we feel pleasure, in part, because of the work done in making that sound possible.

At this point one of the Water Board members would probably say something about getting plenty of pleasure in turning on the faucet.

I'm often at a loss for words when confronted with snide or cynical comments. My hope would be to avoid such a loss for words during an imaginary conversation. Maybe I would just laugh or smile at his comment and continue talking about our system. Another component, I could point out, is our root cellar, which serves both to store root crops and to keep our water supply from freezing. Our eight-by-twelve-foot hole, six feet deep, took me the better part of one winter to excavate using a shovel, an iron pole, a grubbing hoe, and a sledgehammer. I suspect, I would say to the Water Board, that one or all of you might be able to derive pleasure out of a basement you haven't dug yourself, but let me continue with my story. The floor of part of our house covers the cellar, and we enter it via a trap-door and sturdy ladder. As I descend into this new space, I feel lightheaded, the effect of some weight suddenly leaving—in this case, of course, shovelfuls of yellow clay, chunks of limestone rock, gone, my body only going through cool air. To achieve the last seven inches of depth, I had to batter through a limestone rock shelf. Now the last step is luxurious, and I'm standing on the gravel floor, smelling damp earth and rock dust. (A mental note at this point to tell a property valuator that while our house isn't endowed with other dimensions, it nonetheless has depth.)

Now the return: With the first step I'm above the limestone shelf; then I step past that layer of rust-red clay that flaked off like sedimentary rock in flat sheets; then I'm into the realm of blue clay, where, amazingly, root threads from a nearby Osage orange had managed to penetrate; next I'm into yellow clay, where there had been more roots and an occasional big rock; finally, the yellow clay darkens and there are earthworms and grass roots and I complete the last step, now above ground level.

I'm inside our house, next to the foot of our bed, where, as you know, we can hear the tinkling and splashing of water flowing into our cellar tank during a rain.

⌁

On lonely stretches of road, I, to my disappointment, thought almost exclusively about food. In particular, after dipping into Tennessee going west from Middlesboro, I developed a craving for pizza. It began in Morley, where I had intended to eat pizza. When two teenage boys followed me into the pizzeria, however, staring—not asking anything, just staring—and I imagined what my experience would be like with them watching me as I ate, I decided to pass up the chance. The next town, Jellico—although it had a variety of fast food restaurants catering to interstate traffic—had no pizza. There I was soaked by a thunderstorm. Lightning quilted the sky, and the roads, briefly, were rivers. It was really no time to be traveling. Outside town, luckily, there was a campground, and I walked like a leak into the office to check in.

It wasn't until late the next day—after passing through the communities of Newcomb and Capital Hill—that I found a place that served pizza. Up to that point everything reminded me of pizza. A chocolate and peanut butter wafer treat still in its plastic package on the side of the road (which I picked up and ate) reminded me of pizza. Even a beat-up station wagon sitting low to the ground because of the weight of an extraordinarily massive family sitting inside it (all with Slim Jims sticking out of their mouths) reminded me of pizza. Apparently, when traffic was light and I could focus on something other than keeping myself alive, I focused on pizza.

So when I finally sat down to eat pizza in a convenience store deli, I was very happy. Forty miles was a long time for a unicyclist to sustain a craving. I ordered a twelve-inch vegetarian. When I finished that, I felt hungrier, and I thought I had no choice but to order another one, which impressed the store manager. He told me he got full after one that size. He was a big man. The second one didn't have an effect, either. Out of control, I ordered a third pizza. About halfway through it, the first two backed up in my stomach. My whole system braked. I wrapped up the remaining pieces in a plastic bag and after paying for the most expensive meal of my life, walked unsteadily out the door.

At the first house with some land around it, I asked for a place to camp. I must have looked sick. They were kind, let me stay in a field outside their yard.

I went heavily and painfully into my sleeping bag.

Chapter Thirteen

SINCE WE HAVE RECEIVED no response to our letter, we have decided to visit Mr. Gregory. My sister Chris, her husband Joel, and their two daughters, Natalie (age four) and Sophie (age two), were with Jennifer and me in the car as we made the startlingly short drive to his house. We pulled into his driveway. Derelict pieces of farm equipment flanked the gravel road. We were on the ridge top and could see miles of hilly farmland. I felt dizzy. Soon we were pulling in front of a fieldstone house, pretty but for an unkempt appearance. Chest-high weeds hid many of the stones.

Our goal was to again let Mr. Gregory know of our interest in his old woods. And to let him meet us.

To our relief, he was gracious, motioning us inside. Virtually everyone in our county knew Mr. Gregory. It would be safe to say that we were stepping into the house of the most infamous person in the area. Ever since an incident in the early 1980s, when he locked himself up in a Lexington motel room and threatened to commit suicide to protest some aspect of a government tobacco program, he'd been in and out of mental hospitals. He was a known womanizer and gambler and at one point had owned thousands of acres. Land speculation earned him wealth and also trouble with the Internal Revenue Service. Somehow he stayed out of jail. Much of his time was spent in the Philippines, where he owned a high-rise apartment and lived, as the stories went, the life of a playboy.

The inside of his house had as much potential to be pleasing as the outside, yet was as cluttered. Papers, clothes, and snacks were strewn everywhere.

I turned to him and told him I liked the rocks on the outside of his house.

"Come here, young man, I have to show you something."

We all followed him out a door to a long, narrow concrete deck with no railings, possibly the ugliest deck I'd ever seen, but at least one with a view—of the same undulating and populated farmland as we had coming in, as well as the stone back of the house. I noticed that the deck swayed a bit.

"There's only wood under this concrete. I just poured the concrete right over the extended floor joists. Everybody said I shouldn't do it this way, that I needed column supports."

He walked over to the edge and swayed his body.

"Feel that?" he asked.

Well of course we could, for movement had already been detected. Now we felt a little wave of motion that caused us to think of collapse.

So we were relieved to follow him back into the house where we, following his instructions, began clearing space on a couch and a couple of chairs. When Mr. Gregory sat down on an easy chair, the six of us were loosely organized around the oval table that, though practically useless, apparently still had gravitational pull. A wide-screen television playing on a wall thirty feet away flashed its images.

"See this?" Mr. Gregory asked us. He'd picked up a large print of a voluptuous Asian woman. "This is why I keep going back to the Philippines."

He looked younger than seventy-eight, and I wondered if he felt younger. On the table was an opened package of Viagra.

We listened as he talked about his travels and showed us old passports. We asked questions, and he answered us readily. When the phone rang, he told someone to call back later because he was with friends.

As we were leaving, we told him we were still interested in his land and could give him a fair price since there were several of us willing to contribute to the purchase.

"You'd have to have a goldmine to buy it from me in one piece," he said. "What I'd want for it would be too much money just to look at trees. Now before you leave, I want to show you something."

We followed him down a hallway and into a bedroom I figured to be almost the size of Snuggery. A king-sized bed, a bathroom, and a Jacuzzi. Mr. Gregory unfolded the thermal blanket that covered the Jacuzzi, revealing a body of water that seemed equivalent to the amount that our cellar tank could hold. We could make it a little more than a month with the water in this Jacuzzi, I estimated. He flipped a switch and water was blasted across the pool. Natalie and Sophie had never seen anything like this in their short lives and were wide-eyed.

"I got this model," he said, "because of its more powerful jet stream."

~

That same night I had a dream that it was the first normal day after our wedding and honeymoon. Jennifer had gone to work as a developmental interventionist, helping infants and toddlers who had developmental delays. I was in Snuggery, waiting for her return, looking every minute or so up the path where she would come walking. My heart pounded, as if we were about to go on our first date. Yet her return from work and the start of our married life together seemed even more momentous. Then I saw the small blue Toyota the convent had given her as a gift, coming down the path, which was strange because it wasn't possible for a car to get on that path. I ran out to it, intending to wrap my arms around her, welcoming her home. I would tell her that supper was hot in the solar cooker. The car stopped, and I opened the door—and to my fright saw that no one was inside. A song from the radio played, but the words were fading, as if someone were turning down the volume. When the song stopped, the car disappeared—and in its place stood Shadow, our black lab. I was about to look wildly around for Jennifer when Shadow whined. I understood then that I was in danger. So I looked into Shadow's warm, brown eyes. I sank into their hopefulness and generosity.

～

I visited Jennifer for the first time at the convent and then began making that drive once a week. Images swirled in my head during this time, granting me a reckless speed. I attempted landings: on a yellow cardigan one day that tinted her hair a light gold; on our similar temperaments; on our similar trajectories, with her majoring in English at Santa Cruz and volunteering in Latin America and on a continuing search for simplicity and meaning; on a picnic supper by Lake Mary, a creamy hummus before us, the tangy, slightly spicy, nutty flavor that leapt to my brain.

I would return home, sometimes, late at night. One night it was raining when I parked our old gray car at the Duck. I got out, ran to Changing Shack, a bus-stop-like structure that we had clad in slab wood, where boots and jackets were kept.

I pulled on a parka and some rubber boots and stepped back out. The little light at the Duck disappeared as I entered the oak-lined lane back to the cabin, but I knew where to go, how to miss the big puddle at the bottom of Pussy Toes Hill, where to avoid branches.

It was still raining as I made it past Toad Hall, down to the cabin. The dogs didn't hear me as I reached the porch. I stepped inside, where everyone slept, and climbed up the cedar tree to my loft.

～

I would wonder if my family could tell a difference in me while I was seeing Jennifer. Strangely, I didn't want them to see a difference. The same impulse that kept me from after-school activities in high school, or from living on campus at college, or from staying in New York City as a magazine intern, affected me in 1997, and as thrilled as I was, I was also as scared as an eighteen-year-old.

I would best be able to process my visits with Jennifer alone in the field, working on my cedar rail fence.

One such day, while I was digging a posthole, I hit rock and began pounding it with an iron pole. The hole, at times, smoked out acrid limestone dust. I settled into a schedule of rest flanked by bouts of extreme physical exertion.

The rest periods lasted longer. I'd scoop dust and shards and clay chunks from the hole. I'd look out at the hillside across from me, at cedar mixed with the softer greens of new oak, maple, and poplar leaves.

Though I deemed the question too romantically dangerous when I was with Jennifer, I asked it of her now, sitting on the rocky hillside. "How do you want to live?"

I listened, in my mind, to several of her answers. The one that most favored my lifestyle seemed less believable than others.

I stood up and again started pounding my pole against the stubborn rock.

Now I wonder if this fence was worth the effort. Jennifer and I married before I finished it—I'd just made the turn that would bring me around to the very first section—and here is where it stopped, three-fifths finished. Maybe this is just a fence with a very large gate, I sometimes suggest.

The posts and rails are quite weathered now, and those along the north side of the field are green with lichen. I wonder, too, how functional it would have been. With much of it only two rails, a disturbing variety of farm animals would have been able to pass through it, under it, or over it. We would have been left, among all possible farm animals, with only the largest and most sluggish.

Late that afternoon the rock cracked. I kneeled down, reached my hands into the hole, and with the last bit of energy left to me pulled out a thick chunk of limestone, exposing its sharply glittering, blue cut face.

Chapter Fourteen

THE FIELD SPARKLED WITH FROST in the morning—I was glad for the inordinate amount of pizza I'd eaten the day before, which I could no longer feel but imagined had put extra heat in my body. I got up, gathered a few frosty twigs and spent half an hour lighting paper under them before they would burn. I ran out of scrap paper and had to use blank pages from my journal notebook. The strange thought occurred to me that, in doing so, I would reduce the number of experiences I would have on my trip. When at last the water boiled, I poured in two packets of peaches-and-cream oatmeal. The water foamed up to the pot's edge. Soon, eye-level with some of the tallest frozen grasses, I began to spoon hot oatmeal into my mouth. The pot heated my lap.

I'd expected the road to Oneida to be easy; had I been able to lower my expectations for this stretch, I would have been less frustrated. But all of a sudden I found myself assaulted by rushing vehicles, the road no longer having a paved shoulder. I dismounted and began wheeling my unicycle in front of me, feeling foolish. My canteen strap, I noticed, was getting frayed by its metal holders.

After two hours of miserably walking on a gravel shoulder, I finally made it to Oneida. I found a leather shop and walked inside. Would there be a new strap for my canteen? The proprietor showed me a nylon strap that would fit. As I was about to pay for it, he said, "You don't owe me anything. The Lord told me not to charge you." He was, as I found out, a Baptist minister in town. He told me, at length, why he was a Christian.

I listened.

"Can I put my phone number in your book?" he asked.

"Yes."

He looked me steadily in the eye.

"Would you call me if you needed help?"

"Yes." I had the distinct feeling his questions were actually orders.

"It doesn't take much to accept the Lord."

I nodded.

"One thing before you leave," he said. "At the risk of sounding ludicrous, I love you."

I walked away, sweating. Outside Oneida I crossed a barbed wire fence into a field where I finished my pizza. As I ate, I wrapped an old shoelace around the metal clasp on my canteen to prevent it from cutting the new strap. It had slipped my mind to ask the preacher to do something about this problem.

During the day people had told me how treacherous the road was going into Big South Fork National Park. Without thinking, I believed them and dreaded my entrance into the park. Once inside, though, I felt more relaxed than I'd felt all day, the ten-mile-per-hour curves restraining the few cars that did pass. Sometimes cliffs shaded my path. I saw a tulip poplar on a rock ledge, unfurling bright yellow-green leaves at its tips.

With the late afternoon I left the road for the woods. I carried my unicycle. Brushy at the edge, the woods changed farther in, offered tall trees, more spacious growth, the feeling of stepping into an elegant and shadowy room. I took a slant up a small ridge, stopped close to mountain laurel, pine, a big sassafras, and a couple of white oak. The sassafras leaves, which looked like mittens, seemed playful. I'd discovered sassafras trees close to the cabin. If you ripped a sassafras leaf you could smell a spicy lemon scent. Sassafras roots made good tea, which, it was said, could thin your blood. Too much of it, though, it was also said, would kill you.

The backpack off my shoulders, I took my canteen, headed down the slope. A transition in vegetation—oaks replaced by hemlocks—quieted my footsteps. I stepped on brown needles, began to sink slightly with each step. The hemlocks towered above me and darkened the air.

The ground turned soggy. I knelt and smoothed away needles, discovering wet, white sand, which I scooped out. The small hole I made filled with water. I would wait for it to clear.

I heard a waterfall and walked toward it, unsure if I was going in the right direction. I heard it behind me, too. It repeated itself, like hemlock trunks. I went up a runoff branch, careful not to step on any rocks that would make noise. The waterfall was close. I ducked under a hemlock branch, straightened up to see a cliff. And my waterfall: water dripping slowly off a rock ledge. How could a drip sound so loud? I set my canteen under it and waited. Once I'd been in a woods and heard a faint sound that I imagined to be from something loud and dangerous a long way off—only to discover that the sound was within touching distance, two winter-stiff beech leaves tapping against each other.

With a canteen full of drip water, I made my way back to camp, baffled sometimes by rhododendron. I gathered twigs, rolled out my bed. I sat down with my journal.

At dusk I stood up and loudly walked on the forest floor, heading down the ridge on its other side. At the bottom I found more huge hemlocks and another cliff. No waterfalls, but there was a mound of light tan sand at the base of the cliff, the same shape as that conveyor-belt pile of coal outside Middlesboro. I put my hands into it. The particles were so fine my hands sank, almost as if they were going through water. I sat down. How long had it taken cliff, sand, dripping water to make this mound?

Back at my camp I boiled drip water and made rice, ate. Finally I stretched out against the ridge. My eyes closed.

I dreamed that I was with an environmental or social justice group that was very efficient at getting things done. At one point, in a loud voice, I said, "We have got to slow down." Everyone became quiet.

Someone asked if I wanted spring water. I did, but my canteen wouldn't go under the spigot. I looked outside and saw a farm. It began to hail. A cow jumped out of a pond. A kid with bare feet jumped on a pony and began kicking it.

I woke up and remembered where I was and fell back asleep. I was in a car and saw a big fluffy cat turn to get away from me. It ran into the path of another car. I could see terror in its eyes. I sobbed. When my eyes opened, I saw the big sassafras tree. Tears slid down my face.

Dizzy and stunned by dreams, I walked down the slope. Hemlocks rose into a blushing sky. There was clear water in the hole I'd dug. Kneeling, I dipped my cup in the pool and drank. Then I filled my canteen.

The sun turned bright as I pedaled west. It placed my shadow in front of me. I looked like a cartoon. Without words or abstractions, I could see clearly what I was doing, a precise display of my trip. I wished this shadow luck.

꩜

On clear days we look out our kitchen window to see if our solar cooker is facing the sun directly. On a typical sunny day we adjust the cooker every two or three hours. By the end of the day, we're facing west, and the last of the sun is keeping our supper hot.

The thought strikes me that this routine, this arc in our day, can suggest endings and beginnings that are much larger yet, as expected, circular: the passing of one season into another, of youth into middle age, etc. A cynic could point out that it is not cooking with the sun, per se, that ushers in thoughts of one season turning into another, but simply the time it takes for something to cook using this method. An advantage of having traveled on a unicycle is that I'm more immune to such criticism than I would have been. It's second nature now for me to think about supper at the beginning of the day, to look up often at the sky, at any clouds, to be prepared for a shift in the weather, or, if not, the delight of taking out a fully cooked dish at the end of the day. A transition from unicycling to solar cooking is almost seamless.

Our cooker is essentially an insulated box with a glass top. Situated around the glass top are four trapezoidal reflectors that funnel extra sunlight into the box's interior cooking space. Our guests typically do not divine that this contraption is a kitchen appliance, or for that matter, that the yard is a kitchen, a fact that, if recognized, would significantly increase the square footage of our house—though we probably won't attempt to argue that to the property valuator.

~

We don't know what Mr. Gregory means when he says it would take a gold mine for us to buy his property. Being the owner of a small-scale farming equipment business and adept at swinging deals, my brother-in-law, Joel, schedules another visit with him.

~

I made the solar cooker that Jennifer and I use soon after the Cedar Ring Congress in 1997, when I was still living in the cabin with my parents and sisters. I worked in Toad Hall, a workshop/art studio/guest room close to the cabin. Before leaving on my unicycle journey, I'd helped with the construction of Toad Hall; I came home to the completed building. The toad we'd checked on every morning during the construction was still alive and now grandly sheltered.

I'd traded my solar cooker for the use of a tent during the Cedar Ring Congress. It needed to be replaced, and I went about this project, imagining Jennifer at my side.

Start with the inner cardboard box, I mentally explained to her, one big enough to fit two or three pots. Along the two shorter sides of the box, draw lines angled at sixty-seven degrees, making sure the height of the box is just tall enough to fit the pots that will be used. Why sixty-seven degrees? Because for Kentucky, sixty-seven degrees is not too steep to be ineffective in summer, nor too slight for winter. You can make this angle easily by folding a piece of paper twice, as you would in making a paper plane, and creating a right triangle. The larger of the two acute angles in this triangle is sixty-seven degrees.

Cut the angled sides, then horizontally across the high and low ends of the box, creating its final shape. Line the inside with aluminum foil. Place a black tray on the bottom. The cooking will occur here.

A note on cardboard: the cardboard's honeycombed air spaces will trap heat, providing excellent insulation. Once the sun passes through the glass into the cooker, the inner box will contain the rising temperatures, even during an occasional cloud cover.

What do you do on rainy days? I was often asked, though probably wouldn't be by Jennifer, who knew at least something about solar cooking.

Wait, I would say.

My cooker still needed an outer box, top, and reflectors.

∽

Waiting, of course, can help both the solar cook and the unicyclist. I've always thought of it as a good skill or discipline, especially when what you wait for is a known and good thing. If so, pleasure (in the meal, the arrival, the utopia) is deepened; if not, dread is—which is why (forgive me) I must spend a disproportionate amount of time on stories with good endings.

Chapter Fifteen

I SAW IT ENTER A CLIFF, arms first, then seconds later clamber out. It would leave whatever it entered, a cliff, an oak trunk—or whatever it absorbed, a sapling, a leaf—intact, where it had been. If my shadow's span were added to my own height, I measured out extremely long, and my sheer length as I passed under and over trees, through embankments, endowed me with much speed. Thus the remaining mile in the Big South Fork National Park was one of the quickest of my trip, increasing my suspicion that I was only fast in ideal conditions with no one watching.

Immediately past the park boundary, the forest ended. The hills were clear of trees except for rows of planted pines in certain areas. Neat brick houses sat on either side of the road. My shadow lay across mowed grass and was no longer as remarkable to witness. I felt strange, and a feeling came over me that made me remember entering the required junior high dance class for the first time, when I sensed classmates staring at my cheap shoes, and I wondered if anyone could guess I used an outhouse, had no phone. That kind of self-consciousness was compounded in following days by the male role of asking the female to dance, which I did awkwardly and with mixed results, ultimately spending more time in my chair than might be considered possible in a dance class.

Would I be braver now? I hoped I would be. If I knew how to easily express why I was on a unicycle, maybe I could develop confidence.

I had not dared to ask the smartest or the prettiest girls to dance; they tended to be the richest, the ones most appalled by my unstylish, inexpensive clothes, but I did ask one girl who was somewhat smart and somewhat pretty, and she would accept. Then one day, when it was obvious that she was the only girl I ever chose, she said in a loud, frustrated voice the whole class could hear, "He's always choosing me."

Answers. Yet what if the reason for traveling on a unicycle shifted with each locale, as I felt it did traveling from the national park into cleared land? What if I always caught up to an answer a little too late; if, when faced with the question "Why?" I would always respond as I had responded to that Wilkesboro cheerleader: "I'm not sure."

Perhaps, instead of answers, it would be just as realistic to hope for a change in social mores, when, say, vacillation would be seen as cool, and the smart and pretty girls would see someone like me floundering between Point A and Point B and fall in love.

Yes, I thought. Here was another principle for *A Unicyclist's Guide to America*: when it comes to attracting the opposite sex, don't compete with bicyclists.

Now my shadow had withdrawn significantly, barely venturing off the road. I could only imperfectly swallow a mailbox. Soon the rising sun would strip me of all acrobatic prowess. About this time, when I was strange but not awesome, I reeled in two college-aged women sunbathing in lawn chairs, then proceeded with unfortunate slowness to bring them closer, giving them an increasingly better view of me—and me of them, I speculated, if I would look at them directly. Think of a reason to stop and ask a question, I told myself. Yet when I made a right angle to them—the point at which their attention was aimed most precisely at me—I simply kept pedaling.

The piquancy of the moment—that I had come close to communicating with them—oddly encouraged me, so it wasn't with complete disappointment that I reached Highway 127, a busy road. The next roadside sunbathers I chanced upon would provide another opportunity to express bravery, I told myself hopefully.

I took a break in the grass by the intersection, doing nothing. If I traveled 150 miles north, Highway 127 would take me within five miles of my family's cabin. I entertained the notion of returning home. But either the allure of continuing my journey was too great, or the traffic on 127 was too heavy, for after traveling only a few miles homeward I turned off on a county blacktop, heading west toward Byrdstown.

I got back into woods—broken at times by fields. The houses in the area were small, many with wood plank siding. The sun was out bright and hot, though the area seemed less likely to host sunbathers. One of the yards I passed had a stone well, and I stopped for I saw a man sitting on a porch. Chickens pecked about.

Would I be able to fill my canteen? He didn't hear me. He was a very heavy man. When he saw me, though, he stepped off his porch and walked, limping, toward me. He had dirty brown eyes, and his face was covered with the stubble of a new beard. I asked him, again, about getting water.

"That well don't work. You're just as well to get water up the road like I do where it comes a rushin' out the side of a hill."

"This same road? If I follow it, I'll pass this spring?"

He didn't say anything, but I thought I saw him nod. Maybe he didn't hear well.

"I'm aimin' to pull a Pepsi out of the icebox. You want one?"

"Sure." I nodded too.

I sat on the porch with him to drink it. "Tell me," he said, "you look like an intelligent person. Why are you on that funny bike?"

A pause. "Why?" he repeated.

I'd had all morning to prepare for this question. He had sweat on his forehead and was staring at me intently. The way he asked the question didn't suggest he was passing judgment, just wanting an answer.

"I like riding this. I have time to talk to people like you." Only not to college girls in bathing suits. "It doesn't make a difference one way or the other if I take a break."

He didn't respond right away. I wasn't sure that he had heard me. Finally, he said, "I think you are crazy."

I was startled. My answer to the question "why" apparently still needed polishing.

"You're right about that, I guess."

He pointed to his chickens and said, "Look at the least one."

That threw me for a moment.

"Ah, that little one over there," I responded.

"You know, you've got the bluest eyes I've ever seen on anyone. And you're quite the gentleman."

"You're the gentleman, offering me a drink."

We finished our Pepsis. When I walked up to the road to leave, he yelled out to me, "Don't kill no dead snakes. Don't wade in no dry creeks."

"You're crazy," I said.

"You are too," he laughed. "At least I ain't lost."

⟿

On a day after I had recently visited Jennifer, I situated a piece of plywood on my back at the Duck and began, stooped, the trek to Toad Hall. I could have used a vehicle to carry the wood, but I wanted to be immersed in this project at home. I wanted to feel its weight.

A light rain was falling, though I now had a roof of sorts and felt partially indoors. An image reverberated in my mind. The day before, Tim, a Cedar Ring Congress participant, came to visit Trina, and Trina had run from the cabin to greet him, exclaiming, "Timmy!" I'd watched in awe. The emotions my sister expressed openly were the same I now had for Jennifer, and I wondered what it would be like for me to run from Loretto Visitor Parking to the Novitiate Building where Jennifer would be waiting. Even in the sanctuary of my own mind I had a hard time performing the action.

I shifted the roof on my back.

"So do you still like her?" Daddy had asked me that morning. "I think I do," I said.

At Toad Hall, I slid the plywood off my back, onto two straw bales, breathing hard.

The plywood would be used to make the exterior box to my solar cooker. The shape of the outer box would be the same as the interior, but the dimensions would be bigger to allow for insulation between the boxes.

This plywood would also supply the box top, two half-inch strips the length of the plywood to frame the window opening on the box top, and the reflectors.

Mama came in, followed by the dogs—Kibble, Wolf, Bam Bam, and Terry. Kibble went under Mama's desk. The others flopped down on the dirt floor. They knew her routine: one hour of painting in the afternoon after a run through the Wildlife Management Area. Since moving to the woods, Mama had started painting more landscapes and fewer portraits. Now canvases with vibrant greens partially masking the fauna of the woods were hung about Toad Hall.

She sat down, turned on a radio my father had hooked up to an old car battery. Initial static clarified to afternoon classics.

I marked the first cut. With a crosscut saw in hand, and the smells of wet dog, oil paint, linseed oil, and turpentine in the air, I kneeled on what was not a table, drew the saw against the wood, toward me. It vibrated and cut a groove for itself on the line.

The noise of sawing evacuated the Hall every few inches when I stopped for a rest, and our larger and emptier space then would be filled purely—that afternoon—with Dvorak's *New World Symphony*.

⌒

I didn't want to look at my life at the cabin from a distance, through another's eyes, begin to think that candlelight wasn't sufficient lighting, that lowering a bucket into a well to refriger-ate food was distinctly inconvenient, that the water we collected off the roof for washing, yellowish due to pollen and oak tannin, wasn't sanitary, that bathing in the winter—outside, next to a bucket of hot water steaming the cold night air—provided more excitement than a bath ought to have.

I wanted to continue to like this life, not look at it strangely. I'd always talked about my winter baths with fondness, yet I re-strained myself with Jennifer initially, not wanting to scare her. So I didn't mention how the cold would clutch your bare skin until you poured the water, how then you would be released from winter, for an instant, miraculously, in a tropical microcli-mate, a bubble that would last as long as you were pouring water. The pouring of water, of course, stopped as you soaped up, and you would get cold during this stage of the bath. But then the rinse water would flow over you like a warm blanket.

I was fond of how such a bath could swing you around in a complete cycle of sensory experience—but I knew, also, that few would have such a sanguine view, that I, for better or worse, was inside a unicyclist's realm of thinking on this matter and should not assume widespread understanding.

⌒

A lightly traveled road took me through a patchwork of woods and fields. What would the response have been had I talked to the sunbathers? Would I now be carrying, along with the crazy chicken man's laugh, an acceptance among my peers for an un-conventional style—thus a hope I could be attractive to women—or an even bigger gap between them and me?

By late afternoon I left the road for the woods, camped on a rock ledge—then in the morning arrived in Byrdstown, a pretty town with hills and trees. There I ate pancakes and sent my tent home. If it rained I'd just cover up in my sheet of plastic. I felt bold and lightheaded and just slightly anxious about my decision.

Five pounds lighter, I began heading out of town. My plan was to go into Kentucky to get around Dale Hollow Lake. The next community came faster than destinations would usually come to me, prompting me to consider if there might be anything else in my pack I could send away. Static was half in Tennessee and half in Kentucky with no signs of struggle. I talked with a guy sitting on the porch of a closed-down store he used to manage. He told me he didn't believe the road had shoulders going to Albany. Furthermore, he mentioned I'd never make it there on the kind of bike I had. The fact that I had traveled from North Carolina didn't seem to affect his thinking about the matter.

I took off anyway. He was right about the road not having shoulders. I had to be poised for traffic, which wasn't heavy but enough to be always on my mind. Whereas in more relaxed stretches of my journey, I might not have seen her right away, in my alert state on this road I spotted her when she was just a speck in the distance. We gradually consumed the distance between us, and I noticed a woman with a long peach-colored dress, ripped in places, and thick black hair matted in tangles about her head. She had a young figure. How would she react to me? How should I react to her? Just before we passed, she swung a long arm to the ground, tore off the tops of a cluster of wild scallions, and placed them in her mouth. Her teeth were stained green. We passed—with only six feet between us—without her looking in my direction. I dismounted and looked behind me. She moved crookedly and fast, as if with an invisible dance partner. Why didn't she look at me? Did she assume I was normal? I watched as she zigzagged herself into just a speck again.

I continued on to Albany, becoming a speck now to her as well, I supposed. Inside the city limits, a gray Ford pickup stopped, and a man gave me twenty dollars, a donation that made me decide to pedal to Burkesville and pay for a motel. Burkesville, not here, for I thought I should work up to the man's gift. Rejuvenated, I started to pedal out of town, but another car stopped—this time a Lincoln Continental. The automatic window rolled down. An overweight man inside asked, "Got some time?" The next thing I knew, I was staring at a Polaroid camera, which snapped. I saw the face again. "You look like an interesting character," he said, and drove off.

For the next four hours I pedaled steadily, thinking almost exclusively about the room I was going to get. During these four hours I came to the conclusion that I was stupid for not getting a room in Albany. The road was obnoxiously straight. For a unicyclist, a curvy road is better since frequent turns promote an illusion of speed. I pedaled and pedaled and nothing apparently happened. I thought of another principle for *A Unicyclist's Guide to America*: Don't go on a straight road unless you can curb your desire to get someplace. For some of the time I attempted to be observant of the farms, scattered developments, and woods that I passed. I saw clumps of scallions off the road. Wild woman habitat, I thought. I suppressed a desire to eat some. But mostly my mind was already in Burkesville, in a motel room with a soft bed and a shower, miles away from where I was—and the only thing I truly wanted was the cessation of travel.

Arriving in Burkesville, I was as tired as I'd ever been, except for my first day out. I didn't want anybody looking at me, but I sensed a lot of stares. Parents could use me to teach their kids a lesson. "See how haggard that man looks on a unicycle? That could happen to you, too. So remember to always travel on at least two wheels."

The first motel I came to cost forty dollars. Too much. I pedaled another mile into town, which seemed like three miles, stopped at the next motel, a disreputable looking place. Thirty-five dollars. Should I pedal back to the first motel, spend five more dollars for a better place? No, I couldn't do it. I'd rather risk my life than travel one more inch.

The woman at the check-in desk informed me I had sunburned legs.

Chapter Sixteen

IF I WERE TO VENTURE another letter to Mr. Gregory, I'd let him know that the dogwood blossom petals have dropped, as they usually do in the middle of May, and that they organize themselves differently on the ground than redbud blossoms: less like a pool, more like stepping stones, which is how they are on the tree as well. I'd tell him as many particulars as I could about trees, because it's like meeting someone for the first time: once you get to know her, you can start to like her. I'd say that the locust tree blossoms, in sweet-smelling white clusters, have peaked, and that the blossom buds on the blackberry are swelling and streaked with white, about to open. Or that in the poplar canopies tulip blossoms have fully opened, but that we can't see them until they fall into view. Recently, I might mention to him, Jennifer and I were pulling the invasive garlic mustard in the woods. Shadow slept close to us, next to a mayapple patch. When we finished our task, we turned to Shadow and noticed that in the course of an hour several tulip blossoms had fallen around him, one of them on his arthritic right shoulder.

As an aside, I could tell him that we've planted our sweet potatoes and that we are harvesting handfuls of asparagus every day and that I've been thinning apples on our apple trees. He probably already knows that ticks start to crawl this time of year. We check our bodies and Shadow's daily.

Oh, the wood thrush! Does he know the wood thrush? Its song, with its many layers, reminds us of a flute. It is an expression, the most lovely we know, of its preferred old-growth habitat—the downed and growing trees, the chambered light, the hole in a trunk and the solid wood.

He may not know that the wood thrush leaves for Mexico every fall and returns north every spring—to the same woods every time.

⟋

I woke up first thinking I was at home; then I remembered my arduous trek into Burkesville. I wondered why I hadn't arrived more gradually into Burkesville, why I forced a destination that would have happened more naturally a day later. In my scruffier-than-desired room, I counted the miles: thirty, a new record for one day. I vowed that that would never happen again. If I got in the habit of going thirty miles a day, I might at some point begin to covet a bicycle.

I looked at my map. I was heading to see two women, organic gardeners a friend had told me about. They lived outside Altonville. In an attempt to use my unicycle properly, however, I would get there a roundabout way. I would visit Subtle, Kentucky, first.

Soon I was off, pedaling out of town.

"Hi, I want to get on the road to Subtle," I said. I was at a small engine shop on 61N, asking directions from a man in greasy blue jeans.

"What?"

"Subtle, Kentucky."

"Oh, you're talking about 'Subtle,'" he said, pronouncing the "b." "You'll have to go on the road up Subtle Mountain, which will seem like you're in the middle of nowhere, and you are. Then you'll get to the top, and it will seem like you're getting back into the world again."

"How will I know this road when I come to it?"

He paused. "Well, it'll be your only blacktop going to your left by a barn. Right by the barn. Looks almost weird."

I thanked him and pedaled off, only to stop again just past

his shop to read an historical marker. In March 1929, a boring for a salt well caused a huge oil gusher. The oil spilled into the Cumberland River and caught fire, creating a "River of Fire."

In a couple of miles I came to that configuration of a barn and an intersection. How was this weird? I walked up to a man working on a refrigerator on the front porch of a house and asked him if that was the road going to Subtle. I pronounced the "b." He told me that that was the right way, but that I ought to sit down on the front porch and drink some ice water. His name was Jordan Harold. Once I was sitting on a wooden rocking chair, his son stepped out onto the porch and Jordan went into the house and brought out a pitcher of water and three glasses. I found out that Beck's Store, which was on my map, used to be across the road. Several stores had been in the area. People didn't have to go to Burkesville very often, but when they did, they had traveled up Big Runix Creek to get there—the road wasn't built until 1928. A local mill allowed people to grind their own corn.

"Be hard for this young generation to be that independent," Jordan said, looking at his son and smiling.

His son smiled, too. "Who was it out in the garden all day chopping the corn down? Do you remember, Daddy? He was out there, thought we meant corn, so he was chopping the corn down by the weeds."

They couldn't remember who had done that.

"Have you ever raised no farm?"

I told them how I lived in a log cabin.

"You must be kin to these Mennonites."

"Well, no, I'm not Mennonite. Similar though, I guess. Except I've never seen a Mennonite riding a unicycle."

They laughed.

"I read that there was an oil gusher in this area that spilled oil into the river and the whole river caught on fire. Do you know about this?"

Jordan Harold turned in his seat.

"Like the time a man come up the river and I said, 'Where you been?'"

"'Been fishing.'

"'Where'd you get them?'

"'The river caught on fire, burnt the fins off and I got them.'"

A car passed, one of the few I'd seen that day.

"People are a lot lazier than what they used to be," Jordan said. "They ain't able to do nothing, that's all there is to it."

"Daddy, I ain't nearly as stout as you was at my age."

Another car passed.

"There aren't too many cars that go by on this road," I said.

"About as many that goes up that road yonder," Jordan said. "I don't know where they go to. Now that hill you're fixin' to go up, it's a mile I guess from the creek to the top. It's steep too, boys. Your legs'll be feelin' it by the time you get to the top."

My legs were already feeling it, I thought.

"What do you do for a living to travel like this?" the son asked.

I told them about running a game booth.

"Rattlesnake'll get ye around here," the son said.

"I just won't sleep next to anything rattling."

"They might bite ye, then rattle their tail."

I took off. They told me I would recognize Subtle because the store had a big sign that said, "Subtle." In a couple of miles I got to the hill I had been warned about twice. No one had uttered an exaggeration in reference to this hill. As I walked up the steep gravel road that led into a mature woods, my skin turned slippery with sweat and I could feel all the muscles I had strained the previous day. According to the mechanic, I was in the middle of nowhere. The dogwood blossoms floated in their midstory realm. I could angle my body just right with the sun and the shadows, and the blossoms shimmered creamy whiteness. Then the slightest movement would cause me to lose them.

At the top, the woods opened to green fields and a few widely spaced white houses. In another mile I found the store—an old building with a gray tin roof and a long porch. Chipped, white posts supported the porch roof. Half of it was a post office, but both sections were closed. I assumed I was in Subtle. I sat down on a metal bench next to old Pepsi and bread signs and ate lunch, waiting for something I might not have noticed about this town to emerge. Nothing. Three vehicles passed, and that included the UPS truck going up and back. As I ate, drowsiness overtook me. Not allowing myself to fall asleep, I left. A last glance at the store showed me a sign above the porch that had almost faded to nothing: Subtle, Kentucky.

~

Jennifer took me on a long walk during one of my visits, going beyond the convent grounds for part of it. We stepped out onto the road that led to Springfield in one direction, Lebanon in another.

We headed toward Springfield. The air was heavy with pollen and the smell of tar and cut grass. My mind raced, yet was slow, like the road, with curves.

Here we asked about each other's age. I was twenty-nine; she was twenty-eight.

Wild grapevines grew out of a roadside gully, traveling up the trunks and limbs of buckeye and black locust, sometimes entangling our shadows, which the late afternoon sun laid before us. Looking at the road, I could see the entire back of her figure, where her hair met her shoulders, her slender waist, the curve of her hips—and mine too, at the moment absorbing yellow dashes, sometimes losing a hand or a leg to her body. I was taller than she, wiry.

We rounded a bend and our shadows surged up a cleared hillside, swallowing four or five junked cars, then resting on a battered mobile home.

A few more steps gave us a new set of trees that erased this vision, and we were struck instead by the sweet aroma of locust blossoms. Dangling white bunches hung from a locust twisted around a hackberry.

Many in our area, including Mr. Gregory probably, consider the black locust to be a nuisance. It produces formidable thorns; its small leaves create negligible shade and are prone to insect damage; its dark trunk is often twisted and its limbs break off easily. Yet for one week in the spring, the black locust is magnificent with white blossoms.

We have a couple of them growing on our south-facing field, and they always remind me of that Springfield Road walk, years ago.

One other note on the black locust: it makes a hot fire, and its heartwood is a surprising yolk color, given its black-gray bark.

Chapter Seventeen

WILLIAM MORRIS DESCRIBES a vision of a beautiful world in his novel *News From Nowhere*. In a dream, the protagonist journeys into a future England without money, populated by physically strong, beautiful people engaged in work that is artistic and beneficial to society. The protagonist alternates between skepticism and budding hope, inching us into this new world. As readers, we go tentatively as if on ice, yet by the end we find his hope harbored in us as well.

He wakes up, and we fall again into a filthy and inequitably productive London. What went wrong?

The difficulty of returning to a dream is apparent. The goal would be to keep from ever leaving a dream.

Yet how do you keep from leaving a dream? At the very least, I would think, you should remember it while it is occurring. You could tell it or write it or commit it to memory. Then you could tell it again from another angle. Again and again, like carpentry, until that dream is as real as a woodshed, or the early spiderwort underneath the ironwood tree, or the person you love next to you in bed, sleeping. I would think, then, the dream wouldn't disappear.

↬

I unicycled into Altonville much later than I had anticipated, after sunset. Here, teenagers were gathering around their cars in parking lots. In one lot a couple of cars had their radios turned up loud. I'd never hung out like that in high school. I would not have been good at it. Anyway, I gave the teenagers something to look at. One girl yelled to me from across the street: "If you can carry that thing on your back, you can carry me!" Not knowing yet how to talk to girls, I simply waved to her. A couple of blocks later, I thought of a variety of charming and witty responses. I imagined unicycling back there and becoming something of a cult leader for that particular group of highschoolers in that particular lot. I'd teach them to be truly atypical and revolutionary. The girl would fall in love with me, but I would choose to continue with my journey, attempting whatever beautiful and impossible task I'd told them was my mission.

What I did instead that evening was sleep at a Catholic center in Altonville that took in travelers. In the morning I pedaled to the town square to wait for the organic gardeners, Becka Littleton and Fran Parker, who would pick me up there. A hard rain drove me from a park bench to the dry space under some store awnings where the other idle people in Altonville had gathered. Two old men were whittling cedar sticks, making them skinny. Piles of shavings were up to their ankles. The rain pounded on the corrugated metal awning above our heads. I sat down. They told me they had been asked not to make shavings but couldn't see any harm in it. "Did you hear about the guy who pissed in the judge's office and got thirty years of prison?" I hadn't. Mostly they were quiet, intent on the way their knives curled off pungent purple-red wood. They didn't seem to care that I was riding a unicycle.

An old yellow station wagon pulled into a parking space just as the rain stopped. Two women got out of the car. I stood up and wheeled my unicycle down the sidewalk toward them. They were fit-looking women, probably in their thirties.

"Hi," one of them said. "I'm Fran and this is Becka. You must be Mark."

Talking with them on the phone had been awkward, for of course they'd asked me why I was on a unicycle—and I'd thrown out the term "bioregionalism" that Mel Resfield had taught me in North Carolina, thinking that would give some gravitas to my journey. Bioregionalism was the attempt to decentralize and democratize politics and culture so they could be more responsive to particular bioregions. A conversation ensued, which I overheard. "Is our place an example of bioregionalism?" "I don't know. Let him come and he can decide."

On the drive to their place, Fran said, "We were debating whether you would have legs like inverted bowling pins," a comment that prompted me to study my legs surreptitiously. I couldn't tell if anything extraordinary had happened to them. We took a narrow road in and out of woods, until we reached a gravel road that brought us to their house—which couldn't be seen on stepping out of the car due to a profusion of plants and trees in the front yard.

We entered the house, in fact, without me noticing its exterior. Becka and Fran told me they didn't have electricity or running water. They'd built the house out of scrap boards. I could see all its inside space in just a glance or two. They had a cooking stove in the kitchen and a heating stove in the living room, but there were no divisions between the rooms. We were standing in the middle of their house, on rough-cut, board-plank flooring. A sofa was next to the heating stove. Closer to the kitchen, against one of the walls, there was a loom, and across from it, against the facing wall, a desk stacked with books and papers. Kerosene lamps hung on the walls. A cast-iron cooking stove sat in the middle of the kitchen. Shelves held jars of food; pots hung from nails on the wall. A small sink was full of drying dishes.

They pulled out a chair for me, put water on the stove to boil. The space reminded me of my family's new cabin, which I mentioned to them. When the water boiled, my hosts made coffee from dried and ground dandelion roots. A bitter, earthy flavor.

"We call it a dandy drink," Fran said. She had long, light

brown hair. Becka's was short and dark, and she was skinnier and taller than Fran.

Thunder got them up quickly from the couch. My coffee unfinished, I followed them outside to scatter potato eyes on the grass. We covered them with flakes of hay. Becka and Fran assured me that the potatoes would work into the ground and produce. Although there would not be much of a crop, the potatoes would start to loosen the soil, making it easier to turn the area into garden beds later. Over the years their garden had grown like this, incrementally. Bioregionalism would gather its knowledge from people like Becka and Fran. Yet how could this knowledge be translated into political and cultural institutions? They didn't know. Instead, they threw out another term for me: "permaculture." Or, permanent agriculture. That, at least, they knew something about.

I spent the day with them and slept on their couch that night. They slept in the loft. The top part of the stairs folded down from the ceiling, and they slid the bottom part from against the wall where it was kept and latched the two together. The bottom of the assembled stairs rested in the middle of the house, where, during the day, a fold-up card table was placed for dining. A regular table, or any fixture, wouldn't be practical in that spot, unless it could be incorporated into the loft stairs. They'd gone to bed first to give me privacy. I blew out all the wall lamps except the one burning by the couch. I walked outside then, with a toothbrush in my mouth, into complete black. I slowly put one foot in front of the other.

In the middle of the night, the rooster crowed, waking me. Pitch black. I went back to sleep.

At dawn we ate a breakfast of pancakes and home-canned strawberries.

They had seasonal work cutting and housing and stripping tobacco, making just $3,000 to $5,000 a year. "Yet we eat well," Fran said. They produced virtually all of their own food.

Becka said, "If one of us gets an incredible urge for a product, we think about how many hours of tobacco work that would be. A lot of times our desires are curbed."

Before leaving I helped them mulch young broccoli plants with rotted sawdust. Their soil was spongy and black. They told about a neighbor who had told them he could have a nice garden, too, if he had soil like theirs.

"What he didn't understand," Fran said, "is that we add to it every year. This work doesn't end."

I gave them my twig-burning camp stove. I'd been pleased by the absence of my tent. Maybe the absence of a stove would be pleasing as well. I would rely on grocery food that did not need to be cooked. On the drive back to Altonville, they asked me where I was going to end up on my trip. I couldn't tell them because I wasn't sure. I knew that my pack was now closer to thirty pounds than forty.

At the square, the idle people had already started on their cedar sticks. I pointed them out to Becka and Fran as we pulled into a parking space.

We said good-bye. I watched their car pull away, and when it was gone I looked up to see the whittlers watching me. I waved, and they continued whittling, which was foremost in their minds and which needed two hands. I was just something to watch where before perhaps there had been nothing.

↜

I would lean my body against the brace, turning it. The bit would squeak as it mined out red spirals. After drilling a hole into the post a couple of inches deep, I would slide the hewn end of a rail into it.

Easier to just nail the rails to the posts, people had told me.

You're talking to a unicyclist, I should have told them.

Doubts would surface whenever I worked on my fence.

I'd take breaks, pick up handfuls of the red spirals, and bring them to my face. I would breathe in deeply, for an instant cut loose from all other sensation by the sharp, fresh smell.

⟿

After meeting with my brother-in-law, Joel, Mr. Gregory has quoted us a price for his 150-acre property that is at least $100,000 more than we could afford, even with Chris and Joel mortgaging their land and Jennifer and I ours, and even with Trina and her husband Tim and Mama and Daddy contributing $20,000 each. That there is a figure quickens our senses. Yet because it is so high, we find ourselves dodging its sharp thrust at us.

We've decided to query the Kentucky State Nature Preserves Commission to see if they can help.

Chapter Eighteen

IT WAS EASTER SUNDAY, I realized, as I wheeled my unicycle past the whittlers—twelve years since I'd received a unicycle as a gift and had begun learning to ride it. I was on the road, the town square behind me. Then I saw a phone against a convenience store, across the street from me. Impulsively, I walked to the phone and dialed my grandmother's number. Altonville was only a two-hour drive from my family's cabin, as close to home as I'd be. Maybe I'd leave a message with my grandmother for someone in my family to pick me up. I'd visit home for a few days, and then resume traveling.

I let the phone ring probably ten times before hanging up. Someone had parked a car behind me and was waiting. I'd send them a card anyway. I shouldered my backpack, picked up my unicycle, began rolling it back to the road. A viewer would notice a clear sense of direction, a decisiveness. I would let that impression propel me south.

Past Altonville I saw three kids with empty baskets run out of their house, and homesickness struck me again. My parents had kept up a basket-hiding custom for my sisters and me through high school and into college. Our baskets would be hidden in increasingly bizarre places—up the chimney, inside a plastic bag dangling in the outhouse hole, in the middle of the creek in a rubber raft. In the more likely hiding places, my father—ignoring my mother's pleas—would leave notes such as, "Only a stupid person would look here."

The egg-hunting kids didn't see me, and I rounded a bend. The terrain I entered then was essentially flat, yet interrupted at times with short, camelback hills—short enough to tempt me to ride to the top without walking. The pedals would turn hard, and the effort to move them would create an especially non-linear motion.

A difference, I thought, between childhood and adult quests was a difference in boundaries. Kids knew where to look; adults didn't, a distinction that could be related to how swiftly adults went from Objective A to Objective B.

On making it to a summit, I would dismount and stand, holding my unicycle. I'd chosen, essentially, a toy as my means of leaving home a month ago. You could laugh at the way it lent itself to any direction, perhaps more easily if you were a kid in your yard, your parents or siblings watching—but even now, at the improbability of entering adulthood on something that arguably was a flawless symbol of indecision.

The map showed I was headed toward the communities of Mudlick and Flippin, two names that didn't conjure up a notion of efficient progress. I might flounder, have to turn around.

But nothing so cinematic occurred. The only structure in Mudlick was an ancient general store where a woman, so old she looked like the previous owner, poured water from her canteen into mine after telling me the store water was no good.

By the time I got to Flippin, it was dusk. Usually I had a camping spot by that time of day. Just outside Flippin I asked a woman in a trailer if I could camp someplace, but she was frightened, shutting the door. Before going up to the next house, about a half mile away, I put my hat on, thinking a hat would make me look less wild. I walked up to the front porch and rang the doorbell. Through a slit in the curtain, I saw that the evening news was on in a brightly lit living room. The door opened slowly and a young woman peeked out. She said that her father let travelers stay in his barn. He lived a mile up the road in a white stone house. Relieved, I thanked her. It was so dark by that time, though, I had to go up every driveway to see if I could distinguish a white stone house from the prevalent brick houses. Knowing that I didn't have a plausible-sounding story for being on people's driveways after dark, I tried to be quiet.

I asked at a house next to a barn, which looked lighter than others. Luckily, it turned out to be the right one. A man showed me where I could sleep in the barn and how I could turn on a light.

"You know, you're not the only one that's stayed in this barn," he said. I looked around. It was a pretty, bi-level barn with interesting angles. We were on the second level—where hay wagons could be driven in to unload. At the far end was a drop-off to the lower level. "There've been several long-distance bicyclists down this road. You're different from the others, though. One of them was out there taking a picture of a road kill. He said he was writing a book about road kills."

"Why do you get so many long-distance travelers here?" I asked.

"You're on the bikers' cross-country route. That's why you're here, isn't it? This is the bikers' route of America."

Maybe I could veer minutely off course and end up on the unicyclists' route of America.

When he left, I rolled my sleeping bag out in a pile of straw. It began to rain, the first rain without my tent, and it occurred to me on that lonely Easter Sunday how lucky I was to be in a barn, sleeping in straw.

I woke up before sunrise and was pedaling even before I could see how far my shadow leaned to the west. I smelled like straw. Soon the traffic picked up. With a head still so sleepy, I thought it best to turn off on a gravel road. There I saw an old man standing between rows of peas.

He looked up at me.

"All of a sudden, the traffic got bad," I said.

"Those are the seven o'clock cars for the factory up at Fountain Run," he said.

A truck rushed past us on the gravel road.

"That boy, that pickup that just now came by here, he'll get to Fountain Run at seven. He's got cattle down on my place. He's going to check on them. He'll be back here in three or four minutes, get to Fountain Run at seven o'clock.

"I worked in a factory back in 1940 to 1945. We had a war then. You've heard of it, I guess?"

"Yes."

"I made marine boilers, drilled holes, put the pipe in marine boilers. And outside that I've been a farmer for sixty years. It's a nice thing. Some people get rich at it, but most of them just make a living. And I reckon making a living is all. . .you ain't going to take it with you no way. Just as well not to have it. A whole lot of them that's got it didn't get it honest. They stoled it all from the other feller. It's best just to have enough to get through."

He motioned to his peas. "These peas is no-till. Them leaves keeps it from getting hard and keeps the weeds down. Manure is good, too. It holds the moisture. Manure is good for everything. The patch down yonder I plow, but these is no-till."

The same truck rushed by.

"There goes that boy. It's seven o'clock. You can set your watch to it. His car will be in the second or third parking block at the factory. They know to shut the doors when he gets there."

"That first row of peas got the living daylights beat out of them in March. Hail and right in with that you had them cold nights down about twenty degrees. And that was hard on them. But they've turned on in the last few days."

I was so hungry that even though he could have continued talking, I said good-bye to him and on the other side of the gravel road rolled out my sleeping pad and ate breakfast. Most of the traffic died down. One car went by, and in its wake fast food Styrofoam and foil sashayed to the ground.

I pedaled after breakfast in the lull of factory shifts.

In eighth grade shop class, we'd had an assembly line making fold-up chairs. Everybody had a job to do. I operated the countersink. We even had time cards. When we walked in at the beginning of the hour, we punched in, worked an hour, and then left for our next class, not really finishing anything, as far as we were individually involved, that was whole. Before class one day, a guy named Tim sat next to me and started talking. I was happy for the company because usually I was very quiet before class. So I talked with him. Tim was one of the rougher boys in the class. He had a moustache, a significant thing for a guy in junior high. We talked about picking up black walnuts and how stained our hands would get. Tim was trying to tell me his hands would get more stained than mine would. Well, I knew how stained my hands would get, for I'd helped my dad one year fill up a whole pickup, which we took to a walnut buyer on the Kroger parking lot, selling them for twenty dollars. The next thing I knew, I was looking into the stern face of the shop teacher, who told us to come outside with him. Apparently, he had told the class three times to be quiet. Outside, we had to bend over, and he hit our bottoms three times with a paddle. Tim cried a little, but the paddling wasn't as hard for me as telling my parents, who had never hit me. I felt like I had failed them.

The factory sign came into view first, followed by the sign, "Welcome to Fountain Run." I pedaled through a town that seemed dwarfed by the factory, and it struck me as I was leaving that I didn't even know what the factory made. There had been no sign. The pea farmer hadn't told me. Maybe no one in town knew either. I could be a sleuth, I thought—provide a service to a town that didn't know what it was working for. On uncovering the nature of the Fountain Run factory, I'd perhaps cause a hubbub. A unicyclist detective, as the papers would later say, throws a small Kentucky community off-kilter when he reveals to residents the effect of their work.

Maybe my shop teacher would read the article and remember disciplining me. What conclusion would he reach? That he hadn't properly prepared me for the real world?

My mother sent him, the principal, and the superintendent long letters, which I'd not read but could imagine.

Would my shop teacher be happier if, instead of wandering, I now had a factory job? Yet how would a unicyclist perform on an assembly line? The first major adjustment, I speculated, would come while standing close to the conveyor belt, something not unlike a major road. The impulse would be to exit at the next chance. Then, too, the mandate to perform the same motions with each object brought forth by the conveyor belt would run counter to a unicyclist's sense of balance. All the scenarios I could imagine involved a decrease in efficiency and profits for the factory. It was best—and I would include this in *A Unicyclist's Guide to America*—to avoid situations that demanded such unwavering progress.

At some point in my ruminations I missed a bend in the road and was pedaling up a paved private drive. A dog running toward me cued me off. I made a sharp turn (probably left tire marks, I thought later with some amount of pride), and then there was a moment of stillness during which I wondered if I were falling. But I had not lost my balance, and I started pedaling back to the road, which I could now see was only a few yards away. I expected the dog to get my ankle and easily bring me down, perhaps encouraging the animal to do the same with future unicyclists, but I made it to the road safely. The dog was sitting under a pine. It appeared, luckily, that no one else had been watching. My reputation as a unicyclist detective would have been damaged. Unicyclist detectives should never draw additional attention to themselves.

↜

I would wonder, at times, how Jennifer could be interested in someone without the job experiences or skills that society deemed most important. Nonetheless, I knew how to make solar cookers, and I would include that in my résumé to a future society. I had no idea if Jennifer would be responsive to this concept.

SLOWSPOKE

To complete the construction of the solar cooker, place crumpled newspaper on the bottom of the plywood box. Then situate the inner cardboard box on top of the newspaper. Make sure that the inner and outer boxes are level and that their angled sides are parallel. Next place newspaper between the two boxes. Newspaper further insulates the inner box.

Now set the plywood piece with the window opening on top of the two boxes. Check to see that the window opening corresponds with the inner box, that the outer edges of the top piece correspond with the dimensions of the outer box. Nail or screw in place.

Next nail or screw some of the strips of plywood around the window opening and caulk the rest of them to the underside of the glass. The glass should be big enough to fit over the window-opening framework. The strips bonded to the glass should rest flush on the plywood top. If access to the oven is to be through the window, then caulk handles of some sort to the glass. If you choose to make a door in the back of the oven, then caulk the glass in place.

The main body of the solar cooker is now complete, and it can be used at this point, though it will only get up to 250 degrees Fahrenheit. The reflectors will allow the oven temperature to climb over 300 degrees and, on exceptional days, over 350.

The reflectors are made from four trapezoidal pieces of cardboard or plywood lined with aluminum foil or some other reflective surface, each piece joined to two others along its slanted sides. The bases of two of the reflectors will be an inch longer than the width of the glass, and the bases of the other two will be an inch longer than the length of the glass. To make the angled sides, use the same folded paper used in tracing the box angle. For plywood reflectors, join together with removable-pin hinges. For cardboard, sew the sides together.

The reflectors should now fit around the cooker window,

resting on the box top. Situate the cooker so it faces the sun; it is ready to use.

⌒

We are making arrangements for a Kentucky Nature Preserves Commission botanist to come out and look at the woods. Maybe Nature Preserves would be able to help us purchase the property. From the road, as we wrote in our directions, he will walk a quarter mile to the base of a steep hill. An old tractor road is the most gradual way up this hill and winds itself up the hill's south face. Black locust, Osage orange, and wild grape vines abound here. At the top he will come to a small grassy opening. Here he can see a redbud, a grove of white oak, a blackberry thicket, and the continuation of the path. The path heads toward a pond with cattails and goes down a slope to the north of the pond. Here the path is flanked by cedar, but only for a few steps, until the hardwood—sugar maple, ash, oak, and hickory—and a tall understory emerge. A glance to the left will give him a glimpse of the endangered old woods. To the right is the Henbit Forest. In the immediate vicinity is a diverse profusion of plants: black haw, ironwood, black raspberry canes, jewelweed, and coralberry. He will be able to look up to see several mulberries dangling from a sapling about ten feet tall. The path turns, goes up a slight rise, and heads to the entrance trees, the two shagbark hickories. He will pass between them, ducking under a low branch. Upon straightening up he will see that he is in a small area of mowed grass and mulched trees and flower and herb beds. The ground directly ahead slopes almost immediately downhill past plum and redbud and gets swallowed again by woods. To the right, a mowed path leading to the garden goes past highbush blueberries in raised beds and next year's firewood, cut, split, stacked, and covered with tin. To the left, on the east, is our cedar board-and-batten house. Stepping-stones lead him to the back door, which is made out of cedar as well—in the same board-and-batten style as the house—with a clear window. The lever handle is inset a bit, due to the fact that this door we built last winter turned out to be thicker than standard.

He can open the door and feel how heavy it is as it swings on its hinges.

Chapter Nineteen

IN A BAIT SHOP, I ASKED FOR DIRECTIONS to Scottsville and a back-roads route to Franklin. A garrulous man inside put his finger on my map, covering Scottsville, and began telling me how to go—not from the map, which didn't show many of the gravel roads, but from his memory.

"Take a left at Red Hill Church, you'll know it when you see it. It'll zigzag, you go straight, then bear to your left on Gold City Road, go three or four hundred yards and bear to your right. This is Old Franklin Road, it'll take you right in."

By the time he finished, his finger had slid up to Cincinnati. I would ask directions, again, in Scottsville.

I told him how I was traveling, but he took it as a joke. My unicycle was outside the store. And he gave me some friendly advice.

"Most people ain't bad here, but you should talk plain. Country people talk plain. You tell them that you're going from yonder to yonder, that you've come from North Carolina and you're going plumb across this area."

What would happen if I settled down in Scottsville? I wondered.

He lowered his voice. "I don't say this to be mean, but people in these parts don't understand guys with long hair. They don't like it."

My hair was now down to my shoulders and probably garnering the extra attention I'd told myself to avoid.

We walked out together, and when he saw my unicycle he erupted. "You ain't kiddin', are you? Look at that jasper. You mean to tell me you came clear from North Carolina on that thing?"

"I'm afraid so."

"I want to see you ride that thing. You ever get a flat tire? You know, they used to put cornhusks in the wheels of old model cars. They wouldn't have a blow-out, they'd have a shuck-out."

As I was getting on, he said, "Go down to Houchens and tie that jasper up like the Mennonites do with their horses."

"Where are the Mennonites?" I asked.

"There's some where you are going on Old Franklin Road. Did you understand my directions?"

I was already pedaling, but I stuck my hand out.

"Good luck," he yelled.

I put my rain gear on a couple of miles later when a few big drops came down. A man stood in a yard and watched me. I told him I had come from North Carolina and was traveling through the area. Would he know if Scottsville had an upholstery shop where I could get another piece of foam rubber for my seat? He didn't, but said he had a piece to give me and went into his shed. His voice was raspy and quite a contrast, I thought, to the foam he gave me to make my seat soft.

The rain came down harder. In Scottsville I picked up my general delivery letter in the post office and then walked, dripping, into Martha's Diner and ordered an omelet and French fries. A young fellow with a suit and shortly clipped hair let his eyes wander from a newspaper and settle on me. Maybe he was the plant manager at the Fountain Run factory. I didn't let him know that I was aware of him. I opened my damp envelope. Inside were a $400 money order and a letter from Mama. She was volunteer teaching art at an elementary school, using chalkboard drawings and stories, and was telling everybody about my trip. According to her everybody was stunned that I could do such a thing. They'd probably be staring at me right now too, I thought. My food came. Lovely, greasy food. My sister Trina had received a fellowship for graduate study in English at the University of California, Davis. Her twin Chris was becoming proficient in Hindi and while gathering the life stories of Indian women had participated in a protest against a proposed dam. My sisters simultaneously amazed me and made me feel inefficient. Somehow they'd figured out how to do things that brought about discernible results. Daddy was at a festival in Pikeville, Kentucky. Mama had had a hard time with company recently. A friend of a friend asked her if she had a real house in town someplace.

The young professional was getting up to leave, grimacing. Perhaps the inanity of supervising a factory that produced nothing of real benefit for the world was stressful. Walking briskly out, he gave my backpack good berth. It had dripped a pool of water onto the floor.

After lunch I cashed my money order, then left town on a county blacktop road. The rain stopped. In an hour or so, past an ostrich farm and a bend in the road, a Mennonite homestead came into view. Soon I was in a workshop, staring at the gray beard of an elf-shaped man pounding on a piece of metal. Would there be a place to camp? He told me I could sleep in the carriage shed. "My wife has tomato soup for supper if that is good enough for you."

A young Mennonite man then stepped into the shop. He was looking for a part to a cultivator. Fixing horse-drawn equipment, I gathered, was the older Mennonite's business. I went with the two of them to a field where there were two rusted, horse-drawn cultivators. They spoke at first in Dutch but switched to a heavily accented English.

"This is an older model, ain't it, than ours?" the young man asked.

"The part works the same."

After they unbolted it, the young man asked how much it was.

"You don't owe me anything; you've been helping me."

"Are you sure? You've gone to some trouble."

He didn't pay. The generosity was gracefully accepted. The young man left.

As Graybeard (the name I gave him) and I walked to his

house, he pointed out various piles of lumber and parts. "So much work to do here. A lot of times I don't have the energy." We passed a maple tree and made it into a half-mowed yard. "My girls, they were mowing," Graybeard said, "Now, where are they now?"

"Who?" I asked.

"My twin daughters. They're eighteen. They were out here."

As he was opening the door to the house, he mentioned how he was getting hungry. The house was sparsely furnished, which made it look elegant and spacious. A huge cooking stove rested on the hardwood floor of the living room. Handcrafted wooden cabinets and chairs stood against white walls. Graybeard washed his hands in a basin of clean water and dried them on a towel that hung neatly on a hook. He motioned to the washbasin. "If you would like to take anything off your hands," he said. Then we went into the kitchen where a table had been set for two. As soon as he pulled a chair out and sat down, Graybeard said, "This is my wife," although he could not possibly have seen her come in from the back room.

"Hello."

She nodded and motioned for me to sit down. After she put a dandelion salad, bread, tomato soup, a pitcher of thick milk, and a dessert of peaches and pound cake on the table, she left for the back room. I wondered where their eighteen-year-old daughters were.

As we ate, Graybeard's twinkling eyes took me in as he reminisced. If he could change anything, he said, he would have more fully helped a friend of his who had been in need forty years ago. He changed the subject abruptly and easily, telling me that he was taking heart medicine. I wasn't sure where to join his talk; instead I listened.

"I just want to be behind a horse, plowing my field," he said.

After supper I followed Graybeard upstairs, and we carried down a small mattress that I would use in the carriage shed. Outside, we saw his daughters, in long blue dresses and bonnets and black shoes, each pushing a hand mower over the grass. "Linda and Lucy," Graybeard said as we passed. I looked back and saw that they had stopped mowing to go inside, probably to wash dishes. I wondered if they had eaten. Had they been outside because I was inside?

We put the mattress on a table in front of the carriage.

"My name is Elmer Brubacher," Graybeard said.

"Mark Schimmoeller." We shook hands.

"What is your wife's name?" I asked.

"Vivian."

"I was wondering if I could help you out in some way tomorrow. I'd like to work for you."

He pointed to a McCormick horse-drawn mower. "I'll be working on that tomorrow. You can stick around if you like."

I thanked him, happy that I could stay there a little longer. When Graybeard left, I stretched out on the mattress. The harness prongs rested on the wall a couple of feet above me, the wooden carriage wheels only inches away from the mattress.

The morning light both granted the carriage movement and halted it. Graybeard called me in for breakfast—homemade granola cereal and milk, and two fried eggs on thick pieces of bread. Again Vivian didn't sit at the table, and I only caught glimpses of Linda and Lucy in the back room. When I asked Vivian if I could do the dishes, she shook her head. "You are under no obligation to us." She didn't have as thick an accent as Graybeard. Like Linda and Lucy, she wore a bonnet, a dress with an apron, and hard-looking black shoes.

I followed Graybeard out toward the barns and helped him feed horses and water the chickens. Whenever we passed a pile of lumber or scrap metal, he told me what he needed to do with it.

My first job with the McCormick mower was to use two pipe wrenches to tighten a tap on a large bolt. I was glad to do something with my hands. I had to take the bolt back out as well when Graybeard decided that we should grease it. We spent some time that morning looking for parts and tools in his loosely organized shed. Graybeard diligently said something about each piece of metal we happened across. "I like this bolt. I should use it more, but if I did I would not have this bolt."

A truck and trailer pulled into the driveway. "My plow is here," Graybeard said. He put his favorite bolt away and walked outside.

The person driving the truck, Phares Stoffner, lived in a Mennonite community in Lobelville, Tennessee, and made periodic trips to Pennsylvania for people as a way of making money. To get to the plow, we had to unload two horses. Phares tied them to a post next to Graybeard's shop. Graybeard told me to pitchfork the manure out of the trailer.

"How much do I owe you for the manure?" I heard Graybeard ask Phares.

Phares shook his head. He wouldn't charge for that, only for the plow. When I was finished with the manure, Phares came up and helped me wheel the plow off the trailer.

"Look at that," Graybeard said. "That is my plow."

While he was perusing his machine, I ran to the carriage shed to get a wheelbarrow I had seen there. I wheeled it back and forked the manure into it. Phares was talking to Graybeard. "The thing of it is, if you don't spend anything, you don't have to make as much."

Graybeard nodded to Phares, then caught my eye. "The girls will do that. They know where to put it in the garden."

"Can I just dump it in a pile up there?" I asked.

"If you wish."

Phares left, and Graybeard thought it was time for lunch. Linda and Lucy sat at the table with us this time, but Vivian still did not. The prayer before we ate was a minute of silence. We had fried chicken, potatoes, cheese bread, banana bread, and canned strawberries for dessert. Linda and Lucy wouldn't let me wash the dishes either, but I did help to clear the table. Graybeard went outside. I found out that Linda and Lucy and Vivian had spent most of the morning cleaning the attic. The twins had distinctly different features, I decided, but I wasn't sure yet which name went with which face.

I found Graybeard in a field, untangling string from a fence. A cow had dragged it there. He wanted to test a mower he had recently put together and needed a string to make sure the mower teeth were straight.

When we returned to the yard, Lucy was pushing the reel mower across the grass, that task not yet finished. Graybeard recruited her to help us push a big mower he had been working on. Its teeth still didn't move. Graybeard looked up at me. "Now you tell me, what is wrong with this mower?" I exchanged a quick glance with Lucy. She had slightly bigger eyes than Linda, I thought. They were brown. Both Linda and Lucy had attractive features. I told Graybeard I wasn't mechanically inclined. Lucy left, and I stayed with Graybeard as he pondered the newly refurbished and painted mower that nonetheless did not work. Eventually, I asked him if I could work on the lawn for a while. He nodded.

I liked the solid feel of the mower in my hands and the fact that I was saving Linda and Lucy some work. I'd grown up associating grass cutting with noise, so the relative silence of this style of mowing was nice. The mower only worked going forward. I wondered if that would satisfy people interested in continuous progress. I maneuvered around a big maple tree and a small sapling that Graybeard wanted to keep so it could take over when the big tree died. Occasionally I would stop mowing and run down the hill to peer at whatever greasy cog Graybeard was peering at. "One way or the other, we will learn something today," he told me.

Before I finished mowing, Graybeard decided to open the gearbox to another mower to see if we could figure out what was wrong with the one we had rolled down the hill. "This one doesn't have a spring, and it works. Now why is that?" Graybeard decided he wanted to put new bearings in the mower we were staring at. "If we could get that done, I would be happy," he said. We removed the bearings out of one end of the shaft, but when we tried to get the ones on the other end out with a metal pole, nothing came. He yelled for Vivian, and she came out with a pitcher of lemonade.

For a while after our break I was on one side of the mower, filing down a rod, and he was on the other side, digging out his parts. Before we finished with our task, it was time for supper.

We had soup and bread and a wonderfully soft, rich cheese that they called soda cheese. Banana bread for dessert. I passed dishes to Linda and Lucy, who didn't ask for anything they didn't have. During the meal they questioned me for the first time.

"How do you stay balanced?" Linda asked.

Lucy then wanted to know if I had ever heard of Mike King. I hadn't. She ran off and brought back a book Mike King had written—about a trip he took on a wheelchair from Fairbanks, Alaska, to Washington, D.C. With Lucy looking over my shoulder, I opened the book to the photograph section. The man had arms bigger than my legs. It looked like he had a van that traveled with him the whole way. I wondered what that would be like and decided it would be too much like traffic. Perhaps my adventure reminded Lucy more of a wheelchair journey than anything else she could think of.

We finished eating, and I went out with Graybeard to hook a horse up to the carriage. Graybeard wanted to get some ice cream. I think he also wanted me to have the experience of riding in a carriage.

With a blanket covering our legs against mud splatters, and the horse trotting on a gravel road, making a sound like running water, Graybeard pointed out that we had gotten a lot done in a day. I was startled. We had worked on three mowers and hadn't finished with any of them.

"It's not what you get done," he said, "It is the living up to it that is important." The dropping sun had turned a deep red. "Living up to it." The modern version of this phrase would be "live it up"—the same words but in a higher gear, more peril-ously arranged.

I liked Graybeard's version better. Most unicyclists probably would, I thought.

The person who sold ice cream lived outside the Mennonite community. By the time we got there, it was dark. Intense elec-tric lights imprinted the house into the darkness. Graybeard parked the carriage but didn't tie the horses. They would stay still. The freezers with the ice cream were in a welding shop. Graybeard bought a gallon of ice cream and also two ice cream sandwiches for us to have a treat right away. We were about to leave when the proprietor started telling stories about his days as a police officer. Graybeard had to put the ice cream back in the freezer so it wouldn't melt. The electric lights were making my eyes burn. I was too tired to do anything other than nod at some of the owner's more emphatic points. When he found out I was going to dip back down into Tennessee, he said that the rattlesnakes were so bad in the west Tennessee hills that he would have to put sections of stovepipe over his legs when he hiked out there. I nodded. Finally, although it was hard for him to do so, Graybeard said, "Look, Al, my wife, my kids, they're already asleep—I'll pick up the ice cream some other time."

Somehow Graybeard and the horses found their way back through unlit countryside, turning on unmarked gravel roads. Although we couldn't see anything, Graybeard nevertheless pointed out the sights.

"That house there—maybe you can't see it—was built in one day. The whole community came together and built it."

A thick cloud cover must have been blocking all the light from the stars and the moon. Graybeard drove into his drive-way in pitch-blackness. The house had no lights on. Linda, Lucy, and Vivian had already gone to sleep. Graybeard let the horse loose in a field, and we both rolled the carriage into the shed.

The next morning, as I was getting ready to leave, Graybeard slipped me five dollars. I tried not to take it, but he put it in my pocket. I remembered how the young Mennonite man accepted Graybeard's generosity, so I did the same. I shook hands with each of them. None of their hands were smooth. I hoped mine didn't feel too soft, but I imagined they did, drifting most of the day in pure air. The family watched as I mounted my unicycle, swayed a little, and pedaled away.

Chapter Twenty

THE BOTANIST FROM THE Kentucky State Nature Preserves Commission has visited us and Mr. Gregory's property. He taught us more about the old woods, provided names. It's a beech, maple, and ash mesophytic forest. The soil type is a calcareous Eden silty clay loam. The variety of plants, he told us, and the nicely developed understory suggest that the ground has been undisturbed for a long time. The height of the trees is approaching old growth status. Virtually all the low-growing plants indicate a rich moist woods: coral orchid, blue cohosh, goldenseal, beech fern, doll's eyes, trillium, jack-in-the-pulpit, horse balm, jewelweed. The list goes on. He gave us the names in Latin, and we had to ask for their common labels. However, Braun's rockcress—the federally endangered plant that would clinch Nature Preserve's interest in helping us buy the land—isn't here,.

We are still $100,000 short.

∽

All of a sudden I crossed into another bioregion. The world outside Franklin, Kentucky, became flat, occupied by the longest fields I'd seen since the beginning of my journey. Surrounded by them, I didn't seem to be moving, or to be located anywhere. Big machines inched over their ocean-like expanses.

In the late afternoon I walked up to a huge, unblemished white house. I felt like an alien. A short man came from around the barn. After hearing my request to camp, he told me, "No, we're working people hyar," and walked off. I wondered what that meant. At another house down the road a woman told me I'd have to wait and ask the men who were in the fields. I pedaled on. The short guy who had turned me down drove by slowly in a gray truck, staring at me. At the next house a young woman told me I could stay in the guest room and even eat supper with them. "The only thing is," she said, "I'll have to ask my husband when he gets back. I'm sure he'll let you stay, but sometimes he's a little funny."

I decided to risk some time and wait for the husband. A little boy came out of the house and asked, "Why do you have that thing on your back?"

"Can't you tell, he's an adventurer," his mom said, looking at me.

"That's like my house. Everything I need is in there," I told him.

I took it off and sat down in their yard next to a longhaired dog.

The husband pulled up in about a half an hour, and his wife rushed over to explain me. He got out, slammed the door of his truck, and walked over to me. I stood up.

"I'm not comfortable with you here. Not with all that's going on on television."

His wife looked stunned. As I was leaving, she asked me if I wanted some ham sandwiches. I had to quickly find a place to camp, so I told her "no."

I missed Graybeard and his family. Dusk draped itself over me as I continued down the road. At an intersection I walked apprehensively up to a farmhouse, and an elderly couple said I could stay in a nearby field. Grateful, I spread out my stuff in grass already heavy with dew and ate peanut butter and bread in the dark. I didn't light my candle lantern—better not to be seen. Headlights crept up almost to my feet before swerving away. In my single act of bravery that evening, I scooted out past my pad a bit, allowed one foot to get run over by headlights. Daring, I thought. I didn't fall asleep until late—then woke early. I had no desire for people to see me rising out of that field.

I crossed 431 and made it to a virtually untraveled road. A few hills appeared. Perhaps the topographical relief would make the people who lived here a little calmer. This road came to a T-shaped junction, and I turned left and pedaled into Dot, Kentucky, which essentially was the Dot Grocery Store. I walked in. A cashier was making a quilt.

"I must be in Dot, Kentucky," I said to her.

"You're right on top of it."

I laughed. "So I'm not just on the outskirts?"

"Honey, this is Dot, Kentucky, all of it, right here. The downtown, the outskirts, everything. Dot, Kentucky. This is it, period."

Interested, I told her I would like to learn more about Dot, and she directed me to Jay Sharples, a local resident, who was sitting on a bench outside the store. After hearing of my interest, he told me first that he was a distant relative of Daniel Boone before mentioning that there used to be a mill behind the store, on an island in the river. A leap was made then to the subject of local Civil War history, and he seemed to settle in. During a pause I asked how the land was different when he was a kid.

"Tobaccuh has been the most profitable crop. And early time, they raised cotton."

"Have the farms around here always been so huge?"

"Yessir. When I was a kid, three or four men owned most of the countryside." He paused. "You might not believe me if I tell you, I've gone and signed up for night classes. I've had classes in horticulture, landscape architecture, news writing, and even the Bible."

Then he switched from classes to a relative of his, Major John Sharp, who, he said, fought in the Revolutionary War.

Finished with Major John Sharp, he turned on the bench so he was facing me. "I know you like anybody else. Do you believe that Jesus Christ was the son of God according to the Bible?"

"According to the Bible," I responded.

"That's all we got to go by. So many things is real. We just know them things, don't we? They're real. I enjoy talking to you even though we've never met, it's all right."

"I think so too."

"I have traced back the family tree, and I do realize," he laughed softly, "that my old grandfather, he was named for Nathan Bedford Forrest, the general. He's the one they claimed was the least educated of the generals at that time, during the…I call it the War between the States. And he was the man who come from a private to a general, what no other man has ever been able to do. I don't know why, but my grandfather was named for him. And I've always favored him, most undoubtedly."

"Well, you've kind of worked yourself up too, taking classes."

I could tell that he had expected me to say something like that. He put his hands on his knees. "All we can do is work toward what we believe in. When I was just a young boy, one day I looked at a Sears, Roebuck catalogue and saw a Gene Autry guitar. You've heard of Gene Autry, ain't ye?"

"Yes, are you related to him?"

"No, I'm not. But you know I believe Jefferson Davis's kinfolk come to Virginia and places like that. A lot of people I know seem to have some connection with Robert E. Lee. People's kin to him. Sort of funny how things work."

"So you were starting to tell me about this Gene Autry guitar."

He didn't acknowledge that he had changed subjects. Maybe he saw a relation.

"I had this notion to see if I could make music, you know. So I borrowed this guitar. There was two books there. One was *The Art of Songwriting*, and the other was *The Art of Guitar Playing*. I picked that *Art of Guitar Playing* up, and I tried it, looked like I didn't do so good at it, but I just kept on. I got to where I could pick a little bit with somebody, play with them. Wasn't no expert otherwise. But I picked up *The Art of Songwriting*, got to reading it and studying it; I went to writing songs. Just not long ago I got one that I want to tell you about. Got it ready. If I can get somebody to take it from there. I wish I knowed somebody, so I could get that rolling. The name of it is

"Red River Rambling," about this river here. Everybody's heard it. I don't reckon there's anybody made no remark about it, they brag on it. This one guy said, 'You know what you got? You got a hit.' I don't guess you'd know anybody in New York or California who'd be interested in it?"

I didn't, but I told him I would keep my eyes open for him. Red River Rambling. I liked the title. That's what rivers did, I thought, as I pedaled toward Guthrie, Kentucky. And people.

⤳

Though Mr. Gregory's property doesn't meet all of their criteria for purchasing it, the Nature Preserves Commission continues to send out botanists to document the woods. Sometimes we invite them in for water or lemonade. Invariably, they mention how strongly our house smells of cedar. Accustomed to it, we no longer smell it—unless we are gone and return.

When these visitors leave, we feel newly born and vulnerable. Our eyes settle on what theirs settled on, and our life here becomes more boldly traced. That we, over a half mile from the county road, are able to make a living in this small pause in the woods seems freshly incredible. There's no asphalt leading to our house! No power line! No water line! Yet we arrange our life so that what we need can be found here—we can step outside in the morning on dewy grass and fill a bowl with blueberries, from plants we put in the ground three years ago—or given to us, like a downpour that washes into our roof gutters and flows into a tank in our cellar, or sunlight that provides electricity and a way to cook food. (Look at that box with a glass top and reflectors!)

The day I first saw this field I'd been intent on going beyond it, hopefully into more old growth. Now the trees are taller, and the variety is greater. In planting a few this spring—apple, plum, pear, cherry—I had the swirling sensation that I was continuing that path as a young man—yet that now I was doing so with years rather than steps.

~

She whispered something I didn't hear. I moved closer to her. I was in the Guthrie Post Office, attempting to write a postcard home. My companion was an elderly woman who had walked in at the same time I had. She'd shown me already that one of the earpieces of her glasses had broken and mentioned how that wasn't such a bad thing. Being an old woman, she'd said, no one looked at you anyway.

"What?" I asked.

"Remember to pray." She breathed it to my face. I smelled alcohol.

As she was leaving, I told her to have a good day, and she told me to have a good life.

~

It turned completely flat again as I pedaled out of Guthrie— nothing to break the heat that flopped down across long fields and dizzied the air in front of me. The afternoon was bald and relentless; I thought expansively about getting away from the area. I smelled chemicals. Ninety-one degrees, one thermometer said. A drawn-out twelve o'clock whistle signaled the release of factory workers who stared at me as they drove by.

Anxious, I pushed myself to make it past Clarksville, Tennessee. But when I got to the city, the biggest I'd ever attempted on a unicycle, the cars exhausted me and I didn't feel like pushing myself anymore. Close to Austin Peay State University I asked directions to the Salvation Army shelter. On my way there I was stopped by a man who said he was a disc jockey on an early-morning radio show. Before I could agree to the interview, he had his microphone out.

"So, can you tell our listeners why you are riding on a unicycle through Clarksville, Tennessee?"

I knew that, in the context of catchy talk and music, anything I'd say would sound absurd. "Right now I'm headed for the Salvation Army shelter."

"Okay, I didn't know when I saw you. I thought you might be heading toward a bike shop." He chuckled. "Where did you sleep last night?"

"In a field by a road."

"But enough of that, eh? Now you're looking for a roof over your head."

"Well, Clarksville doesn't have any fields."

He chuckled again.

"Listen to him, folks. Now, I just want to know one thing, and anybody who has seen you, I imagine, has the same question. How do you, carrying that big pack and balancing on just one wheel, keep from falling?"

He annoyed me. In another context I would have appreciated the question, for I'd thought a lot about falling. I would have explained how a unicyclist didn't attempt to completely avoid falling, a process set in motion immediately after mounting. Rather, the goal was to keep from falling too far. In fact, a formula could be used in *A Unicyclist's Guide to America*: The act of falling partway plus corrections equals movement.

"Mostly luck," I told the disc jockey.

"Where did you start out?"

"North Carolina."

"And you're going…."

"I don't know. The immediate thing is getting to that shelter before it closes."

"Okay, now, you have a good time in Clarksville, and, listen, don't get a flat."

He shut the recorder off. "Wow, what a stunt. Look, I gotta run. Take it easy." And he left as quickly as he had arrived. I felt that he had practiced some kind of resource extraction on me.

When I arrived at the shelter, the door was locked. I knocked and someone yelled from inside, "What do you want?"

"Shelter for a night."

I was let in, and they gave me a form to fill out—my name, address, why I was there, if I had a criminal record, etc. A volunteer worker put my form in a file labeled "transients." I liked knowing what I was. He told me that no one could go out after nine and lights went out at ten in the bunkrooms. I was free to get something to eat, shower, wash my clothes. Wake-up in the morning was six, and everyone had to do a volunteer chore.

People looked limp. One man was getting in the bunk even though it was only seven o'clock. Others were in a small room close to the registration table, staring at a television with the volume up so high it would be futile to talk. The women's bunkroom was upstairs. As I was going to the kitchen, I heard one of the women say, "I'm going crazy, but I've already been there and back."

We ate beans and wieners and a slice of white bread for supper. Afterward, I showered and washed clothes, and then, with the lights still on, climbed in a bunk. The guy who went to bed early had a transistor radio playing by his pillow. I was writing in my journal when the lights went out. We were to go to sleep.

"Alright men, it's six thirty, supposed to be up by six." I figured out where I was and hurried to get out of bed, sensitive to the reprimand that didn't seem to bother the others.

I asked what my volunteer chore was. The garbage. I took two huge bags out to the dumpster in the parking lot. To get back in, I had to ring a bell. The guy inside closest to the door pretended he didn't know me. I yelled to him that I had spent the night there before I realized he was playing a joke.

"You're welcome to leave any time," the manager said after someone finally let me in.

I signed out and took all my stuff out the door at the same time to prevent being locked out. I figured I was lucky to get out of a place where I had been both locked in and locked out. Out-side, I sat down next to a whiskery-faced man smoking a ciga-rette and re-tied the foam rubber pad to my unicycle seat. He watched me. We let the hot morning sun hit us as we sat for a while in silence. Just as I was getting up to leave, the man who had gone to sleep with his radio came out the door and said breathlessly, "Hey man, you on the radio." He looked at me briefly, as if I were a god, before going back in.

Chapter Twenty-One

NOW THE SWEET, BUZZING, MOIST AIR of summer settles over us. I meant to be prepared for it, but once again I am not. I meant to document the order of events leading up to this screeching and rattling and whistling of insects and tree frogs, this intermittent pinging of bumblebees against windows, these hot days and warm nights, these long strands of pollen from the entrance trees, as intricate as bracelets, falling to the ground; but while I know the progression of white blossoms—plum to serviceberry to dogwood to locust to blackberry—the other openings and blooms were too many to sequence.

Yet I attempt to make the bridge, if only to know that I can return. I want always to know that I can return.

So you might be able to see me, as I put the yellow-blooming spicebush between the plum and redbud blossoms, and the pawpaw blossoms—hanging purple-green helmets—between the redbud and dogwood, applying backward pressure to the pedals of a unicycle, attempting not to go fifty miles per hour. And preparing myself, too, for the next turn—so when the leaves and nuts start to fall, I'll be able to contour my being into the last phase of the year and take that curve into winter—the same one that has spun me here—with better timing than before.

I wonder, too: What day, precisely, did we hear the first spring peeper? The first whippoorwill? See the first lightning bug?

∽

Soon I was on a gravel shoulder next to shattered glass and cars let loose in bunches by traffic lights. Riverside Drive. I pushed my unicycle, sweating, trying to hold my breath. Of all the encounters I'd had in the last few days, Graybeard and the Altonville whittlers surfaced most frequently. They had a manner about them opposite that of Riverside Drive.

I stepped off the shoulder to look at a tree that was unfamiliar to me, one part of a wall of vegetation. The river, I guessed, was behind that wall, out of sight. I couldn't identify the tree.

What did Graybeard and the whittlers have in common? An answer struck me just as another bunch of cars rushed past. Time. What did it mean to have time? You had it or you didn't have it. Yet even if you didn't have it, time still existed. The earth still rotated in space. The fact that so many people were running out of time on a planet whose motion hadn't changed significantly for eons seemed odd to me. It had become cool to have no time, to be busy. If you were busy, you were productive and valued. A unicyclist wouldn't easily be perceived as productive—not given the other available modes of transportation. Yet choosing a unicycle was deliberate, I reminded myself. I didn't want to be rushed.

"And look where it has gotten me," I thought, as I began walking again on the trash-covered, dangerous shoulder of Riverside Drive in Clarksville, Tennessee. For a unicyclist it wasn't good at all to be in a world where there was hardly any time left.

Leaving Clarksville finally, I turned onto a road to Erin, Tennessee—busy but with a wide paved shoulder. It was hot. I filled my canteen in Palmyra and again, about ten miles later, in Cumberland City. Outside Cumberland City I rested under a tree to eat a tomato. I thought of another principle for *A Unicyclist's Guide to America*: In squandering time you demonstrate its availability. An old black man on the other side of the road, pushing a mower across the lawn of a white mansion, yelled to me. With the tomato in my hand, I ran to him. He told me he'd offer me something but said, "The old lady is sick." I told him I was fine. "You got a 'mater, you'll do all right," he said.

That became my mantra going into Erin: I had a 'mater so I'd be all right. And Erin, a pleasingly small and neat town, was quite courteous compared to Clarksville. While I rested on the courthouse lawn, big maples shading me, people from the community walked up to where I was sitting to visit. Someone told me I might be able to get a boat ride at Bee's Bait Shop to get across a huge lake I didn't want to pedal around. And the Superintendant of Public Schools—though I thought at first she was going to reprimand me—bought me a milkshake.

Bee's Bait Shop closed at six o'clock. I looked at the clock on the courthouse: three. I had three hours to go twelve miles. I could do it if I didn't take any long breaks. Ordinarily I didn't combine time and miles, for that started me thinking about speed. Consequently, I found myself rushing—to the extent that it's possible to rush on a unicycle—to Bee's Bait Shop, doing what a unicycle was supposed to keep you from doing.

A couple of miles up the road, when someone with a white shirt and thin red tie and continuous smile stopped me and said, "Do you know that you are a sinner?" I didn't have time to talk, even for a rebuttal. I pedaled until about dusk when the road dipped into water in front of me, where the town of Danville used to be. I'd made it. Half of a grain elevator stuck out of the water about a quarter mile past the shoreline, the only thing visible of the town that had been flooded in the making of Lake Barkley and Kentucky Lake.

Bee's Bait Shop was to my right, and several people had gathered outside the store to watch me.

"I don't think I'll go any farther today," I said, walking toward them. Most of them, I found out later, had been waiting there the past hour or so, wondering when I was going to arrive. "You're not even breathing hard," one of them said. I hoped that I wasn't a disappointment for them. Bee, the young owner of the shop, let me camp in an adjacent shed that night—and in the morning she surprised me by fixing me a breakfast of oatmeal and hot chocolate. She told me she had arranged a boat ride for me.

I sat in the shop with some fishermen. An old man whom everyone called "Mayor," and whom Bee called "cantankerous," asked me if I knew what the Indians said when they first saw the bicycle. I didn't. "White man's crazy as hell—has to sit down to walk," he told me. I wondered what they said when they saw their first unicycle. Maybe just, "White man's crazy as hell," period.

Another fisherman came in and told me he was three quarters of a century old. He mentioned, also, that I would be old by the time I finished my trip. "And it may not be by birthdays either," he said.

At ten o'clock Lew Rogers arrived with a small outboard motorboat. We fit my unicycle and pack in the front of the boat, which sank significantly. Lew told me where to sit and where to face. He seemed confident. I followed his instructions exactly.

As the boat scooted away from the shore, I had the odd feeling I was going up on a Ferris wheel. I had the impression (of course) that the land was getting smaller—but, strangely, I also had that impression of the boat I was in. I gripped its sides tightly. Wind rutted the lake with little waves. The boat bounced. Lew had to turn toward the wind at times and slow the motor. For the most part we were not faced where we had to go. But even moving at an angle like this, we went faster than I could with a unicycle, and by increments the other side of the lake expanded into view. Then we reached the ground.

Lew left me on a boat ramp. My backpack and unicycle lay on the wet concrete like they had been washed up by the lake. I sat down and stared at the water.

Clarksville seemed like a year ago. I felt that I had lost a good portion of my journey. What remained was me sitting on the ramp, staring at the water. Maybe not a bad journey in itself. If someone happened to chance upon me at the moment, I imagined that enough was left out of the picture for it to be quite intriguing.

Intriguing enough to imagine other stories, which may or may not be similar to the one I was in.

Perhaps as I began pedaling away, the two shores approaching each other until (like before) there was a complete stretch of solid ground, my journey would take me again into its whole length.

But for now I felt like just a few strewn details. How, exactly, did I determine which roads to go on, assuming that my presence on the boat ramp wasn't an ending? Would my choice of roads affect the nature of my journey? Where would I be now if I hadn't quit my internship with *The Nation* magazine?

Raindrops prompted me to move. The small roads I chose that day took me through the town of Big Sandy and the tiny community of Mansfield. A little past Mansfield I left the road to camp under three white oaks and a profusion of understory growth. I hung my wet rain gear on branches. The direction decisions I'd made that day were practically automatic, similar to the variations on a straight line I performed unthinkingly while pedaling: if a road was generally heading west, and it was tinier than the one I was on, then I would always choose it.

In the morning I tunneled through undergrowth, making it to the road. The weather had cleared and turned colder overnight. I wobbled at first on my unicycle before gaining its rhythm. A band of mayapples stood at the side of the road, fruit already forming under opened umbrella leaves. At home the mayapple leaves would have just begun spreading out. Mayapples came out of the ground often in chilly weather with their leaves like cloaks wrapped around their stems. The trillium and larkspur would be up at home, too. The thought came to me that I was lucky to have my mind clear of everything except trees and flowers. That would last, I supposed, until the next busy stretch of road.

I'd been thinking about time. At the moment, with no motion greater than my own, I had very little sense of time. Which is to say, also, I had very little sense of distance or my own speed. If cars had come into the picture, passed me, and left me behind, perhaps I would have been forced to think about these matters. But as I was heading into the small community of Henry, the trail of my mind was roundabout, a kind of mental knitting: my arms in the air, a tobacco barn in a green pasture, cows, feet on the pedals, a newly plowed field, the dirt silvery with moisture, canteen across chest, trees along a creek, a revolving wheel, a road taken in short distances at a time. I felt I could be as generous with somebody as Graybeard had been with me.

Thus I passed through the small communities of Henry, Gleason, and Sharon. As those days in western Tennessee went by, one thought did begin to widen greatly in my mind, disproportionate with the others: how to cross the Mississippi River. Somebody told me that the ferry at Hickman, Kentucky, was no longer operating. Other than that ferry, the options for a unicyclist were poor: interstate bridges at Cairo, Illinois, or Dyersburg, Tennessee.

In Sharon I walked up to an Exxon Station to buy a Missouri map. Four guys in greasy blue suits stopped working when they saw me pushing my wheel toward them and walked outside the garage like some kind of Exxon committee to meet me. Two of them asked simultaneously, "Can we help you?" I almost wished that I had a more complicated request. The map I purchased ended up being an old one that showed the Hickman ferry still operating. Not yet interested in the reality of my situation, I chose to be pleased by the map.

That night I dreamed that I walked across a river on a slightly submerged bank or sandbar. On the other side I couldn't find a shore, only cliffs, with no place to walk. I decided to go back across the river, but the sandbar was gone, and somebody told me I would have to wait a long time for another crossing. I said I would try walking across. Before stepping into the water, I saw two of my history professors, perched on the cliffs. I found a rubber duck. With the duck in my hand, I walked over the water to the other side.

SLOWSPOKE

In the morning I passed the road to Dyersburg and realized I had made a decision to head toward a town with no river crossing. A section of the road that took me to Reeves and then Hickman, Kentucky, had abrupt, frequent turns, giving me a pleasant impression of swiftness. Around Reeves the land stretched into long fields crawling with wind-shielded tractors. Metal arms spewing chemicals into the dirt extended from the sides of the tractors. The wind blew dust around me. I tried to hold my breath, as I had done on Riverside Drive. Next to the fields sat big, white houses.

In Reeves I mailed a postcard home and then pedaled out of town where I found some scraggly shade on the side of the road to eat lunch. A field that ended in heat ripples was at my side. Finished, I tossed a banana peel into its long expanse of dirt.

I made it to Hickman, Kentucky, at dusk. The police station arranged a place for me to camp and said that the owners of the ferry—no longer commercially operating—were taking equipment to their Missouri farm in the morning, that I was welcome to ride along.

In the morning I made it to the landing before the ferry owner. A television reporter arrived shortly after me. At first I didn't consider a television interview to be much different from a radio or newspaper interview, but when he trained a camera in my face, everything suddenly seemed unnatural. This wouldn't be like a radio interview at all. I couldn't see the reporter's face. It would be like talking into an answering machine, and I was unskilled at that. So when the red light went on and the reporter motioned with his hand, I didn't do too well. I stumbled over my words. I guessed that I would look nervous and shy on television.

↜

A couple of years ago, Jennifer left for a week-long conference in Washington, D.C., to learn more about autism and to be able to better serve some of her kids in Kentucky's First Steps program.

135

SLOWSPOKE

We had never been separated a whole week. The bed all mine, I would nonetheless sleep on my side, to make room for her.

On my third day alone I heard on National Public Radio's *Morning Edition* that the ivory-billed woodpecker, long thought extinct, was not; a group of scientists on a secret expedition in an Arkansas bayou had seven sightings of what has been called the "Lord God Bird," because of the impulse people have had on seeing one to exclaim, "Lord God, what a bird!" More importantly, the report went on, they caught the woodpecker on video.

I sobbed. I knew very little about the ivory-billed woodpecker, only what *Morning Edition*'s report mentioned. It depended on an old-growth swamp forest; it made a distinctive double knock on wood, a sound that presumably hadn't been heard for decades; it was strikingly impressive in size and in color. I didn't know exactly what it looked like. Our dictionary, which often includes sketches of animals, no longer listed it.

Later, I tried to sort through what made me sad hearing this apparently hopeful report. I picked out reasons like blackberries among thorns: because this bird was alive and because it could become extinct again; because I imagined the bird being shot; because I imagined the joy of the scientists who found it; because I had recently spotted a rose-breasted grosbeak for the first time, and though it was only eight inches long and not close to extinction, it thrilled me, as if, among the more familiar sparrows and chickadees and nuthatches and titmice and cardinals and blue jays and red-bellied woodpeckers and goldfinches, it had just been created, a triangle of red on a white breast, white and black wings, a stubby beak, hopping from branch to branch on the wild plum.

Chapter Twenty-Two

THE FERRY OWNER LOOKED AT ME and told me that to judge distance over water, you bend down and look out between your legs. I kept what I hoped was an inscrutable expression on my face, for I wasn't sure whether he was joking or imparting valuable information.

"I've taken across every kind of traveler you could imagine," he said. "You're the first of your kind though."

I'd never been on such a ship-like vessel—nor on such a big river. A tractor dwarfed my unicycle and backpack. I held on to a rope railing. Perhaps if my television interview had gone well, I would have felt as brave as a pioneer, "the first of my kind." Instead I felt foolish and ill-equipped.

On the Missouri side I had the sensation of releasing someone's hand. The ferry owner left on his tractor. I sat down and ate breakfast. How did you judge distance? You probably had to do something weird to judge it over water. I felt a hundred miles farther from home on this side of the Mississippi than on the Kentucky side, just a quarter mile or so away.

By late morning I was pedaling in Missouri for the first time, following straight, raised roads—levee roads, they called them— through flat, newly plowed fields. The sun beat down hard, the ground only occasionally softened by shade at a field's end or at old homesites by pecan and cottonwood trees. I traveled some distance down a wrong road and when I returned to where I had been and the heat furrowed over me, I didn't feel like traveling any more. Yet I kept on, the area not being good for camping.

Tractors, the only vehicles on the way to New Madrid, took up the entire road. They were responsible, I noticed, for inscribing baby turtles into asphalt. I would leave the road completely when they passed.

Long, skinny fish, like pieces of driftwood—yet alive—floated in an irrigation creek. Three more miles to New Madrid. There I would get a motel, eat in a restaurant. Everything would be lovely—if I could just arrive. The distance between where I was and New Madrid, that scant three miles, had jellied, and I found myself—to a much greater degree than was typical—struggling against immobility. In *A Unicyclist's Guide to America* I would argue against traveling after the air had jellied.

At the city limits finally, I headed toward the closest motel. The destination in sight, I received a burst of energy, which lightened my body, making movement easier. Across the street, a small boy clutched two books and ran as fast as he could, sweat pouring off him. He caught up with me. "You're going to Kansas," he said. "I'm going to CD's."

"Is that a store?" I asked.

"Yeah," he panted. "It's where I go every day after school to get me a coke, 'cause school makes me thirsty."

"Maybe running does, too," I pointed out.

"I got a bike with two wheels, and I ride it everywhere. When I get bigger I'm going to ride it around the world."

"I bet you'd make a good traveler," I told him.

"I will," he said, then sprinted away.

My motel was small and couldn't be considered picturesque but nonetheless was a wonderful place. The thirsty boy would discover how much, in fact, a traveler looked out upon rest—and how much that travel depended on rest or being in place. I bathed and washed my clothes. Then I walked out like a feather to eat in a downtown diner.

As I traveled north on road MM the next morning, the wind came behind me in gusts, pushing me, a much better situation than I had after turning west on Z, heading toward Bernie. Then the wind hit me from the front, hampering my movement. Might as well be in a hilly landscape, I thought. I practiced leaning into the stronger gusts to keep from being blown backward. It took a bit of faith to lean into the wind, sort of like falling back into someone's arms. If the wind shifted too much, or changed intensity too quickly, I would lose my balance and have to step to the ground and start over. Not feeling the wind, the drivers that passed me probably wondered why I was at an odd slant, why I swerved a bit, why my hat was bent over my face.

I retreated inward, and I felt shy—as I had during the television interview on the Mississippi. It was, at least, a good time for shyness. No television cameras, no one at my side. Hopefully, an attractive woman wouldn't materialize, say on a bike. Unicyclists could handle shyness best by being alone, I determined.

A gust brought me to my feet, and I proceeded, walking. The wind blew hard, and I, unable to look at it straight on, had to bow my head. Thus positioned, I was reminded of being in my sleeping bag.

Sometimes I'd dream of walking in the woods and meeting a young woman, who would live in a rustic log cabin also, just a few ridges from my family's cabin. It was the only scenario for falling in love that seemed plausible.

I'd tell her how we finally got planking nailed to the extended floor joist logs, fashioning together a front porch of sorts— which made entering the cabin less of a balancing feat. The roof hung over enough to provide some protection, but with wind the porch would get wet. As we stepped out of boots and into the cabin, we would have to avoid the wet planks. When it rained, we would line up buckets under the porch eave to catch roof drips. Sometimes we'd wash dishes on the porch, using rainwater and buckets, the same method we used inside, there being no sink.

I'd tell her that two mornings after we moved, the milk spoiled—which we knew would happen, but when it did we were reminded again that our lives were going to be very different without electricity. Eventually we would put all of our refrigerator-type foods in a five-gallon bucket and lower it into a deep, stone-lined well, up a short hill from the cabin. We devised a pulley system over the well—the refrigerator door, we called it. Sometimes we'd pull the bucket up and there'd be an orange newt, cool as you please, on the white bucket top.

If she lived in a typical house with a recognizable refrigerator, I would be more reticent, perhaps even nervous.

I mounted again, began riding, my arms out like a wrestler's.

I should refuse, I told myself, to get nervous during a conversation with an imaginary lover.

～

A day or two before the summer solstice, I leapt into the old woods, toward what I thought in my anxiety to be the grinding of a bulldozer. Past the white oak with a coyote hole, through undergrowth and across fallen limbs, between pawpaw, across continents of shadow, to a sugar maple sapling that had been marked once with orange tape. I stopped. If a bulldozer came here, it would not have the benefit of following the trail of tape that Trina and I had removed months ago. It would be coming by memory. Yet when the pounding in my chest lessened, I noticed the sound was more distant than I had thought. In fact, I determined then that the sound was from a bush hog on Abner Lipp's field, two ridges away—and I would not, despite my high level of adrenaline, proceed to defend a patch of tall fescue.

～

That night in a dream I also entered the old woods. Though not running, I was anxious. Shadow walked next to me. We headed directly to the center of the old woods, where I wanted to check on a white ash that had fallen in a windstorm. A hole in its trunk had landed face up and rains had filled the cavity with water, creating a miniature woodland pond. The health of the old woods depended somehow on the ability of this white ash trunk to hold water. My task was to check its water level every day. Every day I would discover that the water level was fine, but with each passing day the need to check it was greater.

We made it to the white ash on this day in my dream, and I saw, instead of a pool of water, a newborn baby—and I knew that this was the baby that Jennifer and I had been trying for years to have. The longing I felt then surprised me, for Jennifer and I had been happy for some time after we'd come at last to accept childlessness. I knew that the baby was safe and healthy, given its relationship with the water. Yet even with my mounting excitement, I remained motionless while Shadow walked over to the baby first. He began to lick it, but then the baby disappeared and Shadow simply lapped from the woodland pond.

Shadow had to lead me back to Snuggery. I recognized our house but wasn't sure if I lived there by myself or with Jennifer.

⤚

Given that the wind had nearly convinced me that I was losing ground, Bernie, Missouri, came as a surprise. With help from the sheriff, I stayed that night in the Baptist meeting hall. In the morning the preacher gave me a Bible, a "seed," as he called it. It weighed as much as the camp stove I gave Becka and Fran, and when I had breakfast up the road in the Elk Community Store, I loosely covered my seed with a day-old newspaper.

I fell again to thinking of a chance meeting with a young woman, who would live just a good walk from my family's cabin—and then chastised myself. It would be just as probable, I thought, to imagine her as a unicyclist, also traveling long distance, meeting me in the next day or so.

In Brosely I tried in vain to get precise directions from a drunk in a tavern. Just up the road at a gas station, however, I received better help. I turned down an unmarked gravel road by a cemetery. About halfway to Road HH, a farmer stopped and told me that the water was up. He grinned. I had two options: I could continue forward and attempt to cross the water, or I could go around it, which would be an additional twelve miles. I wanted the farmer to sway me in one direction or the other, but he didn't embellish, other than grinning, on either of my options. As he left, he threw his arm out in a generous wave.

I decided to continue toward the water. When I reached it, I realized I should have asked the farmer how wide the flooded part was. It looked to me to be about a half mile across. Struck by this vision, I could understand the farmer's grin a little better. As I prepared for my crossing—putting my bathing suit on, wrapping some of my provisions in plastic—a car pulled up, turned around halfway, then stopped, the people inside curious to see what I was doing. That I had an audience made me decide not to look out between my legs to see if I could better judge the water's distance.

If I had had another way to prepare myself, I would have, but I couldn't think of any other action. I just walked into the muddy water, holding my unicycle like some sort of talisman. At least I wouldn't have to worry about traffic. Yet that car at my back was like a television camera. Why was I so affected by people staring at me? The water climbed to my waist, then, to my relief, maintained that depth. Perhaps if I were bearing something more related to water than a unicycle, which I had to shift from arm to arm to relieve muscles—an oar, a broken canoe—I would be less inclined to think that the people in the car were laughing at me. When I was halfway across, the car finally left, and I continued on, making it to the other side.

I guessed that, being west of the Mississippi, I should expect to be exposed to the elements, a prospect that seemed at the moment intimidating. Yet I felt I could deal with the elements better than traffic. Thus far, since crossing the Mississippi, I'd had more tractors pass me than cars. No unicyclists, of either sex.

I changed my clothes, continued pedaling. At the mercy of

the elements, I felt like an adventurer; at the mercy of traffic or stares, I felt like a fool. Perhaps the farther west I traveled, the more of an adventurer I'd become.

In the hour after my crossing, only one vehicle passed me. It stopped. We were just outside Neelyville, surrounded by flat farmland. A farmer got out.

"See that line of trees at the end of the field?" he asked, pointing. He owned seventeen hundred acres.

I could barely see it.

"I've got a dozer there now, going straight down that line."

It seemed, then, that his tone shifted, that he was being aggressive—as if he associated me with that last brushstroke of wild on his horizon, wanting confrontation. It would be a story, I thought, of the bulldozer and the trees, the red diesel truck and the unicycle, the short-haired man and the long-haired youth—and, try as I might, I could think of no outcome to this story favorable to myself. Or to the trees. So I told him I'd better continue on.

But I took those trees with me as I pedaled away from him. I thought of how seemingly immobile they were, yet with a kind of motion, sticking out and catching the eye for the simple reason that nothing else was there to catch the eye.

I would be bigger because of the trees, and they would be with me in my story, moving as fast as they had ever moved, swaying as if in a big storm—but actually only because they unicycled toward Neelyville. It could be a story, I thought, of how the short-haired man in east Missouri found himself outside his red diesel truck, talking to a band of trees, which had been migrating down the road.

In *A Unicyclist's Guide to America*, I would include the warning that unicyclists have no known defenses against aggressive behavior. Except fantasy.

"Neelyville 2 miles." Ploughed fields beyond the sign rippled outward to the horizon, or inward to the road, depending on the glance, and I continued on, feeling by turns belittled by my vehicle and emboldened by it: emboldened, for I'd rendered myself defenseless to the world, a course of action that would seem to suggest, if not foolishness, then audacity. It was conceivable, I thought, that someone could study my wobbliness long enough to discover a corollary of strength. A fantasy would have this observer fall in love with me. A comedy would have her simply fall.

Reaching Neelyville was somewhat like reaching land, and I pedaled up to a woman who seemed quite a bit less dangerous than the farmer. She was planting flowers. An unmowed place behind her house looked like a good place to camp.

"You're early," she said.

"Early?"

"Yeah, usually they come later—last year it was a mule train, year before it was a couple of bicyclists, this year it's you. All going 'cross country. Except they was going the other way. All of them. You're the first going west."

"Why, do you suppose?"

"On account of the wind. Wind's at your back if you go east." I felt stupid and quickly asked another question.

"Who do you think is going to show up next year?"

"I don't know. As long as it's no revolutionary."

"Maybe they'll be on time."

She didn't let me camp. Maybe she let the smarter travelers camp. Outside Neelyville, however, I walked into the Corkwood Natural Area, the first place I'd seen all day without ploughed fields, and found a place to sleep in tall grass. I doubted anybody could see me once I was lying down.

On opening my eyes in the morning, my view was like that of an insect's journey through grasses. I lingered there a few minutes, awake, and navigated wilderness. I made it three feet before losing my way, then allowed myself to be lost. For five minutes? A half an hour? Choosing an option luckily available to me, I then rose from my sleeping bag. Mist hung over spiders' webs that stretched like trapeze artists in the unplowed, grassy field. Where would I go, as a unicyclist, that day?

Into a more hilly terrain, I discovered: the Ozarks. Forested hills flanked me on both sides. The houses were small, often with gardens. I traveled by and over clear, moving water.

One night I slept in an orchard and woke up to a crisp, bright morning. As I pedaled along with the sun climbing my back, every image displaced the fresh air easily and vividly. Like the four wild turkeys that ran across the road and disappeared into the woods. There seemed to be room for everything.

I ate along the banks of the Eleven Point River and watched its strong current of clear water for some time. Disengaging from it, I then noticed in front of me an earthworm, the largest I'd ever seen, at least a foot in length—so large you could begin to think of it as the river in miniature. I'd dissected a worm in high school. Yet no one had taught me how to understand a river. I still didn't understand worms, in fact. You could step into the river and feel its moving weight against your body. You'd feel it acknowledging you and a split second downstream healing itself of the break you posed in its wholeness—but even that semblance of understanding, if you looked for it later, would be gone.

An early summer heat wave has postponed our plans to get a property valuator to appraise our home. Having a valuator walk a half mile through the heavy air would not, we decided, help us get the best valuation for our place.

Yet we go about our days at times imagining someone with a clipboard and a pen at our side. We call him Clipboard—Clip, for short. One of these days was unusually hot. Clip stayed by our side. We got up early to work in the garden while the sun was low. Our garden stood out as an oasis surrounded by brown grass. We hadn't had rain in three weeks. The hay mulch we put on in the spring had kept some moisture in the ground and had saved many of the vegetables, though they had started to produce less. The garden cistern was a third full. Clip would take a note of this, we thought, either on how our water system could handle a mini drought, or on how inadequate it could be with prolonged dryness.

We watered the tomatoes and squash. Up to our waists, the squash had spread out beyond its designated range. To find the original plant mounds, we entered a jungle of bristly stems and leaves with five-gallon buckets of water and stepped carefully to avoid the yellow crookneck and butternut hidden under leaf canopies. The tomatoes that climbed up trellises in designated rows, were, by comparison, easy to water.

With the watering finished, we pulled the garlic that we had planted last October. It had established its roots in the cold months and had come up green and strong in the spring before the other plants. The stems had thickened over the summer and lately had spiraled out with seedscapes pointed in every direction.

We cut the stems and laid the bulbs in the sun to dry.

Late morning, we went inside, sweating. It was quite a bit cooler inside. Clip would possibly make a note here, and we would tell him what we do in the absence of air conditioning, that we keep the windows open at night and close them about midmorning. We shutter the east windows in the morning and the west in the afternoon to keep out the sun. Generous eaves keep the sun out of our large southern windows, and our entrance trees shade us from much of the afternoon sun.

Our other strategy for keeping cool, we would mention, is to frequently pour water over us. Jennifer bathes in a small claw foot bathtub close to a hand pump that brings up cool water from the cellar tank. Next to the hand pump is also a spigot where hot water can flow from a solar hot water tank mounted on the exterior south wall of our house. We positioned this spigot just high enough on the bathroom wall to get a five-gallon bucket under it, low enough so the hot water could flow by gravity. Clipboard would likely note something here, but we would not be sure whether that would be the absence or the presence of hot water.

I would show Clip where I bathe, here by the hydrant pump. I pour earth-cooled water over my hot skin. Jennifer bathes too, only inside with warmer water.

We have a continuing debate over which bathing method better cools off a body. In both cases, the bath stimulated the appetite, and we ate cheese sandwiches with fresh lettuce, tomato, and basil, chips, and home-canned salsa for lunch. At noon the temperature had climbed to ninety-two degrees. I put a pan with oil in the solar cooker. Then we both stretched out on the bed with our books and very little clothing and the pleasurable anticipation of a nap.

Our bed is to the side of the tiled bathing room, a step away from the water pump, two from the bathtub. A plant and bookshelf at the foot of our bed divides our sleeping space from a small dressing area, exactly the width of two dressers. A beige curtain loosely defines one edge of the dressing room and is cut around a floor lamp that serves both the dressing room and living room area. From the bed we can see our small couch, close to the floor lamp and the wood stove; the vertical ladder to the loft, its rungs notched into beams and polished by the grip of our hands; the long, black stove pipe going vertically to the ceiling; our corner kitchen with its large west window, its cabinets and drawers hand-built with planed cedar boards.

We fell asleep emphatically, our eyelids sucked shut like the lids of Mason jars, and in an hour, when we woke up, we felt opened into another day—yet it was even hotter outside: ninety-four degrees.

We peeled and quartered root vegetables from the garden— onions, beets, potatoes, and carrots—and carried them out into the blazing sun to the cooker. When we put the vegetables in the pan, the oil sizzled. Clip would have to note the efficacy of our cooker. We added rosemary sprigs, bay leaves, salt, pepper, stirred it all together, and closed the cooker back up.

Inside again, we wrote letters. When the entrance trees made shade over the house, we sat down with Shadow and pulled ticks off of him. We bathed again in the afternoon.

By supper the temperature had finally begun to drop. Though the cooker had been in the shade for an hour, the roasted vegetables steamed when we took them out and lifted the lid. We ate.

Then with the last light of the day, we went on a stroll, Jennifer already in her pajamas. Holding hands, we walked past the garden and climbed a knoll we call "the Lookout," where we can see a couple of miles past our land to a wooded ridge.

If there's anything spectacular in the sky—a sunset, lightning, a crescent moon—we can see it from here. On this day, the sun set into distant gray clouds streaked with purple. As I occasionally do, against Jennifer's protestations that I will hurt my back, I picked her up and ran a few steps toward Snuggery.

∽

That I'd risen from my spot by the river and the earthworm and continued down the road—without knowing where I would end up that day—was most riverlike, I determined, a thought that soothed me. Here was another principle for *A Unicyclist's Guide to America*: Motion without consideration of beginnings and endings can shelter a unicyclist from time and speed and progress.

Yes. Be a river, I would tell my disciples, who would gather to hear me. Some of them would be carrying unicycles, missing the point. Create a world without beginnings and endings, I would tell them. They would take notes, perhaps, wondering what such a world would look like, how to imagine their lives as a river, and I would not be garrulous, not having experienced such a world myself.

SLOWSPOKE

I would hand out copies of *A Unicyclist's Guide to America*—
then would be at a loss to know what else to do with a group of
disciples. They probably wouldn't realize that those days in the
Ozarks—pleasurable as they were with little traffic and beautiful
scenery—created in me a longing for a restaurant, which I
hoped to find in the small town of Alton. Alton, in effect, would
be the ending of a long restaurant-less stretch, whose beginning
was in New Madrid, Missouri.

Better, I knew, to travel like a river, goalless and present, in
a world without beginnings and endings.

Yet by the time I stepped into the Alton restaurant, my longing was so great, and the ending point so defined, I placed a
double order of pancakes, which ended up being six, each the
size of a large plate. By the time I finished eating, my stomach
felt bloated and painful, a condition that apparently did not help
in the process of balancing on a single wheel, for outside of
town my unicycle shot out from under me, causing me to fall
backward and land on my backpack.

The sky was bright blue. I looked around. No disciples, luckily. On the chance that I would never have a group of disciples,
what in the world would I do with *A Unicyclist's Guide to America*, possibly the only tangible result of my journey, other than
the wound currently on my left hand? Who would be interested? I wondered. In any case I had something else to add to
it: if you find yourself looking up at the sky instead of at the
terrain in front of your wheel, it's likely you have fallen.

I got up. The scrape on my hand was not bad. Keep moving, I
told myself. I was glad that no one had seen me fall. A viewer would
have thought, "What else should he expect, traveling that way?"

I turned off shortly on a gravel road, heading toward West
Plains, Missouri. A few of the rocks were big, so I had to walk,
which was fine with me. Penance for eating too much. The fields
around me were bright green, some of them hosting dairy cows.
Although picturesque, a field of dairy cows did not help my

belly feel less full. In what must have been three or four miles, I reached blacktop again and began to feel better.

The blacktop took me into West Plains, the biggest town I'd visited since Clarksville, Tennessee. Here, I looked for a bike shop but couldn't find one. Nothing was apparently wrong with my unicycle, yet I would have felt better if someone had looked at it. You would think it would need maintenance every several hundred miles. The tire tread was getting thin, but I figured I could make it to Kansas; in fact, given the scarcity of towns on my Missouri route, it looked like I'd have to make it to Kansas.

So although I would have used such a significant town's services for something, I kept on, visiting in the next few days two back-to-the-land families I'd corresponded with before my trip, the first of them just outside West Plains. The Shumachers lived in a secluded valley accessed by a gravel road so steep that it would make the resident, I thought, think twice about leaving home. Prairie and Trellis, in their thirties, had two kids—Forrest, five, and Symphony, three. Off the power grid, they generated their own electricity with solar panels, enough for lights, a refrigerator, and a water pump for irrigating a large garden. For bathing they had an outdoor bathtub set over a fire pit. Prairie, as I discovered, would fill the tub and light its fire before supper, and the entire family, after eating and cleaning up, would climb into the tub for a hot bath before bed.

Comfortable with them—though not to the extent of joining them in their bath—and feeling as if in an oasis, I stayed here two nights and a day, helping in the garden, playing with the kids, and joining them in their dangerously lean and healthy meals. One lunch, especially, was shocking in its simplicity: popcorn sprinkled with nutritional yeast. At one point, after I was shown the strawberry patch in the garden, Forrest told me, "You have two choices. You can either have a strawberry pie or take fresh strawberries with you when you go." On questioning him further, I discovered that he had never had a strawberry pie, that pies in this little oasis were apparently the stuff of dreams.

I grew fond of Forrest, who took it upon himself to show me how to ride a bicycle. He thought I'd only learned how to ride a unicycle. "It's not that hard," Forrest said as he picked up his little bike from the ground. "You just have to remember to put your hands on the handlebars."

He wobbled, crazily at first—then straightened out and coasted down a grassy slope. "You make it look easy," I yelled to him. He ran to a shed and got out a bigger bike, wanting me to try. He showed me how I should get on.

"So I should always keep my hands on the handlebars?" I asked.

"When you first start out," he told me.

I got on and started coasting. "How do I stop this thing?" I yelled to him.

"Use the brakes."

"Where?"

"On the handlebars."

But by that time I had made it to the bottom of the hill. I walked the bike up. I told him that the ride scared me somewhat, that I thought I should stick with my unicycle.

For a while, then, we rode together, with me on my unicycle following Forrest on his little bike. Symphony tried to keep up with us, pedaling a rusted green and yellow tractor.

Before I left the next morning, Forrest said that they might visit me in Kentucky, but that they would have to come in a car or on bikes. I told him that that was okay, if they wanted to risk it like that.

Chapter Twenty-Three

"BUT IF YOU HAD CITY WATER," a water board member might say, "you wouldn't have to skimp as much during a drought."

Saving the planet could very well hinge on a response that he could understand, but I'm at a loss. I know skimping ensures our utter delight during the next rain, but the task of communicating this hits me as Sisyphean.

⤸

The other family I visited in Missouri, the Lucketts, lived just a day and a half of unicycling from the Shumachers, the town of Ava between them.

Outside of Ava, on the day I would arrive at the Lucketts, a shiny red Camaro slowed down, and a woman with long, blond hair and a summer dress leaned toward the passenger window, her left hand steering the car, and asked me where I was going. "I've seen you three times today," she said.

For once I knew where I was headed. "The Lucketts," I said.

"Oh, I know them," she said, but didn't say anything else.

My initial guess was that she wouldn't have much in common with a back-to-the-land family. Now, given the experience I had at the Lucketts, I can see what would lead her to be wary of me.

I hadn't stopped pedaling, and I asked her if she could tell me how fast I was going. She leaned back toward the steering wheel to take a look. "My speedometer says zero," she told me.

A car came up behind us, so she waved and drove off. A bumper sticker said, "Visualize World Peace." I wondered how fast she had to go to visualize movement. She had been embarrassed for me, a reaction I wasn't expecting.

I continued on. Though I expected the Lucketts to be as friendly as the Shumachers, Barry Luckett did not make me feel welcome.

"Do you smoke pot?" he asked me that evening after I'd spent an afternoon working in their garden. We sat in their house trailer, which had a surprising number of electrical appliances given that all their electricity was produced by sunlight. Janie was cooking supper. Their daughter Kathy played video games on a computer.

"No," I responded to him.

"Why?" he asked.

"I've never had the urge."

"Good, that will make mine last longer."

Later he asked me: "You know the best way to carry water?"

"A bucket?" I guessed.

"Nope. A hose."

I began to suspect that he was disdainful of my chosen method of travel, which you could argue was more like carrying water with a bucket than a hose. I left their homestead feeling more foolish than typical and wanting a positive, or at least a neutral, reaction to my journey, as the pretty woman in the fast car had given me, saying just that I was going zero, perhaps embarrassed for me, but not disdainful.

⸙

I walked with Jennifer for the first time on the shady lane between the Duck and the cabin. In minutes she would see my home for the first time.

What would help, I thought, was her experience in Nicaragua. She'd used an outdoor composting toilet there and had hauled water. In Nicaragua she had learned that water had weight. Where was she, I wondered, in the spectrum of living

153

that went from California, where she was born, to Nicaragua?

Hopefully, my family's method of refrigeration wouldn't seem too shocking. We used a pulley to lower a five-gallon bucket with perishable items into a thirty-foot-deep, stone-lined well. The bucket lid would get grimy, but I'd washed it the day before, and now I expected it to be generally clean. Sometimes we'd see snakes between the well rocks. Would that be too rustic an experience? With any luck at all, Jennifer would have encountered snakes from time to time in Nicaraguan refrigerators.

And how would she view the catching of water off the cabin roof into buckets, which we lined up at the side of the cabin and used for washing? Due to tree pollen and lichen and oak tannin, the water was always a bit yellowish.

~

I continued to think of the woman in the Camaro, wondering if I should have responded differently to her question about where I was going. If I had said something to the effect that I wasn't sure where I was going (instead of mentioning the Lucketts), how would she have responded then? The various possibilities I entertained lasted a few miles. If she came by again, I told myself, I would be better prepared for her question, provided that she would ask it again.

But once I began heading into Amish country, I gave up on the possibility of any fast car passing, much less one with a woman inside interested in my travels.

Now before me were two Amish boys standing perfectly still at the top of a hill. One of them held a pitchfork. When I got close enough for them to know they weren't mistaking me for anything else, they went berserk, jumping up and down and shouting boisterously. It looked like they had lost every fundamental, conservative instinct they had. I waved to them.

Without causing further flamboyancy, I pedaled through the Amish community, headed toward Niangula, Missouri. Every few miles I stopped to move a turtle off the road. What could be slower than a turtle on a road, I wondered. I passed through the towns of Niangula and Conway and Long Lane, each one smaller than the one before—so that the sum of Long Lane was a closed general store. No phone. I had tried in Niangula and Conway to call my grandmother to wish her and my mother Happy Mother's Day, but no one answered. I sat for a while on the front porch of the closed store.

The road narrowed out of Long Lane. When the sun dropped, I left it for the high grasses by the Niangula River. I wondered if one day was how long it took, in a turtle's way of thinking, to cross a road. I'd never before tried camping in grass as tall as I was. I couldn't see what I was stepping on. Sometimes my foot sank in a hole or a dip in the ground, and I quickly pulled it back up. If I got too close to the river, the ground became soggy, but the higher elevations weren't flat. I stayed on the rougher, drier ground. Finally I came to a bluff where there was a flat place about the size of my body. I pressed down the high grasses and removed the rocks and spread my stuff out. I sat down and ate almost two dozen oatmeal cookies. Happy Mother's Day, I thought. The continuous flow of water eased the need for me to think about anything in particular. I fell asleep quickly.

I woke up when I heard a big splash. Then another. I sat up, wondering what I had slept with. Nothing else jumped in.

Small roads allowed me to pedal in a kind of trance that day. I didn't think beyond what was immediately in front of me: a hill, a curve, a turtle with its neck stretched out, paddling the road. My reverie was broken only two times—when I had to make brief, quarter-mile skirts on 73 and 65. It was nice that very few people were able to stare at me. When it began to rain, my rain jacket visor prevented me from seeing anything more than a few feet away. I imagined myself being practically invisible.

I wasn't sure exactly how I made the decision to head toward Fort Scott, Kansas, instead of Nevada, Missouri, which was on the Kansas line, but I woke up one morning in Humansville next to a rototiller in a shed someone let me camp in, happy with it. I couldn't believe I was traveling so quickly through Missouri. Maybe I was getting stronger. I hoped that I was being observant enough.

Shade was scarce on the back roads toward Fort Scott. When I passed a tree I often took a break. About noon I even napped under a gnarly Osage orange and absorbed its tattered shade.

Shade gave the ground different options, I noticed, like growing three-petaled purple flowers that I didn't see in the open sun.

In Filley, Missouri, I asked directions at an antique store. "I can see what your problem is right away. You just have one wheel," the owner, Len Dennis, told me. He stood outside his shop.

"I've managed to come all the way from North Carolina," I said.

"You're from North Carolina?"

"Actually, I'm from Kentucky."

"I bet you're lost."

I told him I needed to get to Road CC on gravel roads.

"In other words, you're lost. We haven't had a unicycle traveler yet who has stopped here and hasn't been lost."

Even with his directions, I got turned around and went north once instead of south, which I realized when someone, after I had been walking and pedaling for an hour on gravel roads, pointed in front of me and told me I wasn't too far from Filley, where I had started.

I found a rare patch of woods that afternoon after I got headed in the right direction and made my camp under beech. Would this be my last chance to camp in the woods? My impression of Kansas was that it didn't have many trees.

Before the moon set sometime in the night, it set loose a silver light that dripped from leaf to leaf down to where I was resting. As the moon dropped, the pattern of its touch on my body changed. Eventually, I fell asleep.

When I opened my eyes in the morning, the beech looked farther away than they had at night. I remembered where I was. Kansas! I would get to Kansas that day—and I'd get a motel room to celebrate. Where had my last motel been? I remembered: New Madrid, Missouri, after crossing the Mississippi.

I rushed that day, which is to say I took fewer breaks. By eleven forty, when I was in Moundville buying a package of cinnamon rolls for under a dollar, I had already gone twenty-three miles. A cranky woman who had earlier scuttled my attempt to ask for directions had not even slowed me down. In fact, by sticking her hand out the door and telling me to "get on down the road" and waving a small, wrinkled arm at me, she had done just the opposite.

I was a little too fixed on Kansas to notice much of anything past Moundville. Just flat fields. In two and a half hours of traveling, I arrived at a point where I thought Garland, Kansas, should be, but instead I stared at a sign, "State Road Maintenance Ends." A few yards in front of me, the pavement changed to gravel, and the gravel road, if I looked far enough in the distance, evaporated into fields.

I flagged down a farmer with a four-wheeler strapped to the back of his pickup, and he helped me with directions. "Yep, the roads go just like that," he said after looking at my map. According to him, Garland was a ghost town. No wonder I hadn't seen it. When I found out I was thirteen miles out of Fort Scott instead of six as I had thought, I lost a lot of my energy.

Nothing happened except my desire for the miles to pass. As a unicyclist, I knew I shouldn't long for something up the road, but my tiredness was so great I breached this rule. I simply wanted to be in a motel in Kansas. Not in three or four hours, but now. Or if that were too much to ask, I wanted at least something to happen. Set on blank, hard miles, an encounter of any kind now would be noteworthy. But nothing happened. The terrain remained treeless and flat and the road straight.

Chapter Twenty-Four

IN MY RÉSUMÉ TO A FUTURE SOCIETY, I'd include at least one solar cooker recipe, to show that I could use as well as build these cookers. I'd bank on someone being impressed.

To make a vegetarian burrito filling, I'd say, enough for twelve fat burritos, combine these ingredients in a dark-colored saucepan with a lid:

> 1⅓ cup brown basmati rice
> ½ cup green lentils
> 3½ cups water
> 6 cloves garlic, minced
> 2 tbsps chili powder
> 1 tsp cumin
> 1 tsp oregano
> 2 large carrots, coarsely chopped or grated
> salt and black pepper, to taste

Note that in cooking rice in a solar cooker, you use less water than you would over a conventional stove top.

Place in the solar cooker on a sunny day and adjust the cooker as needed. Using hot mitts, take out the dish when cooked, in 1½–2 hours. Be sure to set the saucepan on a board so it doesn't burn the grass while you are closing back up the cooker.

Knowing when food is cooked, I'd say, depends on experience. A solar cook learns to add time with clouds and shorten it with bright sunlight.

〜

I woke up in a motel room in Fort Scott, Kansas, at a mental standstill. The big, soft room hummed, and my mind went blank. I'd not thought about which direction to head beyond Fort Scott. I'd always considered Kansas to be a unicycling heaven. But what did one do in heaven? It would help to have a map.

I sat up at the edge of my bed and stared at the little lamp on the dresser by the television. Would I run out of water between Kansas towns? I determined that I'd officially left my home terrain. I'd made it out into the world, for what that was worth. My unicycle tire, I noticed, was now completely bald. The lamp blurred into its flowery wallpaper background, and I felt transported to New York City, where I worked, only a year out of college, as an intern for *The Nation* magazine.

Of all the factors that encouraged me to quit my internship—the two-hour commute from Long Island, where I was staying with my mother's cousin, to the office in Manhattan; the claustrophobia I suffered being inside all day, unsure even on clear days where the sun was in the sky; the tedium of fact-checking, which I determined was not suited for my personality—the one that seemed in retrospect the most trivial, involving just ten minutes of my time every day, was the one that plagued me the most. The phone receptionist took a ten-minute break each hour, so the interns took turns staffing the switchboard while she was gone. They gave us a workshop on the switchboard, but I figured I was either less astute than the other interns or starting out with a distinct disadvantage having been brought up in a home without even a single phone line, for I apparently missed some crucial pieces of information.

When someone would call, they typically would need me to transfer their call. I'd start out pretty well.

"Hello, *The Nation* magazine."

"Yes, this is so and so from the *The New York Times*. Is Micah Sifry there?"

I'd look to see if Micah had checked in that day.

"Yes, I'll transfer your call."

Sometimes I'd press the right combination of buttons, and a red light on the switchboard would flash by an appropriate editor's name. If I was lucky, the light would stop flashing. That meant the call had been successfully transferred and answered. Such routine success stories were rare for me.

My main problem was that I didn't know how to retrieve a call that I'd transferred unsuccessfully, a call marked by a continued flashing red light. If I waited long enough, the light would stop flashing. But then I'd get an irate call a few seconds later. I also didn't know how to put someone on hold. So I tried my best to transfer calls to where I knew there would be someone to answer the phone. I hated to send an important-sounding person deep into copyediting, but I'd do it if I had to.

While I was fumbling around with a single call, more calls would come in on other lines, marked by more flashing lights.

I was afraid to ask for help. Then too much time went by, and I couldn't ask for help.

So every day I steeled myself for the ten-minute task. My job was to stop or prevent the flashing red lights. I'd do whatever it took.

My vision solidified again, returning the lamp to its secure place on the dresser top and me to the edge of my bed in a motel room in eastern Kansas, a little worried that Kansas was giving me the same feeling that New York City had.

Though it felt like half a day, immobility in that room may have lasted only a half hour or so. Ultimately, the obvious need to acquire a new tire and a map of Kansas prompted me to make a plan: I would give myself another day for these chores.

Bob's Bike Repair not only changed my tire but aligned my wheel so it would spin straight. If I ever decided where to go I would get there right on. I sent my old tire home. It would take the place of a letter, perhaps.

I spent a good portion of the day studying a newly purchased map. I seemed to be stuck on Eureka, Kansas, but eventually forced my gaze away from this town, which was on the road going to Wichita. My eyes dropped south, away from traffic, and settled on the Chaplin Nature Center. I would go there. The decision was a relief.

As I found out the next morning, the light blue roads on the map were gravel roads, which were fine for traveling—covered with a finely crushed rock—but for the fact that there were no road signs. Intersections were places for major decisions. Straight or right, I'd wonder. Left, I was pretty sure, would head me back to Missouri. Sometimes I would go straight, sometimes right. I came to dread intersections, although they were virtually the only events in my day, and they gave me the sense that I was going at least someplace. In *A Unicyclist's Guide to America,* I would include this thought: stationary objects or landmarks provide meaning for unicyclists. The treeless hills that surrounded me, however, folded into each other as a single organism and could not be considered stationary landmarks. No houses. No cars. I could see for miles if I chose to look up from the road. A few hours deep into this topography, with the sun almost directly overhead, I truly had no sense of direction.

I was relieved to see a house sometime around noon. An elderly woman picked bright green lettuce in a strip of black soil. I walked up to her, and she proved to be an oasis of information. She showed me on the map where we were (still in Kansas, thank goodness!) and filled my canteen and packed up a Snickers bar and other snacks for my afternoon traveling.

In the next couple of days I passed through the small communities of Hepler and Walnut, meeting two long-distance bicyclists outside Walnut. Of course they were going east, the wind at their backs. They showed me maps on their handlebars that mentioned the services each town offered. With that news I resisted a strong impulse to covet handlebars and focused instead on feeling like a pioneer. Highway 96, the bicyclists said, was busy. That day was a hot Saturday, and I pushed myself to get as close to 96 as possible—I would attempt to get my stretch on this road over with on Sunday morning.

I pedaled until dusk, exhausting myself. With the last bit of light, I stepped into tall weeds by the side of the road and dropped my heavy backpack on an old rock foundation. By the time I rolled out my pad and sleeping bag, it was dark. I reached my hand into plastic bags of food and ate what I could find: peanuts, raisins, Ritz crackers, and—my treat—the Snickers bar, which was mostly melted and got smeared over my hands.

I fell asleep but woke up sometime in the night with a big moon over me. How late was it? How early? I decided to get up and travel closer to Highway 96.

Packing up, I was dizzy. I walked to a road filmy with moonlight. Mounting my unicycle would not have been possible, for I even walked clumsily, not sure exactly when my feet would hit the ground. I began to suspect it was only midnight, then was sure of it when it failed to get light.

I could see headlights for miles before the image of me and my backpack and one wheel smashed into the vision of late Saturday-night drivers. Sometimes I hid in the grass beside the road, but mostly I just willed them to pass and return me to the dark. At an intersection that I thought was Highway 96 but that turned out not to be, I lost all of my energy and flopped down for the second time in several hours in tall grass by the side of a road. I slept like I had been run over.

I poked my head out in the morning—a blade of grass bent by a dewdrop, a background of asphalt. Too close to the road! I packed up in a hurry.

Highway 96 was less than a mile away, which meant that my midnight journey had been four miles. Encouraged at first by light traffic, I stopped briefly at a country store. A group of men stared at me like one of them was going to win a bet depending on what I did. Hopefully I would make one of them happy. Hopefully not the one predicting I would collapse in front of the cash register. I bought crunchy peanut butter. Nothing happened.

I continued toward Severy, where I would exit 96. What I had been afraid of happened six miles short of Severy—an increasing number of cars forced me off the road. The roar of one left only to give room in my head for the next. I couldn't notice my own breathing.

So it was that I considered the greasy spoon in Severy to be a sanctuary, that cigarette smoke lacing the air instead of exhaust seemed to be an improvement. I ordered chili and ate it with a positive attitude though the spices were funny, and it didn't settle well in my stomach. I noticed a large billboard across the parking lot: Harris Real Estate. We Sell the Earth.

Despite it all, I was thankful. After lunch I pedaled south on 99, a much quieter road. Intent on finding a place to camp even though it was only noon, I turned on the first gravel road to the west. Then shortly I left the gravel for grassland. I let one hill come between me and the road and then chanced upon a meadow with a pond.

I rolled my sleeping bag out close to the pond, onto ground blanketed with wildflowers. The map showed I could go on small roads west and south for a long time. But now, the time I had to stay in one place billowed, and I went into it gradually, as if into someone's arms.

I had the feeling then that Jennifer and I often have now, when the objectives for our day are clear and the time we have for them is more than adequate, of having our bodies relax into our place and respond, even as we engage in the mundane, to its particulars.

Because I'd given myself a half a day in those grasslands— hours more time than usual for a camp—I went about my chores with pleasure. Indeed, in walking into the pond to get water for washing clothes (grass, not mud underfoot!), then washing them and taking the clean, dripping clothes to a willow to hang them on a branch, motions that brought my body across the body of the land, I felt, I imagined, as one does who is in love.

I discovered wild strawberries between the willow and the pond and harvested them. Sitting cross-legged on my sleeping bag, I put them one by one into my mouth, feeling their slight roughness with my tongue before biting into the sweet and tart fruit.

At dusk I took a bath with a tin cup and pond water and stretched out for the night on a curve of the earth, and as big a sky as I'd ever known on top of me.

Chapter Twenty-Five

JENNIFER WROTE ME A LETTER after visiting my home, saying that she thought my family was living "close to the heart of things." I became intensely happy, but in the days that followed felt that happiness roughened by trepidation, as if I were on a Ferris wheel that had stopped, with me on the top seat.

In one sense I had arrived. Look at the view! Families and couples mingling around the game and food trailers; a carny leaning toward a potential player; pink cotton candy bobbing about in the crowd; a tilt-a-whirl, a scrambler, a carousel, a paratrooper; and then beyond the carnival lot: a busy street, chain restaurants, car dealerships, a bank, and in the distance a hillside, green with trees. Yet as it is on a unicycle with your wheel momentarily stopped, there's less of a feeling of arrival than a need for motion.

I felt suspended between Jennifer and home, and I didn't know how to shift my thoughts to create movement again, so I would not be sitting alone in the sky but carried once more by a functioning ride.

∽

On waking in the morning, I dawdled, not eager to leave my flowering and fruiting grasslands camp. As I remained stretched out in the dewy grasses, two geese flew over my head and landed on the pond. I wondered then if there could be a settlement here that could add to the pond as the geese did.

Thus I daydreamed—but the images I conjured in my mind of a village giving as much as extracting were too storybook or rustic to cross over into present reality. My village dissipated when faced with the modern, brick house and its attached garage, its trash can by the side of the road, its water piped in and sewer piped out, its electrical outlets—and once I was no longer able to imagine a beautiful village, I determined it was time to resume travel.

After pedaling that morning only a short while on a sandy gravel road, I was surrounded by the Flint Hills. Long, sloping, treeless, green hills absorbed my glances and dispersed them. Was this what it meant to be "out west"? Sleepy, I took a lot of breaks. The hills called for that anyway.

My movement sometimes caused the movement of a whole herd of cows, which left all of us, the hills too, going in the same direction.

Close to Latham I caught a highway worker staring off into the horizon. "To me," he said, "This is God's country. Now if only the fences and poles weren't here. You can just imagine what it used to be like, grass above your head, stagecoaches."

The cows, he said, ate the grass down before it seeded. A little farther down the road, I surprised a rancher working on a fence, and he expressed another perspective of the land.

"People say Arkansas and Missouri are so pretty. There are just trees there—you can't see anything. I've spend half my life cutting down trees growing where they shouldn't be growing."

I learned from him that the restaurant in Latham closed in fifty minutes, so for the next two miles I traveled as fast as I could. I had my mind set on ice cream, which I thought would be soothing for my stomach, still mildly upset by the chili. I made it with twenty minutes to spare, and I had enough time to eat six scoops with a piece of homemade pumpkin pie. Nothing could have made me more content. The restaurant workers looked bored. That night while I was camped in a band of Osage orange outside of Smileyburg, it occurred to me that I had a hard time expressing to people the pleasure I experienced from the simplest events, like eating or finding a campsite. What I did at the time always seemed more significant than what I was able to convey.

I was back in flat country. From my sleeping bag, I could see an oil rig continuously pouncing on the earth.

Smileyburg consisted of a shuttered transmission repair shop and a sign with the "Smiley" ripped off its name. Outside this town, a man took my picture from inside his parked pickup. Needing directions, I went over to him. He clearly had not wanted to talk to me, but probably figured he had asked for it by taking my picture. "I pump oil," he said extraneously as I approached him. He was out of breath. Was he more physically involved with pumping oil than was, at first, noticeable? He proved to be no help with directions, only trying to get me on roads he knew about.

A stonemason down the road was a better help—I just had to turn left at the million-dollar Grandview Methodist Church. It would be easy to spot, he said.

In just a few miles I made it to Winfield, Kansas, the town that ranks as my favorite among all I passed through—not for its scenery, but for the unprecedented occurrence of having a bicyclist slow to my pace and travel with me a short distance, something that happened not just once but three times in the course of passing through town. The first cyclist was a chaplain at Winfield State Hospital, and he offered to take me to lunch. We ate at a diner together.

Then, within five minutes of pedaling from the diner, a computer science professor riding home after classes came to my side. He put his bike in the lowest gear, and our paces matched. Along the way he pointed out an oil tank and told me never to climb on top of one because the tops sometimes rusted out. If I were ever to fall in oil, I'd just sink. He stopped at the top of a hill and handed me a cellular phone. Call your family, he told me. It was the first time I'd ever held a cellular phone. The professor probably thought I knew how to use one.

I remembered a story my mother told me, about the first

time I used a regular phone. I was at Grandma's house, talking with my cousin Ralph. When I dropped the receiver to the ground, I became distraught. I picked it up quickly and told Ralph I was sorry and asked him if he was okay. And at *The Nation* they had expected me to work a switchboard.

"Could you dial a number for me?" I asked. Why had I not been able to ask for help in New York? He dialed it, but the connection couldn't be made. "Well, come into my house," he said. "That one there." He pointed to a two-story brick.

I sank into a deep white carpet as I stepped across a room to a cream-colored phone on a polished walnut desk. I demonstrated (thank goodness) my ability to use this phone and said hello to my grandmother. I thanked the professor and was on my way.

When I was out of town and actually glad to be by myself, a young woman on a bike waved me down. She said she had seen me going past the college and wanted to talk to me then, but that I was with another biker.

"I'm a clown," she said. "I'm learning to ride a unicycle now. But I'm not getting anywhere on it. How do you do that? How did you start?"

"I used poles."

She looked at me intently.

"You're welcome to stay at my house tonight. You can sleep on the couch. My husband wouldn't mind. He's a minister."

I thanked her but told her I thought I would just keep traveling.

"Let me go home and do a few chores, and then I can come by with the car, and you can tell me what you've decided."

I thought I had already made a decision, but I agreed to her proposition. I said goodbye to her and pedaled off, surprised at the tenacious grip that Winfield had on me. When she came by an hour later, just as I was getting into a lulling rhythm, I told her I could probably make it to the Chaplin Nature Center—a decision that ended up being a mistake. It turned dark quickly.

If I had known the exact directions to the nature center, I would have attempted the additional four miles; instead, I used somebody's phone to call my clown acquaintance—Jenny Cathery. Although it would be a twenty-minute drive for them, she and her husband agreed to pick me up and bring me back the next day.

Winfield, Kansas, had won, and I found myself entering a modern brick house (for the second time in Winfield) similar to the one that had vanquished my utopian village by the grassland pond.

~

The appraiser did indeed show up to our house carrying a clipboard. He was, unfortunately, sweating a bit after making the walk, though the day was warm, not hot.

We greeted him on the west side of the house. He was retired from the bank but did valuations part-time. "How do you get here ordinarily?" he asked. "The same way you came," we had to tell him.

He had his clipboard out, then. "Any utilities out here? Water, gas, electric, phone line?"

No, in all cases—though we had him step out toward the garden a bit, so he could see our three solar panels, now at their most horizontal position, as it was summer. He could also see the rope I had draped over the roof. I would hold on to this rope when I adjusted the panels, four times a year. Our stovepipe was also visible.

"Wood heat?" he asked.

"Yes, and sunlight," we responded.

We walked him to the south side of the house and explained to him how most of our windows were on the south side, how the low winter sun entered our house, how the higher summer sun was blocked by our eaves. We showed him our solar hot water tank, inside an insulated box with a glass top, mounted on the southeast corner of the house.

"Its capacity?" he asked.

"It is a small RV water heater, fourteen gallons. The water comes out hot. The most we use for a bath is five gallons."

"And to get the water into the house?"

"Gravity."

"To get water back into the tank?"

"Via a hand pump from inside the house."

We moved around to the east side of the house, skirting a round cistern we'd made out of field rock. We pointed out the down spouting from the roof, how we could divert the water to the rock cistern, which we used for summer watering and which could drain into the garden cistern with four hundred feet of hosing, or to a roof washer and piping through the foundation to a cellar tank.

"Size of your cellar tank?"

"Two hundred seventy gallons, but with all of our cisterns we have a three-thousand-gallon capacity."

We pointed out the shed and our compost toilet.

"Septic tank?"

"No, we only have gray water from the kitchen sink, which flows out under this red oak by the shed. Eventually we want to make a tiny wetlands. The compost toilet has a urine drain that flows to a small leach field. The compost that the toilet pro-duces—one wheelbarrow load a year—gets put on fruit trees."

Then we were on the north side. We pointed out the cistern and the gravity hydrant spigot. We pointed to the outdoor bath-room, mentioned that only one member of the household used it—mentioned, too, that our house thus could be considered a two-bathroom. He didn't seem to know that we were joking.

Once we'd circled the house, he took out a tape measure, and we helped him measure the outer dimensions of the house. It would turn out to be, we knew, six hundred square feet. He jotted down the numbers.

We opened the heavy back porch cedar door for him, and

he stepped inside our boot room, a small (seven by twelve) space, where we kept our refrigerator, an herb cabinet, an onion rack, shoes and boots, a filing cabinet, and a ceramic water filter.

We ushered him through the next door, and all three of us were gathered in our little house. He could now see the oiled hardwood floors, the wood stove on its stone hearth, the cedar beams and cabinets, the grain mill, the kitchen counters and sink, the apartment-size propane gas range, the shelves for books, plants, and food, all made out of cedar boards, the bed on the east side of the house, next to the red hand pump and the small claw foot bathtub. He could see a small couch flanked by a plant shelf and a cedar ladder going to the main loft, where the solar batteries were kept. He could see a floor lamp behind the couch and the thin curtain that separated the couch from a small dressing room. He could see the vaulted ceiling and a second, smaller loft above the kitchen area. He could see, too, the addition with its still unfinished floor.

"Is your house finished?"

"We still need to do the floor in the addition, and we want to make a desk and a table."

We offered him lemonade. He declined but thanked us and said he had another property to visit. He would send us his finding.

"Take a second," I said, "and look at our root cellar." I turned on the cellar light and opened the trap door between the dressing room and the bed, and the man with the clipboard peered in. He could see the thick board ladder, the water tank, a tray of recently harvested carrots, the jagged edge of the limestone shelf I'd battered through, and the cooking oils we kept on a remnant of that shelf. Potatoes, we mentioned, store all winter there.

We then walked him out the door. Because he hadn't acknowledged it before, we pointed out the solar cooker and walked over to it. Luckily, the lasagna was just beginning to brown and bubble. We said that we had two kitchens.

"Remember," we said, "two bathrooms and two kitchens."
He smiled this time and walked away.

∽

Inside the Cathery's house were humming appliances, bright lights, soft places to sit, and wall-to-wall carpeting. Amanda and Josh, their kids, were sleeping. Jenny put three potatoes in a microwave and showed me some of her books: *Ventriloquism in a Nutshell* and *On One Wheel*. I wrote down addresses for the Unicycling Society of America and the International Unicycling Federation. What would one do belonging to such organizations?

I startled the Catherys by eating all of my potato, even the skin. At least I imagined them to be startled. Later, Jenny's husband, an overweight man much older than Jenny—who treated her more like a daughter than a wife—used a fork to poke his skin down the sink drain.

Eager for unicycling tips, Jenny took me to a narrow hallway and showed me how she got on her unicycle and held the walls as she moved crookedly forward.

"Try to put more of your weight on the pedals," I told her. "You'll have a little more control over the wheel." Then I suggested something that seemed to help other people, although I wasn't sure why.

"Poise your muscles, but be relaxed at the same time."

Jenny did show some improvement. I was tired. The walls of her house seemed slanted against her.

I slept on their living room couch that night, woke up to the sound of a hair dryer. Amanda walked quickly past my couch to what they called "the pile" in the laundry room, found a pair of perfectly white socks, then went back to her room. I got up, rolled up my sleeping bag, straightened out the couch. Jenny came out of the bathroom with makeup on and her hair curled. I wondered what the occasion was. She had made an image of

Snoopy out of balloons and walked over to give it to me.

"This is for me?" I asked.

"It's yours," she said and smiled at me. She turned and went into the kitchen. How would I put Snoopy in my pack? Maybe I could inadvertently leave it on the couch. Mr. Cathery came in wearing a suit, sat down in his easy chair, and picked up a newspaper. When Amanda came around again, he told her to set the table but said nothing of the sort to Josh, who was younger than Amanda but big enough to help out.

"Somebody forgot to turn the dishwasher on last night," Jenny said from the kitchen, where she was making pancakes.

"Amanda, wash what we need by hand," her father said.

I went into the kitchen and asked Jenny if I could help with the pancakes, but she was clearly uncomfortable with me in the kitchen. Instead, I flipped through one of her clown books while Mr. Cathery made it to the sports section.

The pancakes were very good. Because I put no more syrup on them than what I needed, Jenny mentioned something about me being frugal.

"I also noticed that when you washed your plate last night and when you took a shower, how little you let the water run."

As we were finishing with breakfast, Jenny asked me if she could bike the four miles with me to the Chaplin Nature Center. Had she put on makeup because she wanted to bike with me? That was odd. I told her yes.

"Now, Jenny," her husband said, "you're going to have to pay attention to the roads since you'll be driving back by yourself."

Under skies threatening to rain, Jenny parked the car on the side of the road where they had picked me up, and I helped her take her bike off the top of the car. "I hope this isn't too boring for you," I said. "I go pretty slowly and take a lot of breaks."

Her hair uncurled in the wind. "No, this is exciting," she said.

We walked a short distance to a dirt-road turnoff and began pedaling—Jenny riding over ruts slowly and me maneuvering around them, and both of us trying to keep track of the intersecting dirt roads and landmarks, which were few in an area turned amazingly featureless by industrial agriculture. Thunder banged in the sky when we were about a half mile from the nature center. We both knew that it was time for her to go back, yet we continued on a bit longer—till it got so dark it seemed absurd and even dangerous to go farther together.

"Will you write me?" she asked.

"Yes," I responded.

Abruptly, she said goodbye and turned around and began pedaling back to her car. I stood under the loud sky and watched her get smaller. Then, pedaling again, I accelerated her disappearance.

The naturalist caretaker allowed me to camp on the back porch of the Chaplin Nature Center Visitor's Center, where I arrived just before the black clouds dumped rain. Gerald Wiens even invited me for supper.

Though it was still morning, I felt drained of energy. With the sound of rain on the porch roof, I fell asleep. When I woke two hours later, the rain had stopped, but the trees still dripped. I stepped off the porch and found a trailhead. Take me, I thought. I'll go wherever you go. So the trail and I meandered around big, dripping cottonwood. Some of them would take two or three people to hug. We followed a creek partway, turning when it turned.

The trees thinned out, disappeared. We were in a field of tall grasses. A sign listed big bluestem, sideoats grama, western wheatgrass. As we went along, we swept birds into the sky.

Then the trees regrouped—small at first, gradually taller. Elm, hackberry, locust, and oak. An oak siphoned a squirrel up its trunk. The forest had a disheveled look due to the storm, with twigs, branches, and leaves scattered about, atop much older fallen material. A plaque noted that the massive log off to our right had fallen in 1912.

Again, the trees stopped coming at us and we were in the open—but with sand, not grasses, afoot. Surprisingly, we were on a white sand beach along the Arkansas River. Caught in the center of the beach was a river-drifted tree. A single branch protruded vertically from the gray trunk into clouds.

We were on an island after all. We'd make a turn from this beach, go back into woods, return to the visitor center. We could make the loop again. We'd circle the sanctuary. I clambered aboard the beached tree. The wood felt like bone. I reached down and picked up as much sand as I could hold. I let it trickle out. There was Jenny Cathery leaving on her bike. There she was widening her narrow hallway.

The sand half gone, I narrowed its escape route. Now I could barely see the leak. Yet eventually my hands emptied, and I held nothing.

Back on my porch, I still felt tired. I tried reading the paperback *Small Is Beautiful*, the only book I had packed, but fell asleep. Later, Gerald Wiens gave me a lasagna supper in his house, talked about his job. "Just when you think you know it all," he said, "something will happen unexpectedly in nature and keep you honest."

He treated me also to a pancake breakfast in the morning. Then I pedaled out of my sanctuary. The surrounding wheat fields were flat, although not completely flat. Maybe in a car they would seem completely flat. When the road dipped south for a mile and strong winds buffeted me, I had to get off and walk. Off my unicycle, I was smaller than the wheat, which moved about in long waves. The fuzzy tops caught wind and sun and displayed more colors than I knew the names of.

↜

Those carrots that the property valuator saw, an heirloom variety with deep orange flanks turning purplish at the stems, store well in our root cellar, especially a late fall harvest, when the cellar is cold.

"Experience in building and using root cellars." I would add this to my résumé, the one to be sent out to a new society. I would mention entering the cellar in January and finding carrots still with good color and firmness. We would take them into the kitchen and wash them with a soft brush. We'd cut them and put them in boiling water for a few minutes, and then toss them into a pan with melted butter. For the final touch, we'd sprinkle them with oregano, salt, and freshly milled black pepper.

The résumé could last for pages. This is how they would be in a new society.

The taste of food that we produce and care for ourselves, I might add, is the best we know.

In this dish of January carrots there's a portion of that sweetness that the first fall frost gives the carrots; yet the sweetness is complex enough to suggest the possibility of bitterness, and an image of the feathery green tops comes to mind, how touching them can coat your hand with their sharp smell. Oregano tweaks the carrots' complex sweetness to release in the mouth the feel of a humid summer day.

But in my mind the taste also includes the transition from summer to winter, the change in temperature—not the quick change from day to night, or from month to month, but the change that happens in the earth, in the cellar where they are stored, where it appears that nothing is happening. Yet in the winter the cellar feels like fall; in the summer, like spring.

We taste in this carrot dish the earth's incapacity for being rushed.

Chapter Twenty-Six

IN THE NEXT COUPLE OF DAYS, I coped with the transition of leaving the Chaplin Nature Center for a landscape graphed by roads that formed one-mile square boxes. The next intersection up the road would essentially become my next thought, or so it seemed. I felt I had exactly one mile to defy the logic of the area, but one mile wasn't enough. One of my fantasies, of seeing here a network of small, organic farms, could not be constructed strongly enough in one mile to withstand the calculus of industrial farming: that production and efficiency and size should be maximized at any cost. These assumptions behaved like traffic for me. I wondered, again, if I would be able to carry enough water between Kansas towns, and I thought of going home for the summer and resuming my travels in the fall.

I only spotted the homestead because of a flat tire. On seeing the flat, the first of my trip, my initial reaction was to stare off into space—in this case, across fields to a shelterbelt of trees. Not a woods, just a wide line of trees between fields, like many others I'd seen. Yet this one had a wind turbine that stuck out above the canopy. The blades were turning. Unlike my wheel, I thought.

So in a slightly less distinguished fashion than typical, I arrived at the Pauley's house, pushing a unicycle with a flat tire, and met Phil and Corliss and their kids, Aero, Mesa, and Ladae. Their house was entirely within a band of cedar, locust, hackberry, and cottonwood, not noticeable until you were only steps away from it. As I found out, Phil came here as a kid for solitude and camping. Now he lived here with his family. The wind turbine generated electricity for their house. They had a garden and a small field of organically grown wheat.

I stayed with them two days. Like the Shumachers in Missouri, they had extremely healthy eating habits—to the extent that I wished, for once, that I would visit a family that believed in caloric intake. Phil introduced me to a Victoras Kulvinskas book, and I believe the Pauleys flirted dangerously with Kulvinskas's theory that hemoglobin could function like chlorophyll, that eventually the human body could live off just air and water.

Still, I liked them. I decided I would go home for the summer because I was worried about the heat and resume traveling in the fall from their place. This decision allowed me to visit a friend of the Pauleys. Emerson Trent lived near Hutchinson, Kansas, and could get me—after I visited his farm—to a bus station. An owner of a large, mostly conventional farm, he had not retreated into a shelterbelt as the Pauleys had. As I came to learn, though, he was different from most people psychically. Phil and Corliss told me that when Aero and Mesa were babies, he had accurately judged their characters: Aero would be attracted to the sky, and Mesa to the ground. Indeed, while I was there, Mesa was the one who would escort me to the garden, while Aero preferred to climb trees.

Emerson was a tall man with a cowboy physique and a soft voice. On the morning we left in his truck, he pulled a small, light green leaf off a lamb's quarters and showed it to me.

"This is the first fruit," he said. "It has three times the energy of the older leaves."

We drove thirty minutes to get to his place, a twelve-hundred-acre farm. His first chore on arriving was to back a huge tractor, jointed in the middle like some kind of insect, out of a barn so he could put another tractor in first. When he had the tractor fully backed out, he motioned to me to come up into the cab. I had to climb a ladder to get up there. "This is quite a shock for me, being on eight wheels," I said.

"We just call it a four-wheeler because they are double wheels."

I said I tended to count every wheel.

Then he surprised me. "I'll let you drive it a little." He got out of the driver's seat as I was telling him I had never driven a tractor before, even a small one.

"Go ahead, get over there."

The seat was soft—and quite high above the ground. Emerson told me what to do. As I found out, you didn't have to have a sense of two moving parts to drive it. In fact, it was startlingly easy to maneuver.

As we were eating our first meal together in his L-shaped house, Emerson told me he could sense the energy levels of foods, and that these levels came to him as numbers. A four was good food, like vegetables or eggs; a two was junk, like glazed donuts; a negative four was poison; and a positive twelve was high-energy food, like the first leaves of lamb's quarters. For dessert we had strawberries on top of a pound cake I had taken out of my pack.

"If you'll forgive me," Emerson said, "this pound cake is a two."

I put the dirty dishes into a dishwasher. No place for compost that I could see.

Emerson needed to watch a videotape, *A Course in Miracles*, for a class he was taking, and he asked me if I wanted to watch it with him. I followed him into a huge living room with a wide-screen television, but before I could sit down, he asked me if I would mind washing my jeans. I could use the washing machine. I hadn't thought that my jeans were dirty. I changed into shorts and re-entered the living room, stepping carefully onto the deep white carpet.

That night for the first time since my motel room in Fort Scott, I slept between two sheets. In the morning, Emerson's eighty-two-year-old mother, Frances, arrived to stay a couple of days since the caretaker who lived with her was going on a short trip. As soon as Frances saw me, she thought I was Emerson's son Clinton, despite the fact that Clinton had short, dark hair, and I had long, light brown hair. Additionally, Clinton was clean-shaven, and I had a two-month beard.

"Mom," Emerson said, "this is Mark. He's on a trip across the country on a unicycle."

"Oh, right," she said. "Are you leaving?" She looked at me.

"No, not yet," I answered.

Frances handed Emerson something that looked like a tool kit with her pills in it.

"What pills do I take?" Frances asked.

"Oh, I don't know, Mom," Emerson said.

With his big hands, he opened the medicine box. A couple of pills dropped to the linoleum. "Let's see, Tuesday, noon."

I was close to him, filling up my glass at the sink. Four pills filled that compartment. With a pained look on his face, Emerson handed me two of the pills and told me to wash them down the drain.

"Those two are negative fours," he whispered. "Poisonous."

"Here you go, Mom." He handed her the remaining two pills. "These shouldn't hurt you too bad."

He picked up the two he had dropped, handed them to me. I washed them down the drain.

Later that day, in an event that sent a shock wave through my little unicyclist's soul, Emerson showed me how to operate a dump truck and rode with me and Clinton to a dairy farm where Clinton would operate a tractor with a scoop, and I would take the manure to one of Emerson's fields and dump it in a pile. Chris, a worker, would drive Emerson's other dump truck.

"Farming is a lot more fun since I started doing something good to the land," Emerson told me, referring to the compost pile we were going to make.

"Clinton will sprinkle a little gypsum with each load. That will add calcium to the compost. Leaves would do the same thing, but they're hard to come by.

"I can make a compost that has saline, a mineral that's lacking in soils around here, without ever adding saline.

"How do you know what mineral your compost is making?" I asked.

"I can just sense that," Emerson said after a pause. "But a soil scientist, after testing it, would tell me the same thing. Scientists don't understand this, how elements change into other elements. Compost isn't just what its parts are. It's a forgotten art."

Clinton, Chris, and I had walkie-talkies. Emerson went back to the house where he could listen to our progress. His code name was Number One. On the road between the dairy farm and Emerson's field, the people I passed would wave to me because they recognized Emerson's truck.

After supper Emerson asked me if I knew about ley lines. I didn't. He told me they were unmapped lines of energy that traveled diagonally across the earth. At their intersections were major cultural centers, like Cuzco, Peru, and Manchester, England. Some people could sense them and some people couldn't. I assumed that Emerson was one who could.

"There's a ley line going across my farm. You are supposed to honor them in some way, certainly not plow or drive across them. Priests used to mark them with stone circles. Now ley lines are getting sluggish, sometimes pulsing only once a day. Underground nuclear testing especially has been harmful to them. This is the earth's nervous system we're dealing with."

Clinton left for his fiancée's house. I'd found out that he was studying business agriculture. Frances was still at the table with us—wide-eyed but not focusing on anything.

"What do you think about this, Mom? I'm intuitive, and I've never discussed this with you."

"That's nice." She looked at me. "Are you leaving?"

"Not too much longer now," I told her.

I changed my clothes and joined Emerson in the living room. He told me about his attempt to start a community interested in

181

farming more naturally and intuitively. He called it the Plane-
tary Project. For a variety of reasons, including money, it didn't
work out.

"For one thing," he said, "the people working for us built the
main building with the boards going upside down."

"I don't understand," I said.

"A board is upside down if it's not going the same direction
as it would be going if it were still part of the tree."

I wanted to ask him many questions, but the reserved aura
around him cautioned me. I stayed a half day more, coming into
the awareness that Emerson's mind was incalculable, which
made it interesting, unpredictable, contradictory. A thought
startled me: that I was under his spell, intrigued by him but too
cautious to ask questions. I would probably have done anything
he asked. That last morning he sent me outside to pick three
yarrow leaves. They must be twelves, I thought, his high-power
nutrition. Back inside, like an apprentice, I handed them to him,
and he put them in a teakettle.

After breakfast we walked across a field to his older compost
piles. On the way he pointed out where the ley line crossed
his land. It was plowed over like everywhere else. At one of his
compost piles at the edge of the field, he took two shovelfuls off
the top.

"Look how it's changing," he said. "This was just manure and
straw."

An intent look on his face, he went deeper into his pile. He
wanted to show me how manure and straw came together to
become one thing. It was a lesson, I believed.

His hole was now about two feet deep, slanted toward the
center of the pile. He put the shovel aside and reached in. Most
of his arm disappeared. Oddly, I kept picturing his spotless carpet. His arm came back out, and he turned to me. In his hand
was black dirt.

"See?" he said.

"Yes," I said.

But only minutes later we were kneeling down and looking at an alfalfa field that he had not sprayed with pesticides. We saw first one, then a billion bugs. An initial look of panic on Emerson's face subsided until he appeared calm again.

And I understood then his compost to be a refuge.

⌒

Our kitchen window allows us the perfect glance outside, giving us room off to its side for open shelves of books, music, and glass jars of bulk food.

After only a few years of living here and observing, say, these entrance trees, I realize that waiting for their leaves to change color (or to fall, to be born again) is akin to watching people step off a plane, anticipating a loved one. You understand there's no reason for the event not to happen, yet you are momentarily scared.

A larger window may have given us a view of a white ash close to the entrance trees and the concomitant worry that the emerald ash borer has arrived in our area and is expected to kill every ash tree—but then we might not have been able to avert our gaze to a jar of pinto beans or a copy of Wendell Berry's book, *What Are People For?* and toward that which we could arrange, decide upon, restock.

⌒

Emerson Trent had dropped me off at the Prairie Festival in Salina, and I was among seventy other campers—yet was the only one with a sleeping bag wrapped in a thick sheet of plastic, which was held down by a unicycle. The others had tents. Emerson had recommended the festival. When it was over I would go home for the summer.

It struck me that this would be the biggest social event of my journey. A shadow of self-consciousness passed over me. I wondered if I should shave off my small beard or cut my hair. Or hide my unicycle.

Yet my unicycle caught the attention of a neighboring camper named Robert, who also lived in a neighboring state, Tennessee. What I remember about Robert is a piece of information he gave me, which I took as a gift. He said that a study showed that with all the time Americans spend with their cars, including time in traffic jams, time at work to pay for them, time to fill out insurance forms, the average American travels about two miles per hour. If I, then, pedaled along at four miles per hour, I buzzed along twice as fast as the average American! Next thing you'd know, there'd be a unicyclist as a cartoon-strip superhero.

The speakers, workshops, and tours during the festival put me in a daze. A lot of what I had thought about during my trip was amplified by the people around me.

"The accumulation of speed is something in this society that is death-oriented," said David Orr, a professor at Oberlin College.

Another point in his speech:

"Our schools' architecture needs to change. Schools train minds to think like factories. We need to do away with hallways."

And another:

"Our education should be about our proper place in the world. A lot of times we need to know what we don't need to know."

Afterward, I headed to a workshop on the medicinal uses of prairie plants, passing on the way a compost toilet that had been dubbed "World Headquarters."

Yarrow, yucca, purple coneflower. Each plant had something to offer. They had 220 species of plants at the Land Institute and were still adding to the list.

"Learning the plants around you and beginning to use them can become one of the most important political acts you can undertake."

A prairie tour was next. We followed our guide to a place at the bottom of a small hill. The guide stretched his arm in front of him.

"I brought you here to show you a place where you can see nothing but horizon and grasses. This is what the early pioneers found for days on end."

"The prairie is self-regulating and energy self-sufficient. Because of a huge array of plant species, there aren't epidemics in prairies as there are in wheat fields. No erosion either because the roots of some of the grasses and legumes and composites go down over twenty feet. A prairie actually makes soil. We think that's remarkable, so we're trying to learn from it, use it as a model. We ask certain questions, like what is here, what is required of us, and what can it help us do."

We found out about a project to cross sorghum with Johnson grass to create a perennial crop. With such a crop, farmers wouldn't have to break ground, reducing the chances for erosion.

Wes Jackson, director of the Land Institute, was the first speaker after the prairie tour.

"We should not be technological fundamentalists, accepting new products or technologies without first scrutinizing the social, agricultural, political, and ecological implications. What is stunning about our age is the efficiency with which we have thought the world to pieces. We're playing fast and loose with the parts. We claim that we know more than ever before because we've identified certain parts of the atom. Yet we still don't know the first thing about living on this planet. We need to look at the whole thing, not just at its components. Imagine yourself very small, in a plant cell, exploring. Some of what you would find would be alive, but some of it would be dead. If you looked at the whole cell, though, a top-down view, you would recognize all of it as being alive."

That was it for the speakers. It was almost suppertime. I walked back to my odd camp, stretched out on my sleeping bag. My eyes stung a little when I closed them. Nothing appeared, just a tissue of colors.

"The accumulation of speed is something in this society that is death-oriented."

"The efficiency with which we have thought the world to pieces."

Maybe the answer was in not thinking. Just recognizing an array of sensations. Just being. Like a prairie.

I ate a few things out of my pack and then took a shower in an outdoor shower stall. A black tank heated the water by absorbing sunlight.

A barn dance was the next event. I wasn't a good dancer. But what scared me more was asking someone to dance.

Later that night as I edged close to the person I wanted to dance with, a bright-faced energetic intern at the Land Institute, my resolve failed. I told myself I'd ask her during the next round. The next round came, and she walked away. I followed her, pretending to look for another person. Luckily, there was a big crowd. For the next two rounds, I walked short distances or stood still, moving as frequently as she did, almost making a complete circle. At one point I convinced myself I was already dancing with her. At about the fifth round, I finally asked her to dance, but my words came out faster than my resolve, so they seemed alien to me and inappropriate. But she said, "Sure, you want to dance one," like it was nothing.

When we got to the floor, the caller said, "Now you all are ready for a hard one," his voice amplified by four loudspeakers.

The dance was about as bad as I feared it would be. I seemed not to be able to concentrate on the moves, so my partner had to lead me. When it was over I didn't ask for another dance.

Ironically, then, I left that festival feeling more isolated than when I arrived. Robert drove me to the Greyhound bus station. There, the officials looked warily at my unicycle. Eventually, they said I could check it, but at my own risk.

Soon I was on my way to Kansas City, seated next to a woman who was telling me she liked to go to bed when she wanted to and get up when she wanted to. I wasn't sure what brought that on. We were on one of those roads that had so often scared me. She was a teacher.

"Why, I had one student who just wouldn't do the work. That's the plain truth. I had to take her aside and, you know, talk to her, one on one. I said to her if she didn't do her work, she wouldn't get a job, you know, wouldn't be able to buy a car."

Before we reached the Flint Hills, it got dark. The land gone, we could only see towns, like Manhattan.

I should have joked with that intern somehow, I thought, about my dancing ability. I should have told her how good a dance partner I could be on my unicycle.

"I know someone here in Manhattan who likes blue flowers. He keeps his yard picture-perfect, like the kind you see in magazines."

I thought she had fallen asleep. Abilene, Kansas, where Eisenhower was born. It looked similar to Manhattan, at least around the bus station. I couldn't believe how fast we were traveling.

A Peace Corps friend of my parents, Jack Vetter, picked me up in Kansas City. After what seemed to be a lifetime with my seat partner, Jack's understated, quieter manner appealed to me a great deal.

At a Mexican restaurant Jack told me of a couple of his attempts to ask women out. "I got bopped down," he said. "But I'm being rejected by a better class of women."

I stayed a couple of days with him. On the last day he introduced me to a friend of his, Roger Fulton, an inventor and mechanical engineer who tended to follow his whims, most of which were not marketable, and thus he was out of a job and making it from day to day. He called himself the Earthworm Castings Company. The closest he had come to commercial success was when a company narrowly rejected his patent for a folding bicycle.

When he saw my unicycle, Roger began tapping on a calculator. He looked at me after his calculation and told me where I would have been at that point if I had had a two-inch bigger wheel.

Roger maintained a path from the living room to the kitchen, but otherwise he was a tolerant man with his space, with books, papers, loose bicycle wheels and frames randomly arranged. I noticed a four-set volume on a bookcase: *Ingenious Mechanisms for Designers and Inventors*.

"This is a chamber of horrors," he said. "It's ninety-eight percent chaos and two percent clutter. Come here, I want to show you something."

We stepped down into his basement shop, a space so crowded that we had to pass through part of it sideways. There were enough machine tools and parts to build a bicycle or an automobile. From a jumble of bike frames he pulled out something that wasn't a bike or a unicycle.

"Let's go out on the street," he said.

Turning around, I knocked over a can of bolts.

"I've got to clean up in here," Roger said. "You know the one thing that's practical about a unicycle?"

I was bending down, picking up the bolts. "For one thing," I said, "you can use your hands."

"That's right. Well, with this thing I've taken care of that. I call it the Pyramid. It's as difficult as a unicycle but doesn't have any of the benefits of a unicycle."

We made it to the street, where I got a good look at his contraption. It had two wheels, but they were close enough together, I saw, to make the riding of it precarious. And it had handlebars, but they were backward somehow.

"You get on it backward," Roger said, "and you steer by putting your hands behind you."

Clearly, a different species of bicycle.

"Go ahead, try it."

I stepped up backward on it, an approach to a bike that so puzzled me that I didn't pay attention to Roger telling me that the steering was very sensitive. I turned a little too hard and fell off. The next time I did a little better.

"What do you think?" he asked, beaming.

"There's no sense to it," I said.

His smile continued. We put it away. He referred to it as a "whimscycle," the generic name for all the flaky bicycles he made. Pyramid was the specific name. Whimscycle Pyramid.

In the plane the next morning, I closed my eyes as the ground rushed out from under me. I had the impression we were falling. Instead, the plane left the ground. Captivated, I looked down. Lots of swimming pools. Highways everywhere, spiraling sometimes. No wonder some intersections were called cloverleaves. From my perspective up high, a top-down view, where everything around the loops could be seen too, they looked like loose knots.

Chapter Twenty-Seven

RETURNING HOME MIDWAY on my unicycle journey fit a pattern I'd demonstrated often: foraying into the world and retreating back to what was familiar, safe, hopeful. I did this in choosing a college within commuting distance of my house. And in moving to New York, then quickly returning home again. Somehow I rationalized living at home until I was thirty-one.

Surrounded by woods, I may have become a more hopeful person than I should have become.

And in leaving home at thirty-one I didn't go far—only as far, in fact, as I had wandered as a young man. Even now, with most of my time devoted to the land Jennifer and I own, I know the exact distance between our place and my parents' cabin, and I can describe the cross-country route by heart. I step over a strand of rusted wire to the northeast of our house, into Mr. Gregory's property, at the edge of the cove where the old trees are. If I go downhill at this point, maneuvering around person-sized elm and buckeye saplings and spicebushes, the trees begin to soar, and I am in another realm—defined by borders, of course, but extravagantly spacious inside, as in a child's mind during imaginative play. Fallen trunks and limbs are everywhere, and I step over them, sit on them. I enter a pawpaw patch and look up at its little canopy. Here is a forest by itself! The light is dimmer, only threads of sunlight here and there. If I grew up only here, I would know very little of the larger world, for the pawpaw leaves are broad and long and keep the view of the outer forest mostly hidden. A mayapple patch is at my feet. If I were a smaller creature, I could go under yet another canopy, look up at mayapple leaves shaped like a crawdad's pincers.

I see a half-moon of pressed-down vegetation where a deer slept. Nearby, a doll's eye plant is growing. It has seeded out. And look! Dolls' eyes! White orbs with black dots as pupils!

I can stay within the pawpaw forest, I discover, if I continue downhill. Is this how the deer went? I slip my body between slender trunks. I come to a wet-weather streambed. I cross with a clanking of a rock, and I'm out of my subforest, into the main, staring at the trunk of a white ash. This one! The one that Jennifer and I roughly estimated, using the thumb-and-body boy scout trick, to be eighty feet from the ground to where it first branches out. From my vantage point here, though, I can't see it rise beyond a layer of sugar maple leaves. I'm a child again, for I want to hug this trunk like it's the leg of Mama or Daddy. On this side of the trunk, there's a cluster of blue cohosh, a low-growing bush with leaves like a dog's footprint, and with seeds the same color and size as blueberries, only poisonous. I'll make a note to tell Jennifer: blue cohosh next to the big white ash.

But on the way to my parents' cabin, I usually don't detour into the old-growth cove. Why, I wonder, does becoming an adult always usher in—even here in the woods—certain pressures to get to places on time, to accomplish a certain amount in a day? But I flank the old growth during my hike, and I am brushed with its presence. I pass the white oak with the coyote hole (at least a hole big enough for a coyote) in its base. A stone's throw from this oak, the ridge slopes downhill to Long Branch, and I pass a white ash that has changed growth directions at least two times in its hundred years of living. Now it appears like a dancer, bending and leaping and coming to a standstill.

I pass the Dutchman's breeches that come out early in the spring and cross a wet-weather stream that empties into Long Branch. I've left the old section of woods and am in a young, bottomland forest, along Long Branch. The best place to cross is here, on a pile of water-swept rocks. A walnut on the other bank has a protruding root that is a step up. On the other side of the creek, I walk between walnut, elm, hackberry, ash-leaf maple, red oak, and ragweed until I get to the large downed tree that years ago gave me hope of discovering old growth. Here there are patches of fire pink and trout-leaf lily. I angle up a slope and pass through the collapse of an old cabin foundation. A minute later I'm in a twiggy cedar woods.

Soon another fence: I cross it and I'm in Abner Lipp's cow field. I walk up a long cleared slope. At the top I'm hit by wind; I turn, let my vision glide over where I've been. Then I go down the hill on the other side, through black locust and rutted cow trails. At the bottom is Poe Branch, easily jumped over. If there's a breeze, a metal gate leading to Mitchell's property sometimes clangs against a post. The next fence I cross takes me into my sister Chris and brother-in-law Joel's land. I follow a long, narrow valley to Duck Bottom and the site of my unfinished fence project. Then uphill again. I pass by a ten-by-fifteen-foot structure where Chris and Joel lived the first four years of their marriage. With sides made out of split cedar logs and clay, it has a definite rustic feel. A large picture window adds a touch of elegance and a theme other than decomposition. They dubbed it Uppity Shack. Farther up, I come to where they live now in an earth-bermed house. A trail takes me to Lost Owl Road, which in one direction leads to the Wildlife Management Area and in the other to the Duck. From the Duck, of course, I go past the Changing Shack, down the hardwood-lined road to Toad Hall and a slope to the cabin. This hike takes forty minutes.

My question is this: if one part of the map is lost—say the big woods are clear-cut and become indecipherable with brambles and sunlight—then is the whole route lost? Would there be no way to return home or to be a child again?

৵

My unicycle preceded me in making an appearance at the airport in Lexington, Kentucky. From a distance, I could see my parents and Trina, who were facing the conveyor belt, pointing at it. I immediately wanted to correct its position, for the wheel was more up than down, propped on a brown suitcase. It looked as if it had just thrown somebody and kept on going.

In stepping up to it I would be claiming involvement in this particular story. I would be the man thrown by the unicycle and not, say, the man in the suit, checking his watch and ultimately claiming a suitcase with a pull-out handle and wheels for brisk walking, on the way to a meeting.

Soon my parents and Trina were hugging me.

"You're actually real," Trina said.

Which was funny because I felt myself slipping into an almost dreamlike existence while I was at home for the summer. After being in Kansas, the more intricately green world of Kentucky shocked me. I went into it as if into camouflage.

The change for my sister Chris must have been even more dramatic; she returned from India nine days after my return. When she saw her luggage at the airport, she lunged for it, accustomed to Indian crowds. We had to point out to her that there were only a few people waiting. She laughed, lightheaded, between two continents.

She walked into our eighteen-by-twenty-two-foot cabin and cried because we had so much space. She wrote in our family's woods journal and signed her entries, as if still writing us letters. In one entry she wrote, "I find that suddenly I make comments that people think are funny and have strange English sentences come out of my mouth and can be completely amazed at a completely ordinary scene—like at the fair where we helped Daddy, where there were parking spaces for cars, where the kids were all clean and pink and where the women walked around by themselves."

If someone had asked me what I was doing that summer, I wouldn't have had a precise answer. I probably would have said I was working with my father, but I spent more time in the woods than I did helping him. I didn't take my basketball game out. If society hadn't been whispering in my ear that I was being irresponsible, I think I would have been completely happy that summer.

For the most part I was able to separate my life in the woods from the outside world. It helped that there were no houses within sight, that there were few human-caused noises, that at night an unbroken darkness set off the stars, the moon, that it would be possible to hear, say, a wild turkey gobble punctuated by a pileated woodpecker on a hollow oak.

I did, nonetheless, write to the first woman I'd ever kissed, a smart, shy, and pretty English major in my same class in college. But in sending a letter to Rachel, I now wonder if, instead of defining myself, I was only fading into memory.

I'd found her note to me in my car as I was about to leave campus for home. Incredulous, I read that she liked me. Thus began two weeks of delirious happiness for me but apparent disappointment for her, for at the end of this period she told me she was returning to her former boyfriend, a tall soccer player. The kiss that she gave me on our last date was not, as I'd thought, a deepening of our relationship, but instead a farewell.

Yet after college, we continued to correspond. She took a job in Chicago as an editorial assistant at a publishing house, and one day I received a letter from her inviting me to visit. I drove up in a snowstorm, happy again. The first thing that struck me on seeing her was that she had cut off her long hair and had a businesswoman's short trim. I told her that she had become more professional. She told me that she had become more responsible. She said she could get me a job at the same publishing house, but she didn't let me kiss her or even take her hand—and I wasn't sure I wanted to with this very different person.

Yet once again I found myself writing her a letter, this time after the first stage of my unicycle journey. I suppose I simply wanted her to know that instead of working in a publishing house, I was an adventurer, traveling on a unicycle. I put forth that I was happy.

Meanwhile, I spent hours hiking in the woods, much of this

time in the old growth I'd discovered. I'd bring back leaves to be identified—a slippery elm, a mulberry, a rusty black haw. I came to learn all the trees and to know which were common, which were rare. I found an endangered ginseng plant. A patch of goldenseal.

One day a wild turkey chased me. Another day I saw a black snake emerge from a pond I'd just chanced upon, its mouth stretched over part of a frog, which it held aloft. The snake's mouth became quite large as it traveled over the rough skin of its catch. Even as it was disappearing, the frog honked. It sounded like a foghorn.

Then, too, were the less extraordinary events, though still striking in some way, such as the young persimmon I came upon, covered in small, bell-shaped blossoms and bumblebees.

On sunny days we cooked meals in our homebuilt solar cooker. I took over much of the solar meal preparations, and I kept a solar cooking log. In it I included not only recipes but also detailed notes on changing cloud formations. I became convinced that a solar chef should be able to predict the quantity and quality of sunlight in a day. My observation of clouds, I thought, would help me learn this skill, which I knew wouldn't be counted as a résumé builder but would be helpful in my own world, in knowing when to put in a low-bake granola, or when to bake lasagna, or when to boil beans, or when not to cook.

It turned hot and muggy part of the summer. I put a bucket of water in the root cellar so I'd have something cool to pour over me at the end of the day. Some afternoons we'd pull the refrigerator bucket out of the well and take sips of cool mint tea.

Our compost heap steamed, which gave me an idea that led to a culinary failure. I poured lemon cake batter in a cast-iron pan, put a good lid on it, and buried it in the compost. It didn't bake.

Increasingly, I began thinking of my unicycle journey, which I would continue. Though everything I did that summer seemed to establish me inside a cocoon, I was ready for another foray into the bigger world. I wrote a letter to Roger Fulton, asking him if he could build a unicycle that would hold water under the seat and that had a slightly bigger wheel. I would be traveling into unpopulated areas and needed to carry enough water to make the long distances between towns.

One night I was walking by the pond close to the cabin when my solar light touched on the biggest frog I'd ever seen. The circle of light was barely big enough to cover its body. It stayed still until I moved the light off its skin, and then it leapt hugely, slapping the water. Past the pond I moved my light off the trail onto white mushrooms lifting last year's oak leaves off the ground. I stood still. Bullfrogs trumpeted at the banks of the pond.

I included this in the letter I wrote to Rachel, along with a multitude of other things. She didn't write back. I'm not sure why she didn't write back.

Strong winds during a midsummer storm toppled a shagbark hickory on the ridge where we picked blackberries. Inspired by the pliable branches suddenly within touch, I cut off a few and took them back to the cabin. Using a hand drill and wooden pegs, I fit a few pieces together, not resulting in anything useful. I then wove smaller branches into the larger rudimentary structure, and it began to seem finished, whatever it was. Trina turned it over, and to my surprise it stood up like a magazine table. At the same time it looked like a running creature. I put it in my loft and called it the "wild turkey."

It could be that Rachel thought I was too childlike to ever function well in society.

The potato beds bulged during the summer, and we dug them in August, hauling them in crates to a dark root cellar.

I dreamed one night that I was walking the long way back to the cabin and came to a part of the woods that had been bulldozed. I began to dig and my shovel cut through some red root, which I thought was bloodroot. On looking more closely, though, I saw that it was a cedar tree with sawed-off branches. I began to get eaten up by mosquitoes.

Then I was with my family on a high ridge. I was holding a copy of *Wild Earth* magazine. We began walking toward a man who wanted us to work in the mines. I was about to turn around, but he took my *Wild Earth* so I had to go with him.

Soon we were on our knees, crawling under a mountain. Already scared by how much our passageway was shrinking, I was planning to quit as soon as we got to the smaller tunnels.

I woke up startled. I lit a candle, and the shadows its small flame made coupled with the shadows of the moon. Papers had just about covered up my wild turkey. Scrap paper, notebooks, clothes, empty matchboxes, books were strewn about me.

I seemed to have dreams every night. In one of them, the path I walked every day took me by our fire pit, which had turned into a canyon. A cedar log lay at the canyon's edge. It could be moved either for fuel or for a bridge. Famished, I moved it, intending to cook a meal, but ending up with a bridge across the canyon. I stepped on the bridge and began taking the first few steps.

In another, I went out looking for mushrooms and came back with a rotten log.

Daddy and I started building a shed, which we would call Toad Hall. We found dead or dying cedar trees and cut them up to use for the perimeter posts. We drilled holes in these posts to bolt on crossbeams, our bodies leaning against hand drills, our slowly turning bits making the sound of crunching snow as they brought up spiraled wood shavings.

Enough time had lapsed for my trip, once again, to seem flimsily constructed. Yet I began to clamber aboard, for August had turned into September. Some leaves had already fallen, and I peered through new openings in the woods, as if through binoculars. What I saw was not in focus—and on the night I was packing to leave I couldn't make the adjustment from home to travel.

Candlelight, again, toyed with the walls, deepening them. Using an axe and a hatchet, Daddy and I had notched the ends of the logs so they'd grip each other in the corners. One log would roll into place onto another. I would remember many of them, where exactly they'd been in the woods. Now I wished my own journey could slip so easily onto something solid. I didn't know what would bring clarity: gathering closer what was distant in my mind—unicycling in Kansas—or fading out that bigger context to focus on what was within touch, to step from one clear image to another, heading toward what was a blur.

$\backsim$

The red numbers of a digital clock hung on a minute at a time without slipping. For the moment, 7:43. It struck me that I disliked the clock. I sat in Roger Fulton's living room while he worked below me in the basement. He didn't want company and was feeling rushed to finish my unicycle. He had thought of an elegant solution for carrying extra water: essentially, he had carved out three holes in the aluminum frame, each of them big enough to hold a one-liter plastic bottle. He had also found a two-inch bigger wheel, and he showed me precisely what difference this would make: for every mile I would have to turn the bigger wheel 775.6 times, quite a bit fewer than the 840.3 revolutions I had been making each mile on my twenty-four-inch wheel. Mathematically, things were looking good for my journey.

Now he was attaching the seat. I heard a grinder. A tiny fan by my side sat on a stack of books on an oblong, dusty table where it swiveled in a 180-degree arc. I had told Roger I was going to write in my journal, but my attention wandered. In a corner formed by a bookshelf and a wall, a cobweb-colored cat slept, its tail almost touching Volume I of *Ingenious Mechanisms for Designers and Inventors*. I pulled out a book next to it: *Design for the Real World* by Victor Papanek. Its cover showed an Arab man bent over with a television on his back. I returned it to the shelf, not opening it. Eight liters of Cost Cutter diet cola lined the hallway between the living room and kitchen. On the same table as the fan sat a yellow spiral notebook. I wanted to be traveling, yet found myself waiting for two days. Or 2,880 minutes.

Yet soon enough I was on the Pauley's driveway, my left foot on the left pedal, ready to mount my new unicycle. Phil, Corliss, Mesa, and Ladae watched. Aero, surprisingly, would travel with me for one day. He was at my side now, sitting on his bike.

Roger had made my new seat a little high, which made mounting it more difficult, but I was able to do so without falling, and, with everyone watching, we were off. We rounded a bend—out of sight, thankfully, of the Pauley's house—and I hit a bump and fell off my unicycle, landing on my feet. Aero got off his bike and waited while I awkwardly got back on. I experienced a low-level dread, worrying about the height of the new unicycle, the weight of the pack on my shoulders, Aero's emotional state. A little distance and time, however, diffused some of these worries. Once situated on it, I liked the new rhythm of my unicycle, its longer stride. I liked, also, that Roger had put a container of tools in one of the frame holes under the seat—all the tools I would need, he said, to repair my unicycle. In my pocket was a stack of his Earthworm Castings Company business cards, to be handed out to those interested in my custom-built wheel. Though I would have been happy to distribute them, no one during my journey expressed much interest in Roger's invention.

We were in flatter country. That was good, I supposed. The long, straight fields accentuated movements that weren't straight, like my path, or a tiny dust whirlwind that spun down a long stretch of soil, or the pheasants that brought our attention suddenly to a dozen different places in the sky.

At a grocery in Munfordville I asked Aero how he was doing—if he wanted to keep traveling. He did. We called his home, and I let him talk to Corliss. He practically whispered into the phone, as if Corliss were only inches away.

I picked out a long loaf of bread. Aero stood by the cookie section.

"Mommy told me that pecan sandies are more good for you than other cookies," he said.

"You can get some cookies," I told him.

Still, he was sheepish about buying them. At the checkout I was thinking of where to put the bread in my backpack, not realizing until I saw the cashier's concerned look that I was squeezing the loaf to a smaller size. Usually I had the sense to do that after I had paid for it.

"Oh, I don't care about the shape of the bread," I told her.

Aero fit his cookies in a pouch on his handlebars. We ate lunch outside the store. The day became hot, but we moved steadily along. Sometimes I got too close to Aero's back wheel and had to tell him to move a little faster. Every mile or so he reached into his handlebar pouch and ate a cookie. Once when we were close, he turned around and said, "Wimps are people who use cars all the time." A school bus passed, and we could see kids looking out the window, laughing, which upset the homeschooled Aero. I told him that they were laughing at me not him.

Aero never complained about anything, never even suggested that we take a break. I was the one who led us into a small creek-side woods at midafternoon so we could rest. My shoulders were sore. We sat on the bank and ate apples and granola bars. Afterward, Aero climbed to the top of a small creek-bank elm, making it sway as if in a storm.

When he got down, he picked up his apple core and threw it in the creek. I tossed mine in too, and we watched them float out of sight.

"Look, we're still traveling," I said to him.

Fencerows, where trees sometimes were allowed to grow, offered our only chance for camping that evening. The problem would be in trekking across the flat, bare fields, which would frame us. As we were debating whether or not to cross one of these long fields, a farmer stopped and asked if we needed help. He told us we could go five poles down the road, turn to the right, and we would come to an abandoned homesite where we could camp. I gave Aero the job of counting the poles, and we made it to a relatively wide area of trees.

While I sat on my sleeping bag, making notes in my journal and spreading peanut butter on bread, which I re-shaped into square slices, Aero bounced around, waving a locust stick.

In the morning when he had filled his little backpack, my companion stepped back from it and looked at me. "It's regained consciousness," he said. We made it to Catherine about nine o'clock. When his family arrived, Aero, before doing anything else, gave his brother and sister the rest of his cookies. I said goodbye to them and watched until their car was out of sight. As soon as I couldn't see it (on that flat stretch, it looked like it was going down a drain), I had the impression that I had landed hard in Catherine, Kansas.

Chapter Twenty-Eight

FROM OUR KITCHEN WINDOW, I could have told the Water Board, we can see our outdoor canning stove between the entrance trees and blueberry beds. We built the stove out of rock and bricks, a piece of steel, and a found terracotta chimney. It gets the afternoon shade.

There's more work, I'd say, in canning this way, as there is in harvesting your own water. I'd describe how I go out into the woods with a bucksaw and a hatchet and cut up dead cedar saplings. In areas now overtaken by hardwood, dead cedar wood, both standing and downed, is everywhere. After I gather an armload, I carry it to the stove or to a wheelbarrow. I breathe in the smell of newly cut cedar.

The Water Board would ask what this has to do with a water line. But it's all related.

A week ago, we set up a card table under the entrance trees, two shagbark hickories to the west of our house. These trees make a solid shade, and we sat in this shade, a bucket of Roma tomatoes next to us, good for making sauces and salsas. Elliptical, they fit in the hand easily. We cut off the stem ends and squeezed the juice and seeds out. We then cut up the remaining tomato into the canning pot. Midway through the tomato cutting, as is typical, I lit the fire. My matchstick flame doubled itself on crumpled newspaper and stretched upward into a scaffolding of twigs and larger wood. At this point, we could hear the pop of the fire and see smoke drifting from the chimney as we worked. It was late summer and dry; some of the hickory leaves were brown and curled. A breeze rustled them. Occasionally, we heard the slow rip of a hickory nut that would fall from a treetop and hit branches and leaves as it descended, ultimately, to the ground, which was bumpy with both the nuts and their hulls. Some of the hulls still encased the nuts; some of them were quartered by the fall or by squirrels. The hull fragments looked like toy boats, the bunches of browned hickory leaves their broken masts.

In late summer we are sometimes unmoored by the noticeably longer shadows—by midday we already seem to be upon the end of the day. Indeed, as we canned, we could have been at any point in time. It could have been this morning, or it could have been last year. We picked handfuls of basil and oregano and cut up onions to add to the sauce last year, too.

When I looked up at one point to see Jennifer standing by our rock stove, her long blond hair held in a clasp as she stirred the thickening sauce, a column of smoke behind her obscuring the immediate background, I saw us together as an old couple, and I saw us together in our first days of marriage, and when we were dating, and though I was looking at her in the present moment, the vividness of the scene was such that it pierced out of the present.

Finally, of course, we poured the sauce into sterilized jars, capped them, and put the jars back into a boiling bath for twenty minutes. Then we removed them and lined them up on a makeshift cedar board table. Soon the lids popped as the jars sealed themselves.

I should add that when we use this sauce for lasagna or spaghetti or soup or pizza or spicy lentils and rice, we are bringing into our meal a flavor full enough to include sunlight, wood, sky, smoke, hands stained by and smelling of basil, a hickory nut falling from a tree top, love, bubbling water, and of course tomatoes, onions, oregano, basil, and salt.

I can't argue that buying a can of tomato sauce at Kroger is more convenient, as is having city water over rainwater. And so the only recourse left to me in making my argument with the Water Board is to do as I've done and move the boundaries of the discussion.

~

I've been more affected by the former banker's valuation of our house than I would have thought possible. Clipboard only valued Snuggery at $5,000, about what we spent on materials to build it. Since it is now clear that we can't get enough money from the bank, we send letters to everyone we know, including Cedar Ring Congress participants, asking if anyone would want to purchase part of Mr. Gregory's property.

~

I looked about me a few minutes after the Pauleys left and was startled by a small crowd.

"We've never seen anyone ride one, except on television," someone said, as if to explain.

I'd better go, I thought. A bit insecure about the height of my new unicycle, I wished I could launch down the road in private. Luckily, I made it up okay and after a few wobbles began pedaling south in a relatively direct manner. The townspeople's stares sticky on my back, I put my hand out in an approximation of a wave, kept pedaling. It took about a mile, I guessed, to get beyond the elasticity of their attention.

I stopped often because of my sore shoulders, thus having numerous occasions to practice mounting my taller unicycle. I think I got better at it. It helped, I discovered, to talk to myself during the process.

I noticed very little that would suggest I was moving. Eventually, though, what had been distant hills were now before me, large. A black object stood on top of the closest one, and I wondered what it would turn out to be, a process of discernment that took three or four miles. Then an oil-pumping rig defined itself for me. Such a sight usually was not that pleasant for me, but given my approach to it this time—slow enough for me to have developed a relationship with it—it seemed less ugly. Anyway, it was certainly one of the major events of my day. I wondered, briefly, about how I would communicate a fondness for an oilrig to my family.

The landscape, I soon noticed, became studded with oilrigs. I reached Medicine Lodge by midafternoon. There, while I was pedaling on Main Street, a man in a white apron came running out of the barbershop, motioning for me. Had my hair really gotten too long? I went over to him, followed him into the shop.

"My son rides a six-foot-high unicycle in the parade," he explained. Two little boys were waiting for him in the shop, one of them in the barber's chair, which he spun around. "Sit down," he said to me, motioning to a chair. He pulled a book and a photo album off of a bookshelf and handed them to me. "I wrote that book," he said.

I looked at it. *How Indian Tools Were Knapped Out of Flint* by Richard E. Earnest. "And that album has some pictures of my son." He opened it to the right page. "Look at that cowboy hat and chaps," he said. "He figured he was liable to get throwed. But this ain't nothing for him. He's mowed the lawn riding a unicycle. He's rode down stairs."

On the same page there were pictures of Richard Earnest in buckskin, knapping out an arrowhead.

"I can make anything the Indians made," he said. He was talking over the head of the boy in his chair. "We're in the middle of a country where you can spit and the wind will blow it back to you around the world. Some people are scared of it because of the unknown, but I am excited because of what I don't know. That's why I explore. I go out every weekend and just survive, eating what's around me to eat, seeing what I can discover. I can walk right out there and live for thirty days and you'd never know anything different had happened to me."

"What would you take with you?" I asked.

"I sure as hell wouldn't take a unicycle. I'd take tools, but if you challenged me and put enough money on it, I could go out there naked and live."

He gave his customer another spin on the chair.

"You start to learn things, like yucca can help you out with food and clothing. You can't learn anything by not trying to live. I tell you, if you eat too many crickets, you'll get sick. And another thing, don't eat what you rely on for a water supplement. Like snakes, for example."

He was already finished with the first boy. I wondered what these kids thought of their barber. The second boy looked like he had just had a haircut.

"People are on the fast roads and can't see what's out there, what there already is. They're too interested in making money and in things you can't eat."

When he was finished with the second boy's hair and the boys left, he turned around his window sign so that "Open" faced us.

"Being a barber means that sometimes you become connected to everybody else's problems. That's why I like going out into the hills. Because there I'm on my own, in my own world. A lot of people, their complaints about the hills are, 'I don't like the dust, it's too hot.' They got a whole bunch of complaints. That stuff don't bother me. I accept all of that. It might take me a little longer to go that way, but I'll go that way just to see what it looks like. And then go back in half an hour to look at it when the sun changes to make it look different."

He was putting away his tools. "We have long-tailed cats here. I've run into them; they don't bother me. If I come up to an animal, I'll talk to it. I've walked up as close as I am to you to a coon. If it's just me, they won't run. Another person would scare them. I can call any animal."

Suddenly a guttural, mewing sound emanated from him. Then silence. "That was a raccoon," he said. A neat array of hair-trimming tools hung on a wall behind him.

"Or how about a beaver?" he asked, and he made a high-pitched sound that echoed. He smiled. "That's to get him to come up and splash water on you."

"Or a rabbit squeal?" A high, thin scream. "One time I did that, a horned owl swooped down and tried to carry me off."

At sunset that day, I saw an owl perched on a silo, and I wondered if Richard Earnest could make its call. I had camped by an old barn. The sun for the moment hung between grass heads, a liquidy red. It sank, and the owl, now a silhouette, swooped to the ground, then back to its perch. I thought I saw its glowing eyes. Soon it was too dark to see them.

As I was getting into my sleeping bag, I wondered how I could describe the owl and the sunset to someone. And the barn, for that matter, the field. In telling the story of an owl, I'd have to put together a whole world.

I wished Aero could be with me to experience this camp. Or my family. Would Rachel be interested in this camp? She would have been in college. The instant I thought of her, though, I became weary of thinking of her. Instead, I imagined someone ahead of me, a future Rachel.

I would tell this Rachel what it was like from day to day, as I approached her. And, in fact, the telling of my journey would be the making of it, the way forward. Thus I fell asleep with the fanciful notion that if she didn't exist only in a future utopia (or if I didn't), I was bound to meet her.

⤳

One late summer evening Jennifer and I joined a family potluck in the valley below Snuggery, where Trina and Tim live. We found out from Chris that Mr. Gregory had agreed to meet with Joel for a one-on-one talk, which gave us all a burst of energy. After supper, I picked up Eric, Trina and Tim's youngest boy—Phillip's brother—and Jennifer picked up Sophie, Chris and Joel's youngest girl—Natalie's sister—and we began running, Phillip and Natalie trying to catch us and rescue their siblings. Eric and Sophie's mouths were opened wide, laughing. I pivoted to avoid Phillip, but he caught up with me and grabbed my leg.

"Stop, thief," Phillip cried, his face flushed, bright-eyed.

Chapter Twenty-Nine

THE HILLS BETWEEN MEDICINE LODGE and Coldwater stretched out before me, broadly sloping and treeless, like ocean waves but for the fact (for me) they hardly moved. A car was a single dot for an eternity before eventually rushing past. Would a driver, I wondered, experience these hills as actual waves, one coming after another?

The wind would bend me, like the grasses, a little off my path, but was not strong enough to be frustrating or exhausting, and I would feel, if not like a speed demon, then at least transported by the rhythms around me, joined in this way to the landscape. Again, I wondered how to describe the feeling I had. What did being joined with the landscape mean? I wished I could communicate my travels with the clarity of an animal cry.

"Here I am!" I would cry to the wind. And the wind would take my words soaring into disappearance.

Then the echo in my head that the wind couldn't erase: "Here I am!"

I passed through the small town of Coldwater without noticing a single person. A pay phone made me wonder if I should make a call to let someone know I'd arrived. But then the town was behind me. I camped that night on a grassy hillside.

The next day the wind kicked up, and I turned off onto a dirt road. With ruts and blowing sand, it took all the skill I could muster to stay up, and sometimes I couldn't. I imagined the sky watching me as if it were a kid with an eye close to a laboring ant.

Power lines that stretched for miles strummed long howls out of the wind. At one of the only trees I came to that day, a small locust, I took a break. Gusts shook the tree's shade over me. I wrote in my pocket notebook that the wind was tousling me but crossed that verb out. "Bullying" seemed better but inaccurate also.

When I couldn't go any farther that day, I left the road and began a long walk up a broadly sloping hill, reaching the top and continuing until my body gradually disappeared from the road's vision. There I stopped. My gear sank into the high grasses, goldenrod. Prairie continued as far as I could see, the sky on top of it.

I lay on my back and saw storm clouds enter one corner of the vast sky. Once in, they swelled, gaining surface area. I'd never had such an intimate viewing of a thunderstorm. I zipped up the bivy sack that covered my sleeping bag and situated its head flap. Soon the storm lay on me, bolting and banging and pelting the earth with rain, and it seemed to me foolish that I wasn't at least in a tent. Whether I lived or died was a matter of chance. Yet I wanted strongly to live.

So when the storm passed and I woke into a new day, I felt grateful, even despite wet gear and the smell of mold on my clothing. That morning I came upon a gas station grocery in Ashland and bought provisions—a good thing, for shortly afterward I came to a sign: "Open Range. Livestock has right of way. Driver held responsible."—and began pedaling into the most unpopulated area yet of my travels. I think in a sixty-mile stretch I passed through only one community. And given the experience I had in Englewood, Kansas, I was glad the area was sparsely populated. There, two men in a stupor on a sagging porch had yelled for me to come over, and, stupidly, I did. Almost immediately I began to get mired in their slurred sentences. They offered me anything they imagined I wanted, including a shower, a woman, a beer, and I had to come up with ways of declining their generosity. They liked my beer excuse best: "If I had a beer, I'd fall off that thing," I said. "Amazing," one of them said, his favorite and perhaps only word in his vocabulary. The other kept asking if I had money. Eventually, I just walked away, which they didn't like, and began pedaling down the road. "Amazing," the one guy boomed, lost in that word. Because of my pace, they could not have guessed I was running away from them.

I liked it better without people. Things were what they were. Like that red butte off the road a way, just beginning to cast shade. I walked to it, sat down on a small ledge that held both light and shadow. Minutes passed. The light eventually spilled over the edge. The butte then clothed me in shade.

At dusk a large coyote appeared from behind the butte, at a good pace in spite of a limp. An older, male coyote, I speculated. When he saw me, he stopped and sat down. We stared at each other. Some time passed. That shade that had come over me touched the coyote and by increments covered his bright body—and it was as if then we dwelled under the same blanket, for just that little bit of time.

After dark, he howled—and was answered by a coyote behind me. Then by a coyote to my right and a coyote to my left. With this sudden immersion into wildness, I shivered but was not afraid, as I had been in the thunderstorm. If I were Richard Earnest, I thought, I'd howl, too. Howl and yip. And they'd listen. They'd hear I only had one wheel on the ground, tangential to America, arms opened wide, adjusting the horizon to help ease myself into it. They'd take my cry on as their own, until the din in the night air was solid, like the surface of a table, where you could set a dream.

Of course in the morning anything abstract would be gone. But you might find, as I did, the sun coming up behind a craggy butte, the clean smell of sage, a red rock that fits nicely in your palm and feels good to squeeze.

The road from my camp turned ninety degrees north, and I pedaled into a landscape less sharply irregular than where I'd been, wavier. High clouds blunted the sun, the air only dusted with light. Looking behind me, I wouldn't recognize terrain I'd just crossed. When I passed a sign for cars going the other way,

I turned out of curiosity and read "Dead End."

The wind kicked up, but most of it came from behind me, batting me along nicely. I passed a few hundred yards of fence with old cowboy boots pulled down over every post top. The boots, I thought, of people who had died going the other way. Besides a farmer on a tractor, the only person I saw on those dirt roads was an old woman who waved me down from inside her car and told me in a shaky voice never to leave the main road.

〜

Surely, we say to ourselves, people wouldn't cut down trees at their peak with fall colors. Look at the yellows, oranges, and reds of the sugar maple!

The maple leaves have started to fall, their vibrant colors passing on to poplar and pignut hickory, and we begin to venture further into new terrain. We want to map this season, what slips away, what appears. We want to place ourselves here on this ridge top, with the woods around us, with our garden and fruit trees and flowers and herbs, with our dog, our nieces and nephews. We want to tell it, again and again, what we already have, like it's a story we read from beginning to ending, then back to the beginning again, until it's known by heart.

The beech, we rediscovered this year, can harbor many colors on the same tree: green, brown, orange, yellow, the yellows and oranges often brilliant, like those on the maple or poplar. Soon we will turn our attention from brilliant colors to the satin browns and reds of the oak family. These colors make us think of pleasant days and thrillingly cool nights and winter teas.

Sassafras trees turn a beautiful orange this time of year. We split their roots into pieces and store them in jars for a supply of winter tea—with caps on the jars so our house isn't flooded with the pungent, root-beer smell of them.

SLOWSPOKE

~

I arrived in Kismet, the largest community I'd seen since Ashland, Kansas, and stepped down from my unicycle. In front of me was a grocery. But first I bent over to read a newspaper's headlines. Anyone viewing would have thought it curious how intently I stared at that newspaper, and perhaps would have noticed my tangled hair and the red dust that coated my clothing and skin.

A sign mentioned that the grocery was scheduled to permanently close in two days. I was going plenty fast through Kansas, I thought, to have made it here in time.

I walked inside and a woman looked up from a paperback romance, surprised. The shelves, I noticed, were almost bare, and there were no customers.

"Can I help you?" she asked.

The Englewood drunks had asked me the same thing. How many days ago had that been? My words to them were the last I'd spoken to anyone.

Now maybe I should speak to her in an exotic and imaginary language and transport the two of us into a purely fictional realm.

Instead, I heard myself saying: "A jar of peanut butter?" .

"Sorry, we're out," she said.

I'd been too sanguine about my pace through Kansas, I thought. Had I been on a bicycle, I surely would have secured peanut butter from this establishment.

Instead, I picked up a can of bean spread and a loaf of bread. Soon I was out of town with some provisions and the news that Bill Clinton led in the presidential polls. A small bridge took me over the dry bed of the Cimarron River. Oil pumps were scattered everywhere. I saw a field drained before my eyes of prairie dogs, their tails, wiggling, the last to disappear underground. That evening a family let me spend the night in a camper by their house. Their directions in the morning led me through someone's back yard before I got to blacktop. I passed directly under a basketball goal. No one seemed to be home. Once on the blacktop, I went south to 51, a busy road, and stopped at the intersection to eat breakfast. A cop pulled up, a brusque fellow. He asked me immediately for ID. I had to look through several plastic bags before I remembered where I had put my driver's license. The cop didn't believe me when I told him he was the first person who had asked me for an identification. When I asked him if there was a way without traffic to Elkhart, Kansas, he couldn't help me. He left, and I finished my breakfast, feeling guilty.

Even with a paved shoulder, 51 was too busy for me. The wind blew hair in my face, making it harder to pedal straight, and it hid the noise of vehicles until they were suddenly behind me and blasting past.

Labile, I exited on Hooker-Moscow Road, but when two semis rushed past me, I changed my mind, returned to 51.

Two miles outside Hugoton the wind and the traffic overwhelmed me. I dismounted. I felt bedraggled, and my shoulders ached. The thought of getting a milkshake in Hugoton kept me going, but after arriving I couldn't find one. A clerk at a convenience store seemed disdainful of me.

Pedaling out of town, I ran over a sandbur and got a flat tire. Luckily, I was only steps away from a golf course maintenance garage. Yet once I got the tire fixed, I decided to quit for the day. The first house I knocked at attracted me because of a nicely arranged flowerbed. There, a woman with stylish hair opened the door and skillfully directed me to some other place where I could ask about camping.

I stopped next at a more modest house. A man with a sooty face opened the door and told me I could camp wherever I wanted. He said he would rather go cross-country on a horse.

I camped amid dry cow patties and mosquitoes. Natural gas fires burned in the distance. In the morning I stepped carefully over an electric fence, leaving two owls perched on a dead tree in the middle of the field.

I'd been worried about Highway 56 going to Elkhart—that its traffic would be another impediment, like yesterday's wind or flat tire, that would keep me that much longer from a town where I would receive a money order and letters from my family. I'd also promised myself a motel in Elkhart, since it was so close to Oklahoma. The elements of bliss in my mind were threefold, all of them centered in Elkhart: a room with a shower and a bed, a meal in a restaurant, news from home. A few days ago, my map to bliss may not have existed. But luckily I'd suffered enough for it to now be clear.

To my relief, Highway 56 was only lightly traveled—but as I settled in to the long stretch, I discovered that the road never turned or curved. About noon I stopped looking at the big expanses in front of me, for I felt them drowning me. Instead, I kept my attention just a few feet in front of my wheel. The dotted lines, I discovered then, would zip—relatively speaking—past me. By this measurement of progress, I had a truly impressive afternoon. Then within five miles of Elkhart, I saw a corn plant busting its way out of asphalt on the broken shoulder of the road, and I knew I could make it. Boldly, I looked the whole way to town and pedaled toward it. And arrived.

I booked a room at a motel. Soon I was backing into a newly unlocked room, pulling my unicycle after me. Inside, I let my pack slide off my shoulders and thump to the floor, peeled my clothes off my body and—as was customary with me in a motel room since childhood, I supposed—jumped once or twice on the bed. Afterward, I took a long shower.

Refreshed, then, and light-shouldered, I went outside. Although strip-mall development with monotonous box architecture dominated the town, I did chores with relatively good spirits. I bought a map of New Mexico, which included the section of Oklahoma I needed, picked up a money order and a couple of letters from Mama at the post office, bought a thick new piece of foam rubber for my unicycle seat, and stepped into a small café, intent on an omelet, hash browns, and a milkshake, what I'd decided would be my dream meal. I was the only customer in the café, which was managed by an attractive woman about my age. After I placed my order, she said she'd seen me on my unicycle and asked where I was going. When was the last time anyone, much less an attractive woman, had asked me anything about my trip? She asked, also, some kind of follow-up question. The fact that she didn't then continue the conversation failed to disturb me, for I imagined the silence between us to be meaningful.

I left the café with a full stomach and returned to my motel room. Once faced with the prospect of an evening of rest, however, I realized that more than anything I wanted to be with the woman in the café. The geography of my bliss had become more complicated.

As I was heading to the phone, I told myself to not think about what I was doing, to just do it.

While dialing, though, I hastily designed my approach, complete with an escape route. She answered the phone.

"Hi, I was there earlier. I'm the one who's riding a unicycle."

"Oh yeah, hi."

"I can't seem to find a small notebook of mine. I was wondering if I left it in there."

"Hold on, let me look."

My face burned. If she said yes to a date, I couldn't very well offer to drive, and the town dissuaded walking. She came on again.

"I don't see it here."

I paused. "Okay, it's probably in my backpack someplace. Thanks."

I hung up and lay on the bed until my breathing returned to normal.

What distressed me was how perfectly matched I was with my unicycle. Every once in a while, I thought, I'd like to do something surprising, like go somewhere quickly, or take the most direct route possible, or tell someone I like her.

I walked by the café in the morning to see if it was open. No. Then I left town. I crossed into Oklahoma, on the road to Boise City. Having a new piece of foam rubber helped significantly. On one stretch I pedaled four miles without needing to take a walking break, a personal record.

In two days of traveling I traversed the Oklahoma panhandle. Not too much happened. I spent a large part of my day, I realized, wondering when my next eating break would be, or where I would sleep that night. That my thoughts weren't more complex than this disappointed me at times. Generally, though, I was thankful that traffic was light enough that I could think at all. On the road to Boise City more people honked or waved than during any other stretch of my journey.

In Boise City I slept in the Methodist Church meeting hall—the logistics arranged by the sheriff—and the next morning headed north to Black Mesa State Park. I passed a turn-off to Wheeless, Oklahoma, and although the idea of visiting Wheeless appealed to me, I continued on to the state park—one way that morning that I, perhaps, avoided needless risk.

The landscape changed, and so did my thoughts about the woman in the Elkhart café. I'd been distressed by my timidity, for I'd wanted to be with her. While I was in Elkhart, she was a big thought in my mind. Now I looked up, surprised to see mesas in the distance, tall grasses. Inches at a time, some things grew, some shrank. A Santa Fe trail marker. We needed margins, I thought, to give us perspective—uncluttered spaces, whether physically, as in wilderness, or mentally, as in a respite from thinking too much about a person or a problem. These two kinds of margins could be related. What would have happened, I wondered, if I had stayed for a longer period of time in Elkhart? The café woman, or rather my fumbling reaction to her, was like a knot in my head. How would I have dealt with that knot, so close to the café that had caused it? Would I have had the space to loop one end of a tangled mental rope through itself and back out, laying it down a little longer and freer each time? A good thing about traveling, I decided, was that you created margins for yourself. You found enough space to lay your mind out freer than what it was.

I'd entered a narrow lane into the state park. Then, too, given the way I was traveling, I was probably somebody else's margin, helpful to somebody in the same way the juniper-clad mesas were now helpful to me. A sign appeared: "Cattleguard 400 ft." My wheel turned fifty-three times between the sign and the cattle guard. If I had also counted the seconds, and if I had any inclination to deal with fractions, I would have been able to calculate my speed.

The young park ranger was quite surprised I had made it to the park by midafternoon. Six years ago he had made the same twenty-seven-mile trek from Boise City but started at sunrise and didn't arrive until after dark, exhausted. He had hiked. Moreover, he didn't have the camping fee, so he told the ranger that he would work for the fee. The ranger could either sympathize with him or get the police, Peter Aiken knew, but he had to gamble because he couldn't go one step farther. Ever since then, he had been working at Black Mesa State Park, living in a tent. His dream, he told me, was to own an acre of land and build a sod house.

Probably thinking I was as bad off as he had been six years ago, Peter told me about a cave where I could sleep and not pay the fee. The only problem was there would be mosquitoes. I assured him I could afford the six dollars. I paid and left just as the owners of a Winnebago stepped into the office.

I set up camp at the far end of the park. Newly lightened with my pack off, I crossed a nearby fence. Dry grass crinkled under my feet. I stepped around chollo, currant bush, and a silvery-leaved plant I didn't know; and passed little gullies, which the land swallowed behind me—I would turn around and see flat ground.

When, at dusk, I returned to my camp, Peter Aiken surprised me with a visit. He carried a chunk of flint and bone from a deer antler, said he thought I might be interested in seeing someone knap a point. He told me he found a lot of arrowheads, too.

"People ask me how I find arrowheads. I tell them that they should try to get lost first."

He hit the flint with short, precise strokes. He seemed to be just a few years older than me. Thirty, maybe. He had a wild yet serene aura about him.

"If the system collapsed, say we ran out of fossil fuels for our engines, then what would we do? If you think of all the ramifications of what happens if you don't have petroleum, it just shuts down everything as we know it. But there will be people who survive. Ultimately survival means being outside the monetary system. There's no more money. There's no more K-Mart stores."

He held up his deer antler bone and flint.

"I mean, if this was all you had. You take away the trash barrels and electrical lines. If this was all you had. If somebody threw you out in…This is it. What are you going to do? It's possible to survive and to live reasonably comfortably too, I think. I don't think the Indians…I don't think they starved to death at all. I think they did real well. I think they must have spent more time enjoying themselves than we do. They lived in all these caves around here. There's evidence that they lived here for a long time. They liked it here."

The way he paused while he spoke gave me the impression that he didn't often talk at length to people.

"I love this country. And I hate to ask people for money just for sleeping on the ground. You know, if they're driving a big RV and carry their poop around with them, I don't mind charging them. The Indians thought that the funniest thing about white men who traveled in trains was that they carried their toilets with them.

"When I come out here, I had never give the Indian culture a second thought. I had spent at least a third of my life addicted to heroin, and I finally went into treatment. Even after I got out of treatment, I just couldn't be myself. I was real dissatisfied with life, and I just took off walking down the road, and I didn't know where I was going, and I didn't care.

"I didn't prepare at all. I was going...basically it was alternative suicide. I was going to kill myself, but I thought, no, I'll just walk down the road and let the road do me in. I mean, I'll either do myself in, or I'll get over this. There's got to be something different out there. And I'm going to find it one way or the other. And I come out here and I found life was just a little different. It was a little better. Not perfect, but..."

Some of the irregular edges of the chunk of flint had been knocked away.

"Anyway, I found a couple of arrowheads, and I was just really intrigued by them, and I thought the Indians had some kind of magic. I mean, they were almost magical because...how did they do it? They knew something I didn't know, and I wanted to know what that thing is that they knew. And so I read a couple of books about how they make arrowheads...

"I picked up my antler bone and started chipping so it's not a mystery to me anymore. And I'm not so crazy about hunting them. I used to be insane, you know, about hunting arrowheads. It's like gold fever. But I'm not that way anymore, because it's not a mystery to me. Now I can see one and just leave it."

His antler struck a large plane of flint off the block. He picked it up and continued talking.

"This is a scraper. It would cut off a piece of meat. You have a working edge here. A lot of the artifacts you find out here will be no more than this. This is a crappy piece of flint anyway, but this would serve a lot of purposes. It's a kitchen utensil. You could use it as a butter knife.

"What I haven't done yet is take off naked into the woods. I mean, if you're going to be self-sufficient, that's the epitome of doing it. I haven't done that yet.

"You're fixing to go into some unbelievably beautiful country.

From Kenton to Folsom. When I first came out here, I thought this was the greatest place in the world. There are places out here...they haven't changed. They're the way they've always been. You expect to see a mammoth come walking out.

"When I left Tulsa, I basically...I had a car and I basically just gave it away. I renounced all my material possessions. I didn't want them anymore."

The dusk air had darkened.

"I dropped out in Tulsa, and I just took off walking. Kind of like the aborigines who go on walkabouts. Have you heard of a walkabout?"

"No."

"When they decide that life has just become too complicated or whatever, they'll go on a walkabout, and they'll keep walking until they figure something out. I guess what I did was the equivalent of a walkabout. I said I'm going to keep walking until I find something of value. 'Cause I found no value living in a big city. Everything was so phony. I lived in Tulsa for years.

"I just thought there has got to be something more. There's got to be something more than working your whole life just to pay rent. You know I would get off work, go home, watch sitcoms. I don't want to watch sitcoms anymore. I want to do something different. And so I come out here. This is kind of halfway. I'm meeting the Clovis Man halfway. The Clovis people were an ancient culture around here. I'm not completely out of it, but I'm headed in the right direction. I still have to go back to town to get boots and socks."

Now he couldn't see well enough to knap. The flint had become pointed but was unfinished. He stuck his bone hammer behind his belt, the newly shaped flint into a pouch at his waist.

"Guard your food so the raccoons don't get it," he said. As he was leaving, he handed me something. I felt that it was a small arrowhead.

"I made that," Peter said. "The Indians would use that for small game or birds."

He walked away into the night. I ran my thumb over the craters and edges of the arrowhead.

That night I dreamed that my water bottles escaped from my unicycle and rolled away from me. I had to run down suburban streets to head them off.

Chapter Thirty

WE ARE LIKE TOURISTS needing to take one last picture. Some of these trees go up sixty feet or more before branching out. No trees in the area are taller than they are. Stepping under them, we feel transformed. Beech, maple, and ash dominate the forest, with numerous oak and hickory and poplar scattered within. Also, there are a couple of elm, a couple of walnut, and at least one black gum and one basswood. The forest has a complex and highly developed understory of spicebush, pawpaw, and maple-leaf viburnum. Every time we enter this forest we feel a hush, the effect perhaps of the various plant stories. The noise of a woodpecker, even several trees away, is resounding here. In no other place does my mind roam as easily, both in the sense of daydreaming, and in the sense of having an answer arrive, of suddenly knowing how to arrange my day, or how to phrase a thought. Connections, either fanciful or practical, are more easily made here.

In late fall, with most of the leaves gone, we can step out our back door and see deep into these woods. The door on the north side of the house faces these woods. I built it out of solid cedar boards around a triple-paned window. I sanded and oiled its entire surface. It would fit on no other house because of the uniquely askew rough opening it occupies.

We open this thick door and find ourselves in a small, unheated boot room. There's a coat rack made out of a cedar limb.

"Everything that should be here is here," the botanist for the Nature Preserves Commission told us, referring to the understory growth in the old woods. Invasive plant species that are choking out the native flora in many areas of the state—garlic mustard, Japanese grass, honeysuckle—are not found here.

We open an interior door and step into the heated area of the house. We see the red pump. It's mounted on a slab of red oak I chain-sawed out of a large, fallen tree. The slab has three stool-like legs, made from the branches of the same tree, supporting it. The handle of the pump is gracefully curved, with a nice place for the hand.

I'm reminded of a beech that stands in the old woods. It has a number of pileated woodpecker holes in its trunk, and two of the holes line up in such a way that if you are standing downhill from it and looking east, you can see straight through the tree. I was startled once by the proof of hollowness in something I'd thought solid. An instant later, I'd followed the trunk of the tree upward to its canopy and—instead of flaking bark and pith— found the fine-limbed upper structure of a tree that, indeed, was still alive.

⤳

In leaving Black Mesa State Park in the morning, I climbed, walking, an extremely steep hill that wound around boulders. At the top I looked out at the view, surprised to see how small the park was. In just a few steps I'd pull brown hills and mesas over its cleft of green, and you'd not know an oasis existed. I reached in my pocket for Peter Aiken's arrowhead, held it up in front of me. Wherever it was, it pointed, like a compass in this sense—useful if you didn't have a particular destination in mind. At the moment it directed my attention to a sky tilted east with a rising sun.

Tall grasses flanked the narrow road. In a few minutes the land fell: below me, an immense valley. The mesas scattered about its floor had started gathering their morning shadows. At the place where the road began its descent, I had the feeling that I was going over a lip, into a mouth. Lean back a little, keep a good hold on the pedals, I told myself. With my arms out wide

I made the descent. I'd only rarely look up at the vista, for it dizzied me. Boulders perched on the sides of cliffs, just off the road, armless.

If I thought Kansas, with its large, unpopulated expanses, had the capacity to diminish objects in its midst, then New Mexico and that stretch of Oklahoma past the state park turned out to be beyond anything I was expecting, astonishingly real— vivid, beautiful, scary—yet like a dreamscape as well, blurry since I couldn't take it all in at once, just one bit at a time. I'd not quite had that experience before in my travels: looking out so far into the world, seeing so much of it at once that I thought planet more than scenery, evolution more than birth date, God more than myself. Lift my eyes and I could see the world as readily dissolving as solidifying. At the moment, given my descent on a curvy road, I chose a six-foot take on the scene, keeping my world within grasp.

At the New Mexico state line, just outside Kenton, Oklahoma, where a closed grocery sported yesterday's newspaper in a stand and I wasn't able, anywhere, to top off my water bottles, I surprised myself by shouting as loudly as I could. Here was my voice, I thought, even as silence began healing itself over the intrusion.

I looked on my map and saw that it was sixty miles to Folsom, New Mexico. Mesas, many clad green with piñon and juniper, stretched out so far in front of me that in the end they seemed flat. Focus in closer, I told myself. A juniper stood just off the road, loaded with blue berries. I walked to it, put one of its berries in my mouth. It had a resiny, gigantic taste. I spit the berry out, resumed traveling. The taste faded gradually.

My Earthworm Castings Company water bottles sloshed under the seat, not quite full, and I started taking smaller sips. In an hour or so, the pavement ended, and the wind kicked up, a bad combination. I had to watch for big rocks. By midafternoon I began counting mile markers, an activity that was for a unicyclist somewhat boring and virtually uneventful.

Finally, not quite halfway to Folsom, I made my camp—partially up a mesa, beneath piñon pine, a quiet spot. Only one car had passed that day, and I'd seen the dust it had raised for miles. Now I watched the sunset, cracking piñon nuts and eating them along with bread and Skippy peanut butter—meeting the Clovis Man halfway, as Peter Aiken had said. I tried not to drink much water. Clovis Man would have probably known how to find water. This camp must have been one of the quietest I had, for the small noises I would make, like the cracking of piñon nuts, magnified themselves a thousandfold. The unzipping of my backpack was an avalanche.

By dusk I'd generated a small mountain of piñon nut hulls. It disappeared a while later, along with most other particulars. What remained that night were the big forms: trees blotching out portions of the sky, the sky gripped by mesas, sleep submerging consciousness.

The effect of the sun in the morning through juniper needles was symphonic, and I left with light and shadows swinging in my head. Though still long and rough at times, this day's stretch to Folsom seemed easier. I didn't start counting mile markers. The morning sun at one point hit a band of cottonwood, turning them golden. A creek, flowing between boulders below the road, absorbed the same brilliant color. It was well into October, I realized, a little startled.

During one of my afternoon breaks, I sat on porous metamorphic rock just outside Folsom. My feet dangled in a small creek. Water flowed past them a short distance before falling off a ledge. Twenty feet below, a pool of water perpetually gathered.

Folsom didn't have a grocery. I only had nuts and raisins and bread left in my pack. No peanut butter. Luckily, however, a restaurant was open. I filled my bottles and ate a big meal. A food server, sensing the importance of the meal, brought me an extra basket of chips.

Three miles south of town I left the road to head up a small, volcano-formed mountain, picking a route that let junipers and piñon pines hide me from the road, though, really, no one was going by. I had to crawl sometimes, pushing my unicycle in front of me.

At a flat place near the top, I put my gear down and looked around, sweating. In just one day the landscape had changed dramatically. To my left, a treeless plain stretched for miles before an upsurge of mountains. In front of me, the Capulin Volcano. To my right, more forested slopes, but still the combination of plain and mountain. This terrain, with its lumbering, irregular gait, was more unpredictable than the mesa country between Kenton and Folsom. You could imagine megafauna. Why did some of the slopes have trees while others were bare? Why were some of the mountains rounded and others pointed? It occurred to me that I was inside yesterday's blurred horizon, turning it tangible: a boulder three feet from me; fallen, weathered sticks; some kind of scrub oak that I could reach out and touch with my left hand; sweat starting to dry under my arms.

I picked up a stick. I liked its grayness, its ridges, how it both curved and forked, like something in the midst of a decision. I liked the little bit of weight it had, the slight roughness. I liked knowing that I could break it, and it would make a particular sound. That it could give me a splinter. Yet northern New Mexico seemed to ask for more than specifics. Look at the way your voice didn't last, how it dissolved into a larger entity, whatever that was. Look at the way a stick in your hand began to expand in significance, representing everything you could lay your eyes on. The feeling here, perhaps, was like the one a cat has approaching a mirror for the first time, seeing a reflection that is so exact that it is confusing and oddly inaccurate. The cat doesn't linger. I dropped the stick. Chilly now, I prepared for bed.

In the morning, I couldn't mount my unicycle because the road slanted up too steeply. I walked a mile. At the top I turned and saw that one of the mountains I had passed, which had looked smooth-topped, actually had a huge crater at its top. It had gotten behind me so swiftly.

I pedaled downhill the remaining distance to Capulin, into an imprecise and shocking landscape. The bases of mountains and volcanoes melted before they met the rangeland, leaving you unsure of their start. Rounded and pointed peaks descended to points that could be either distant or close.

Luckily Capulin had a gas station food mart. Though it had a poor selection—no peanut butter, for example—I purchased an array of groceries, which came to $17.29. That my needs in that grocery translated to the exact cost of $17.29 reassured me. It felt good that I had done something quite specific and practical, like spend exactly that amount, before heading out on eighty miles of back roads to Roy, New Mexico, the site of the next grocery, which hopefully would be larger.

At the edge of town, I asked directions from two guys, who expressed surprise upon realizing my route, said I was now off the back roads. They told me to turn south once I got to the other side of Palo Blanco Mountain, called "Seven Sisters" by locals. I would surely know the mountain once I had seen it, they said. They asked if I had warm clothes.

At noon it was cool and windy with dark clouds in the sky, and I went, flimsily, into another immense landscape. I passed a mountain I had seen from my camping spot, and it appeared just as distant, just as hard to tell where it began and where it ended as it had in the morning. Even up close, it appeared velvety.

Off to my left, some distance away, two herds of antelope grazed. The three closest to me bounded away when I drew near, then stopped, waiting for me to get close again. And when I did, they ran away again. I followed them or was pulled by them, threaded forward.

When I turned south at Seven Sisters Mountain—which did turn out to be easily recognizable—the wind whacked me, and the rocks became bigger. The road had turned into an obstacle course or a maze, the wind like invisible walls. I was lucky to move at all. When a gust pushed me entirely off the road, I quit. I stepped into a wilderness of boulders and juniper trees and countless smaller rocks. I walked ten minutes before I found a patch of rock-free ground big enough to roll out my sleeping bag. By then I had a feeling of being sheltered, a result of passing through, what seemed to me, dozens of entranceways.

In my sleeping bag, I looked past boulders and juniper branches to the sunset, a deep red, and saw irregular, dark clouds and pointed mountains in the distance.

The winds turned into gales, which lodged themselves against my bivy sack. I wondered if the dead juniper close to me would hold up. I pulled my head flap over, covering myself. Lightning flashed. I wanted the storm to come and pass. A few times I stuck my head out into the big sky, curious to see what was happening. No stars. It was very chilly, though I was warm in my bag. The wind billowed the loose material of the bivy sack. Evergreens swayed. Good to be in a field anchored by boulders. Finally I heard the first few patters of rain. I secured the head flap and turned on my side, curling my body.

In the morning I looked outside, stunned to see two inches of snow on the ground, blowing snow in the sky. To be in my underpants seemed absurd and dangerous. A little frightened, I decided to stay holed up for the day.

Only half-awake most of the time, I took hours to do a few chores. Around midmorning I finally unzipped both bags and peed into the snow, lying down. Feeling somewhat active, I then stuck my arm outside, quickly brushed the snow off the backpack and unzipped the side pouch, retrieving Honey-Nut Cheerios and peanuts. The rest of my $17.29 purchase was on the other side of the backpack, out of reach.

It took some time for my bag to warm up again. I pulled long johns, pants, two shirts, and a pair of socks out of my sleeping bag sack—which I had used to stuff into a pillow—and dressed myself, squirming.

I ate breakfast in bed, without some of its associations with luxury. I'd make a funnel with my left hand and pour food through it to my mouth. Chewing made an incredibly loud noise in my head, though I suspected someone just two feet away would hear nothing but the storm.

I drifted into sleep, the bags of food on either side of me. At some point that day I put my shoes on and got up and stepped dizzily outside. My unicycle looked dead. I shook the snow off it and quickly unscrewed the tops to the water bottles. When I tipped the unicycle, some water flowed out of them. For much of the morning I'd worried about water freezing and cracking the water bottles. Then I relieved myself a few steps from the sleeping bag, my back to the wind. One last chore: the bag of fig bars. As I was returning to my sleeping bag, a big gust nearly knocked me over.

I stayed holed up the rest of that day and night. I'd gone from being able to see hundreds of miles in any direction to approximately three inches in front of me, synthetic blue fabric keeping my vision much to myself. Here, I supposed, there was no horizon-line vagueness—no horizon line at all, in fact. Create a small enough world for yourself and you could know its boundaries. Was this the feeling Peter Aiken had living in Tulsa? I wondered if it was harmful to breathe in your own breath.

Every once in a while I'd ask myself if I was warm and then hope that that perceived warmth was not an illusion.

Had I ever been with myself for such a long stretch of time? Stupid question. I realized, then, to what extent I'd been traveling with another presence, say wind, a landscape, traffic, a rock on the road coming up. I'd go about the day often wondering who I was in relation to other objects. Some things grew clear, some faded.

On my second night, the wind abated and I lay awake, planning my exit. I'd look out to check the sky. A gibbous moon hung in it. I waited until it set, dozing at times. Then I put my hat and gloves on. I sat up and put my rain jacket on over my other clothes. Standing up, I swayed and quickly sat back down, putting my legs into the sleeping bag's nest of warm air. It was cold but not as windy, with still about two inches of snow on the ground. I ate sitting up, attempting the task with my gloves on. Bean spread on bread. Corn nuts. Fig bars. I made another attempt to get up, this time putting my shoes on first. Though unsteady still, this time I remained standing. Feeling fragile, I walked over rocks and peed. On impulse, I did fifty jumping jacks for warmth.

I packed up and with just a blush of light in the east, I headed carefully out onto snowy rocks toward the road. In twenty minutes I made it. Newly born to the road, I set off walking. By three miles most of the snow on the road had melted.

When I was able to mount, balance, then move—a little at first, then more surely, gathering toward me a small incline—I felt euphoric. Movement delighted me, and I had boundless energy that day. "Hit the road, Jack," I sang at the top of my voice.

As I traveled, volcanoes faded at my back and I entered flatter terrain, surrounded by grasslands with herds of antelope and cows. Snow began sliding off vertical objects, clumping to the ground and melting. As a result, perhaps, I noticed the town of Farley, some distance off. I drew nearer, absorbed in the wonderful process of motion. At its outskirts, I noticed that its parked cars were junked cars, that some of the houses didn't have roofs, that there were no people. The term "ghost town" came to me late, precisely when three skinny dogs rounded a corner, causing me to jump. I pedaled quickly out of town.

I devoured the miles. Late in the day I pedaled into Kiowa National Grasslands, where it proved difficult to find a camping spot. Of all the features that could hide someone who wished not to be seen—trees, volcanoes, hills, boulders, snowstorms—Kiowa National Grasslands had none of them. Then I spotted an erosion gully some distance from the road, deep enough to keep me under the ground's surface. In *A Unicyclist's Guide to America*, I would include erosion gullies as possible campsites. After traveling fifty miles, the most I'd ever traveled in one day, making it practically to Roy, New Mexico, where there was a grocery, I disappeared into the range.

In the morning I rose out of the earth, made it to Roy. After traveling 150 miles into New Mexico, the restaurant in Roy was the second I'd seen in the state, the post office the third, and the grocery the first full-fledged one I'd found. The grocery even had an array of peanut butter, but I decided not to buy any—a decision that ended up being a mistake—because Wagon Round, thirty miles up the road, also had a grocery. I thought that the idea of peanut butter up the road would be more of an incentive to pedal than a jar in my pack. Maybe I would get a motel in Wagon Round and call a college friend.

Roy sat at the edge of a huge canyon, which I soon began descending. I stayed on my unicycle for most of the way, pressing heavily against the eager pedals. I attempted not to look too deep into the canyon.

From the bottom, I climbed two miles to get to the top. I walked. Once past the steep part, the road still climbed, although gradually enough to let me ride my wheel. The wind kicked up. Every turn of the wheel seemed to create that much more road. When the wind stopped briefly, making the pedals suddenly easy to turn, my distress turned to delight.

"You're faster than an inchworm," I heard myself saying, a little louder than a whisper.

Perhaps, I thought, something more dramatic than that: "Okay, you're faster than a girl doing hopscotch."

When the wind picked up again, my hat blew off. I was always glad that no one was around when my hat flew off, causing my hair to fly around, get in my eyes.

The road still climbed. I thought again of calling a friend that night.

I heard a judge's voice: "I pronounce you guilty of riding one wheel."

"Yes, sir."

"For the next ten years you will push two wheels up and down the main street of this town."

"Yes, Your Honor."

When I approached a mile marker, I would squint my eyes and look away. About five miles out of Wagon Round, however, I treated myself to a mile marker, hoping that I was actually closer than five miles. I wasn't: seven miles out. But still, the last stretch.

"You've begun a great pounce into Wagon Round."

Despite the expectations I had for it (or, rather, because of them), Wagon Round disappointed me. I blamed Interstate 25 and its ceaseless noise. I blamed, too, Wagon Round's lack of a real motel. It only had four rooms behind a Chevron Food Mart, each of them facing the Interstate and each without a phone, and I chose not to rent one of them. The Food Mart had no peanut butter. I remembered my last spoonful of peanut butter, at my camp between Kenton and Folsom. Skippy Honey Butter. Instead, I bought corn nuts and more fig bars and told myself Cima, New Mexico, fifty miles away, would have peanut butter.

As I was leaving, a woman with long, dark hair greeted me and welcomed me to Wagon Round. She said that she had done a lot of traveling as well and was envious of me. I told her that people usually felt pity toward me. She gave me her address and told me to visit if I passed by.

A mile out of Wagon Round I climbed a hill and found a place by a boulder and a single large juniper. That night I dreamed I was in a room with several people watching television. Everyone sat. I was on my unicycle, trying to balance in place. Someone pointed out that I could sit down on the couch. I said I wasn't used to being in a house.

If I opened my eyes during the night, I'd see the moon at some point in its arc across the sky, and I'd be glad I wasn't in a motel room behind a gas station, even if it had had a phone. I was glad, too, I wasn't in a snowstorm. If you were enclosed either way, you wouldn't have that experience of being with the moon as it rolled over. And what experience was that? I wasn't sure, unless I said the obvious: that I went to sleep with it on one side of my body, its face close to mine as it first came up; that it rose high above me before falling to my other side, close again; that there was brightness involved and a patterning with lights and shadows.

I pedaled into high range in the morning, passing bands of antelope. I said "hello" to them, lengthening the "o" sound.

A baby elk (nonetheless a large creature) leapt from the grasses in front of me. Apparently thinking it couldn't jump a nearby fence, it found itself trapped between the fence and the road. Later, when four semis passed me and I thought about the little elk running quickly out of space, I became angry, but my anger was directed at something so abstract and large that it turned to sadness. I didn't want animals to be trapped. And it wasn't as simple as humans denying animals habitat, though that was part of the problem. It was also a problem of humans feeling enclosed as well, inside the demands of deadlines, having to deliver something as fast as possible between two points, to do more, all the time.

Chapter Thirty-One

I STAYED A NIGHT with Julie Berkstrand and her family. Julie was the woman who had greeted me in Wagon Round, and she told me now about a mountain wilderness family that lived outside Cima, New Mexico, thinking I might be interested in visiting them.

Before arriving in Cima, I began seeing lakes and tall trees, the first tall trees I'd seen since the Chaplin Nature Center in Kansas. A Hispanic town, Cima was one of the friendliest of my journey. Nearly everyone waved. A full-sized grocery, nicely stocked with peanut butter and other foods, also buoyed me. I loaded up, unsure if I was visiting the wilderness family or heading more directly west. The checkout woman helped with my decision. She knew their name, the Leavens, and the location of their homestead, somewhere past Truxton and Aspen Lake, which were on my map. Outside the grocery, I hesitated, but took the road that headed toward the Leavens.

I made it, exhausted, to Aspen Lake—a day's traveling, I guessed, from the Leavens' place. At my camp, through pine needles and flaming aspen leaves, I could see the lake. I had enough light to write in my journal; then I did nothing. The balance of light changed from the sun to the moon, which came up hugely and suddenly, like an instant bonfire, or headlights.

The event that happened next could serve as a cautionary tale for unicyclists. I'd refrained that afternoon from opening my newly purchased jar of peanut butter, thinking it would be all the more pleasurable to eat at my camp at the end of the day.

Thus that skunk that sauntered out of a moon shadow only a body-length away from where I sat on my sleeping bag, a newly opened jar of Shurfine Super Crunch before me, could serve this warning: that the postponement of appetites or destinations or passions for the purpose of increasing the pleasure of these fulfillments can be taken to an extreme.

Look at the unicyclist hurriedly screwing on the peanut butter lid and then abandoning his camp. Look at him feebly throwing a pine cone at the skunk. Look at him dropping all resistance with the skunk's raised tail. How pathetic! Look at him simply watching the skunk eat a whole bag of fig bars.

A Unicyclist's Guide to America would mention that the art of unicycling is knowing, in part, when to give in to desire.

༄

The Leavens supposedly lived at the end of the rocky road past Aspen Lake, but the road forked that morning before it ended. Guessing, I turned left. The mountain, becoming steep, fell against me as I walked. Every few steps I stopped to rest. There were blue spruce and aspen as well as pine. Some of the trees were huge. It took two hours to reach the top—an alpine meadow with two lakes, a soft, flat stretch of aspen-leaved ground where I was able to ride my unicycle briefly—but no wilderness family.

Back down, through that very thin air. I wanted urgently to cross that fine line to sleep. But I kept going till I made it to the fork in the road. There I stretched out, my head resting against the backpack. I ate a banana with peanut butter. I napped.

I rose still tired. The other direction climbed gradually for maybe a mile and opened to a sunlit meadow. Two horseback riders appeared in a flash in the middle of the meadow, behind a herd of sheep. I saw two boys with bare feet, riding bareback. They wheeled their horses in whichever direction the sheep were going. Motionless, I watched. They didn't see me. Swerving around a bend, they emptied the meadow except for two large, fluffy, white sheep dogs that walked slowly over to where I was standing. I stroked them, wondering if the shepherds would return. I let a few minutes pass and then followed their path.

I made it to a large wooden cross that stood at the bend in the meadow. From there I could see a rail-fence corral with the sheep already in it, looking amazingly calm. A small log house with a rusty tin roof came into view. In a few more steps I could see a young woman in buckskin taking a baby out of a tub of water. She looked up and saw me and went quickly into the house. Soon a man with a beard and a woman with long, thick brown hair came out of the house. Several tow-headed kids, barefoot, their hair going in all directions, followed. A four- or five-year-old girl with red cheeks was clinging to her mother's long skirt, and a couple of boys behind their mother peeked at me.

The whole family had gathered, as if waiting for a speech.

"Hello, I'm doing a little traveling," I said. I hadn't talked to many people in New Mexico. The kids looked at my unicycle more than at me. Although it probably didn't need to be emphasized, I lifted it up. A couple of the kids smiled, but the father remained expressionless. I said something about attempting to visit people living for something other than what our consumer society deemed was important. After what seemed to be a long pause, the father spoke.

"You've come to the right place. We've discovered the joy of being real, the joy of being together, and the joy of being poor, living by Christ. Let me introduce you to everybody.

"This is Jerusalem," he said, ruffling the hair of the little girl still clinging to her mother's skirt.

"And Moses. Where are you Moses?"

A little boy made an appearance from behind his mother.

"Israel." A slightly older boy who reminded me of an elf.

"David." The blondest boy of the bunch. I noticed that they all had leather pouches at their waists.

"Joshua." Thin and sturdy-looking, like all of them.

"And Joseph, our eldest son.

"Elizabeth, here, is our eldest daughter." She was the one I had first seen giving a baby a bath.

"The baby is in the house. I'm John, and this is my wife, Salina."

They had just returned from the Santa Fe flea market, where the air had hit them, they said, like a sledgehammer. They were tired, John said, and were ending the day by unpacking and getting baths. He said I must be tired too, climbing so high on a unicycle, something he didn't think had ever been done before. The only people who had ever chanced on their homestead before had been lost. Because I wasn't Christian, I couldn't come into their house, but I could camp—Joseph would show me where—and the whole family would camp outside with me, nearby.

I went off with Joseph to my camp, a clearing inside a stand of blue spruce, with a circle of rocks around a fire pit. Joseph left, and I lay down on my mat. The afternoon sun, shredded by spruce needles, accumulated on my back, and I fell asleep.

David woke me and gave me a stained cup of tea with slightly discolored chunks of ice. The ice, he said, was the last from the icehouse. After I drank the tea, Jerusalem, the little girl, walked to me, stuck her arm out. Her hand dropped an apple into my hand, and she ran away. I looked at the apple in my hand, surprised.

Later, Joseph showed me how he milked Jonas, the milk cow, letting me try but quickly taking over again when he saw I was ineffective, saying that it took some practice. Israel and David showed me the contents of the leather pouches at their belts. A compass, a pocketknife, flint and steel and tinder, a whistle. "Survival pouches," Israel said proudly. Already David was striking the flint and steel together on the tinder. When part of the tinder glowed, he cupped his hands and blew gently. A flame sprang up. "It's easy," he said, "once you get used to it."

After the fire-making and cow-milking lessons, Joseph took me to the horse lot so we could ride horses. Jerusalem came running behind us.

"What are you supposed to be doing?" Joseph asked her.

"Nothing. Helping you."

We got to a horse. "Usually we ride bareback," Joseph said. He put his hands on the horse's lower neck and flung himself up. He quickly got back down and asked me to try it.

"Let me show him how I can do it," Jerusalem said. Before Joseph could respond, she leaped up, grabbed the horse's halter, dangled there for a moment before beginning an incredible trek across the horse's face to the high point of its neck where she slid down to the back and stopped, facing the horse's rump. She began to turn around and would have slipped off the horse if Joseph had not propped her up.

I gawked at her.

"Jerusalem." David came running up to us. "You're supposed to milk Jonas with Moses."

Joseph caught her slide off the horse, setting her on the ground, and she went away running.

I mounted the horse like Joseph had, thinking of Starlight. David and Joseph mounted two others, and we left the corral into a big, late-afternoon sky. They started trotting immediately, and my horse went along without waiting for any direction from me. We went past the cross and down a hill. A branch I didn't see in time scraped across my nose. We slowed down at the bottom to let the horses cross the creek. The other side was rocky. David turned around.

"You want to gallop?"

"Maybe we ought to find a better place," I responded, worried about the rocks.

"This is the best we got."

He and Joseph galloped off. I clung to my horse as it took off too, trying not to think of the rocks or the logs that we would miraculously miss or jump. We flew. Finally, a steep wooded slope stopped our gallop. David looked at me. "We figured if you could stay on a unicycle, you could stay on a horse."

That evening Salina cooked a meal at the fire pit by my camp.

Everyone gathered around. The fire completed a circle, tossing light generously among us. Jerusalem sat in her mother's lap. Israel and Moses leaned against their father.

Somehow Salina cooked pan pizza and apple pie for everybody. The youngest kids ate first, followed by the oldest, with adults being last. John got out a guitar, began singing hymns. Every once in a while we could hear wind rustling the tops of aspen trees, but it never hit us, sitting where we were, surrounded by blue spruce. John told me they had been kicked out of churches, perceived as too radically following Jesus's example. A rich person isn't Christian, he said. He wondered about me, if I'd had any faith training, and although I perceived this question and others that followed as being too directive, I nonetheless decided that I liked him and his family, how close they were. John thought God had sent me to their family and hoped God would help them understand why. I hoped that, too.

I woke up in the morning to the sound of laughter. Their big St. Bernard dog that they had told me about but that I hadn't yet seen lay just a few feet away from me. Her name, I knew, was Mountain Mama. She was huge, droopy, and happy-looking. Then I saw her blind, blue-eyed, wildly furred puppy named Samson walking toward Mountain Mama and me in a gait that reminded me of a toddler's. At that moment one of the kids called his name repeatedly, and Samson eagerly changed his direction. His name had been turned into a trail.

I walked into the woods. Aspen, pine, spruce. Rotten logs. In just a few steps I couldn't see any clearings. All directions seemed similar. I turned around and came out of the woods at a cylindrical tank just above my campsite. I saw John, and he told me that they stored wheat in that tank. Unground wheat, which lasted longer. "Planning is so critical here," he said. "And what we are doing with wheat preparation is, on a different level, similar to the work we are doing for eternal preparation."

He asked me if I wanted to go on a hay run with him to

Truxton, about five miles from Aspen Lake. They didn't yet have the winter's supply for their livestock.

"How are you going?" I asked.

"By truck." We walked down the hill just past the fire pit, and he pointed out where the truck was. What I had first thought was a wooden shack had—I finally noticed—wheels, and an ancient, weathered hood. Blocks chalked the wheels. It faced downhill, toward the cross.

"It's where we live when we're at the flea market."

"How often do you go to that?"

"About two or three times a year, to sell wool or extra produce. We make about $1,000 a year, which is enough for us. In the world a family our size needs $1,000 a month. Or a week."

I told him I would go with him. David and Jerusalem wanted to come, too. Before we left, Salina gave us each a slice of banana bread. She would kill a rooster while we were gone.

With Jerusalem sitting between John and me, and David standing on the running board by his father's window, we began—after that motor turned over and caught with a kind of geologic slowness—a steady, unicycle-slow lurch down the side of the mountain. John pointed out the first bend in the road past the cross and the sheep meadow. He called it "Miracle Corner."

"Our transmission fell out here once, which we considered to be a miracle because we were so close to home. Whenever we reach this point, coming back from wherever we are coming from, we consider it a miracle."

He angled the truck between two huge boulders.

"It's a relief to get home because there's a growing wickedness out in the world. This has been pre-ordained. It's in the Bible.

"I don't try to make things better in the world. I concentrate on my family."

David, I noticed, kept his eyes in the woods.

"He sees bear before any of us," John said. "He saw a grizzly bear. You know where you made that wrong turn and ended up on top of the mountain? Right up there in the meadow. And he's been chased by a bobcat while he was on his horse."

"Rosehips," David said and jumped off the running board, picking some tiny red berries off a bush. He hopped back on the truck. "You can eat them," he said, popping them into his mouth.

"There's Tribulation Tree." John pointed to a towering blue spruce. "That's one of our wood piles against the tree. We seem to break down or get stuck a lot here. The lower side of the tree stays dry no matter how hard it rains."

I was beginning to wonder what our chances were for making it into town. The truck, when John had to ease it into a particularly large rut, made the sound of a tree beginning a crash to the ground. Nonetheless, Jerusalem managed to fall asleep, her head resting against her father's lap. When the road began an even steeper and rockier descent, John brought the truck almost to a halt.

"We call this area the Staircase. It didn't take much revelation to name."

The brakes, I sensed, were like hands gripping whatever they could find.

"Christianity comes at a cost," John said as the truck tipped downward.

Apparently, being carried down a staircase was a calming thing for Jerusalem. She continued to sleep.

I put my right hand on the dashboard as the truck angled even more steeply downward.

"At the bottom there's a place we call the Valley of the Shadow of Death because with just a little rain the truck slips into these huge ruts."

We were going more slowly than I had gone pushing my unicycle uphill. The front wheels dropped over a rock ledge, and something banged against the underside of the truck. John accelerated and the truck lurched forward, making it all the way over the ledge.

In the Valley of the Shadow of Death, whenever John eased off the brakes, we moved just inches at a time, making it past deep ruts. After that section, the road improved somewhat. I recognized the one stretch where I had been able to ride my unicycle. When we got to a hill overlooking Truxton, John stopped the truck. Jerusalem sat up.

"This is the Valley of Temptation," John said. He closed his eyes and was silent for a moment. Before continuing on, he made David get inside the truck, said it was dangerous being on the paved road. With all of us up front, we rumbled into the community, which seemed bigger to me than it had before.

We drove past the church and down a country road about a mile before getting to the farm where the Leavens bought their hay. John knew how to place the bales to use the space most efficiently. I handed them to him, and the farmer who was selling the bales counted as we worked. Sometimes he looked at me strangely, like I had gone to the other side.

Shortly after leaving Truxton, we turned off the road we had arrived on and started climbing a different slope. John said that we were taking a way home that was longer but not quite as steep.

"This is Rescue Mountain," John said. "Our timing chain broke here in the dead of winter last year. I sent Joseph and Joshua home to tell everyone what had happened, and that night, lo and behold, Salina and all the kids arrived with horses, food, blankets. We camped out a week there before we got the truck fixed, and the whole time we were there not one person stopped to see if we needed help."

To my surprise, the old logging road that we were on emptied into that alpine meadow I had found after making the wrong turn.

"There's where I saw the grizzly." David pointed to where the valley dipped into a lake. "It was bigger than a horse."

John then horrified me when he turned down the same steep, boulder-strewn slope that had worn me out walking up.

"You think this is possible?" I asked, an alternative to my first reaction, which was to yell stop.

"Lord willing."

Jerusalem crawled over my lap, wanting to sit by the door, but I put her back between John and me. Five minutes later the truck lurched sideways, and the door flung open. John told me how to shut it so it couldn't open. He didn't seem disturbed.

We headed down an area that looked just as bad, or worse, than the Staircase. They had done some repair work, rolling small boulders into huge ruts. The left front wheel of the truck dropped into a ditch and the truck lurched sideways again. "How often does Salina kill a rooster?" I asked irrelevantly, an effort to stop my mind from crashing us. Two or three times a year, I found out. I held on to Jerusalem. John tugged the large steering wheel to the right. We continued to move in this way for another fifteen minutes.

By the time we reached the fork at the bottom, I was exhausted. Shortly, we arrived at the meadow where I had seen Joseph and Joshua herding sheep. At the cross John stuck his head out of the window and whooped: "Wuuuu...Jesus!" From the house, the response: "Wuuuuu...Jesus!" Elizabeth and Joseph came running, smiles on their faces.

The kids took off running—David toward the woods and Jerusalem just running—and I marveled at their strength and spirit. I followed David.

"Where are you going?" I yelled to him.

"To find firewood."

"I'll help."

We entered the woods together. "Is this just your job, or does everyone help?" I asked.

"Even the little 'uns help with the cooking firewood. Just whoever's not doing something."

Soon our arms were full of dead branches, which we brought to the firepot. Everyone gathered around, sitting on stump chairs. My eyes fixed on a tropical-looking bird perched on Elizabeth's shoulder. Even at dusk it was brilliant.

"That's Earthquake," David said. "He can talk in complete sentences when he wants to."

"I'm already surprised by him," I said.

That evening I informed the Leavens that I wanted to go cross-country to Senales instead of backtracking to Cima. John said I'd have to cross the Lopez Wilderness. They would take me partway, to the headwaters of the Lopez River. The whole family would go. But first they needed to harvest the root crops.

The next day, the little kids would squeal when a shovel turned over an exceptionally large beet or carrot or rutabaga, scramble to be the first to put it in a burlap sack. The whole family worked in the garden, the older people with shovels or carrying the full bags away.

Later that day I sat with Salina by the outdoor firepot, washing and slicing potatoes for her so she could nurse the baby. I worked more slowly than she did. David told me not to worry about getting the potatoes so clean. "We eat dirt all the time," he said.

When enough were cut, I slid them into sizzling lard. Salina waited until they were partially blackened before taking them off. We cooked three batches.

The magnitude of what the Leavens were doing—trekking into the wilderness with me with kids, three horses and a donkey, the Saint Bernards, Jonas the milk cow, Earthquake, baby rabbits—dawned on me the morning of our departure. The packing for the trip took place in the clearing by the cross. I mostly watched. Israel and Jerusalem were placing bunnies in a wool-lined milk bucket. John and Elizabeth opened a yellow-leaved animal-packing manual to help them remember the diamond hitch they would use on Jonas. Joshua, in charge of the baby Hosanna, placed her on the donkey Bethel's saddle. The saddle slipped and Joshua had to lunge to catch Hosanna, while the others continued what they were doing. David pulled the calf toward Jonas. Salina had put the pail of rabbits in a box and tried to place it behind the saddle of her horse. John saw her and yelled out. "Somebody help Mama tie the rabbits on." Jerusalem, free from her chore with the rabbits, had managed to scramble on Bethel. She motioned for me to come over. "Move Bethel over there," she told me, pointing to where Mountain Mama was lying. Israel came running toward us and said that Jerusalem was only trying to get a ride out of me.

"Earthquake can go on somebody's shoulder," one of the kids yelled in a high voice.

"Mark," John called, "We're about ready for your pack and unicycle."

They strapped them to the milk cow. Moses handed me a bowl of milk and cornflakes. "The milk's still warm from Jonas," he said.

Our caravan left midmorning. I walked behind Jonas, carrying a stick. It was good, I decided, to do something to move my unicycle along. In just a few minutes, the mountain reared in front of us, and our trail had to wind back and forth just to keep itself placed against steep slopes. The animals' feet slipped on the rocks. The rabbit box slid, stopping the caravan. John tied it to the front of the saddle so Salina could hold it. Jonas began to slow. I apparently did not hit her hard enough, because Joseph switched with me. I pulled her instead. Rock ledges made tall steps in the trail.

We came upon two elk hunters, who stepped off the path. They watched us.

"Look," one of them said to the other, "They've even got a pack steer."

John said something about getting three gallons of milk a day out of that pack steer.

Up and up and up. I worried that Jonas was going to die. Her whole body sank in and out as she breathed. Foam from her mouth dripped off in long streams.

The woods thinned and we came to a slope of boulders, which were so numerous as to appear moving. Usually snow covered this area, John said. We spread out, each of us picking a way among rocks, still climbing. A half an hour passed. David made it to the top first. Soon we all did. A broad, flat plain of rocks and short dried grasses stretched before us. Being higher than anything else, we could see no mountain peaks on the horizon.

Moving again after a short break, I stepped on the ground as if it were delicate, as if being so close to the clouds made it less substantial. I could also have been dizzy. We reached a fir tree forest and kept going. I had thought for some reason that this wilderness would have trails with markers, but apparently the Leavens knew where they were going and were comfortably spread out in the blue-green dark shadows. We seemed to walk for hours. Then the trees gave way to a narrow valley with a small stream—the headwaters of the Lopez River, John said. The temperature had plunged. We chose to camp a few steps inside the woods. I put on my sweater and gloves, walked to the stream to fill my canteen with clear, cold water.

At the camp I spread out my sleeping bag and bivy sack. Then I looked for firewood. The branches of fir brushed me as I walked deeper into the woods. My feet sank in the spongy ground. Needles crackled. I could only see the big forms of things. Turning around, I saw that trees had neatly sealed the opening I had come through. I felt the ground for sticks, gathering an armload.

Salina and Elizabeth had a fire going and were cooking potatoes and rice. We all sat down. An idea struck me, and I ran to my pack, retrieving the Shurfine peanut butter and bread. I sat back down, the warmth of the fire at my front. Each piece of bread needed to be unfolded. I used my pocketknife to spread the peanut butter. The first sandwich went to Jerusalem. I couldn't believe how cold my back was, how hot my front. The next one to Moses. Then Israel, David, Joshua, Joseph, Elizabeth, Salina, and John. Then me.

The rice and potatoes warmed us. I appreciated the lard. We watched the last of the sticks burn down to coals. Then I helped Joseph and David place fire-warmed rocks around Earthquake's cage. To insulate the warmth around the stunning bird, they produced a small blanket, draping it over the rock-mounded cage.

In the morning I put my rain gear over every article of clothing I had to keep warm. The Leavens were up to see me off. John gave me a compass and a trail map that I didn't think would be useful because I had yet to see a trail. Senales, he told me, was to our north and west. He also gave me strips of white cloth to help them follow me if I didn't make it to Senales and call their neighbors in three days' time. He gave me a Bible too, and I wanted to tell him please no, you've given me the words already by doing them. You've given me the closeness of your family, your generosity. But I accepted it and put the extra weight in my pack. Salina gave me an irregular chunk of cheese, wrapped in brown paper.

I hugged the smaller people first and worked my way up. Some of them held tight. I could feel the horse-climbing muscles in Jerusalem's arms. Toward the end I was crying, and I turned away from them with blurry eyes. For the first time in my life, I stepped out alone into a wilderness. When I reached the bend in the valley, I heard, "Wuuu...Jesus!" and turned around to see the whole family still there, watching me. I waved and walked on, letting a pile of boulders ease between us.

⁓

The angling and patterning of our indoor light in our house across a day and across the seasons is reminiscent of the forest. So, too, are the native wood and stone that we used in the building, the rain and sunlight that we store and use. A less tangible but nonetheless noticeable connection also exists: a simple elegance, a sense, as in a forest, of nothing out of place, a purpose for everything here.

We depend on the forest to help us ask questions, even ones small in scope. How could this cupboard be as functional as possible? How could it be built best with the materials at hand? How should it relate with the rest of the wall?

SLOWSPOKE

⌐⁓

A cold wind hit me as I climbed out of the valley to a treeless, rocky plain. Gusts squeezed between my pack and body, whistling. I turned around to confirm that none of the Leavens followed. I took out the compass then, glad no one could see me use it so soon. As if to keep from being blown off-course, I cupped my hands around the instrument's thin needle, which floated before idly pointing north. So, north and west, the direction Senales was supposed to be. I looked up to see in the distance the start of a fir tree forest. I walked toward it.

As they grew bigger, the fir trees appeared clad in animal fur. Drawing still closer to them, I saw spaces between the trees, openings for me to enter this body of wilderness.

At its edge I tied a strip of cloth to a tree limb. White on green. I liked the contrast. I liked, also, my blue raincoat between the plain and the forest, by the white cloth on the green branch.

I stepped into a blue-green darkness. I stood, letting my eyes adjust. How would they ever be able to track me? A step away was a log on the ground as high as my knees. Another one lay close to it. Another one, further off. Sun streaks that managed to slip fir needles and land on the forest floor were so rare as to appear accidental, like spills.

I'd always looked at mountains from a distance, seen them as background. Though I dimly recognized the beauty, I was, foremost, afraid.

I placed my unicycle on the other side of the first log and attempted to step over the log. The backpack shifted on my shoulders, and I lost balance. I sat down and pivoted my body to the other side. My unicycle had lost much if not all of its use. It would have made as much sense to carry an oar, a steering wheel, a golf club.

The trees, I noticed, had fallen in any direction, creating a labyrinth. I'd go twenty steps and have to cross another one. Sometimes instead of climbing over them, I'd walk down their

249

long lengths, going around them, the effect being a kind of travel somewhat like unicycle travel. Fear gave me the urge to pass through the forest quickly, but the forest kept me going slowly.

Every few minutes I'd check my compass. Always pointing in one direction, the needle began to seem absurd and unreliable, yet I continued, generally, to follow it, even abandoning an elk trail when it meandered too far south.

Clear water that flowed over rocks came to me only as a concept. Water. I should drink, eat. I forced myself to sit. Shortly, I was moving again. Some of the newly downed trees ushered in roads of sunlight, but mostly the forest was dimly lit. It opened once to a small glade, and I stepped into the opening carefully, as if easing into someone's vision, squinting my eyes against sudden brightness. Partially hidden, a small stream ran through dried grasses. It took one long step to span it. Watching the grasses, I traversed the glade. At its edge, I looked behind me: the view was the same I'd had on entering the glade. One more step forward and I'd be gone from the opening. I tied a white strip to a branch.

For the next hour or so, the forest continued as it had been, though the trees began to thin. Then they ended, and I looked out, astonished, at the scene before me, a wilderness ripped open wide: grassy valleys with boulders, lakes holding as steady as frogs' eyes in unlikely, high places, sky, shadows, wind.

Any direction I went, even northwest, I'd have to climb. Immediately before me was a forest of miniature trees, about waist-high. I tied a strip to one of the treetops. Carrying my unicycle like a guitar, I then entered the miniature forest. Canopies clutched at my legs as I planted them blind between trunks, my pace either like an ant's or a giant's, depending on the focus.

I reached a slope, and the trees ended. The slope didn't appear steep. Within minutes, though, I was on my hands and knees, barely moving. The grass rippled below, for an instant revealing a small lake. I put my unicycle in front of me for balance and worked myself toward it. The slope steadily steepened. All at once

I couldn't move, up or down. If I so much as moved a finger, the pebbles would slip under me, and I would slide down the mountain. My heart pounded. I had never been unable to move before. Somewhere the wind blew, for clouds hurried across the sky and the valley grass undulated. Luckily the wind wasn't hitting me.

Time passed. Nothing happened, which was good. I thought of a proverb I'd learned in a high-school Spanish class. *Vísteme despacio que estoy de prisa.* Dress me slowly for I am in a hurry. I thought of big things—the sky, the mountain—and small things—the way a rock pressed into my right thigh. Still, I didn't move. I didn't dare look up more than a couple of inches.

In my mind, I envisioned a several-mile-long rope, fabricated with the strips I'd tied to trees and shrubs in the wilderness, my every step in arriving here part of a long whole. I could, I fantasized, slide down this rope to various points in my past. At any point, a slight alteration of direction could have rescued me from this mountain. I could slide down only to the base of the mountain and take another route. Or I could travel all the way to college graduation and attempt then to keep up better with my friends, most of whom probably had fallen in love by now, married, found good jobs. Or to junior high, when a classmate came up to me and sternly advised me to get a job and purchase a good pair of shoes. I would see the warnings not to go off-course. I would see how inevitable it was—given my persistent angling toward the fanciful or utopian, toward that which didn't exist—that I would end up here with a unicycle, on the side of this mountain.

Something plunked above me. I looked up slowly and saw that Peter Aiken's arrowhead had dropped out of the pouch under my unicycle seat. It stayed where it landed, a good sign. It pointed at nothing in particular. Due south, it looked like. At its tip was a patch of light sand roughened by rock fragments.

In a re-written junior high script, I would have told that classmate that I wanted to stay home and build forts and read books and ride horses. I wouldn't have agreed with him about the job and the shoes.

SLOWSPOKE

I moved my right leg, which felt numb. I moved it out from under my left leg and waited for the avalanche of feeling to pass. I hadn't slipped yet. I pushed my unicycle forward and wiggled toward it. Once up to my unicycle, I reached uphill and grasped a woody-stemmed plant. I pulled myself forward and eventually used the plant as a foothold.

Chapter Thirty-Two

IMAGINE OUR HOUSE BEFORE SUNRISE on a clear, cold morning, eighteen degrees. The temperature inside would be just under sixty degrees, the fire not yet lit. Insulated well, our house only requires a fire a few hours a day. I usually get up first, turn a light on, get dressed. I go out into the cold boot room and slip shoes on and open the cedar door. The ground is crunchy under my feet as I step outside. I inhale fresh cold air, walk to the edge of the forest, look up at the stars and branches, and pee.

Back inside, I kneel down by the stove and a tray of wood I'd set on the rock hearth the night before. First, I lay strips of newspaper between two firebricks at the bottom of the stove. Then I place four pieces of kindling, tic-tac-toe style, across the firebricks and newspaper. A few months ago on a summer afternoon I'd split scrap cedar boards and filled two large bags with the splintery strips. Next, I stack bigger pieces of wood on the kindling, until the stove is full. This wood is Osage orange, or hedgeapple as we sometimes call it, a heavy, twisted, stringy wood with a yellow heart. An invasive, it grows on parts of our land and burns longer and hotter than other hardwood. It pops and sparkles. I'd cut, split, and stacked this wood at the end of the previous winter, about a pickup truck load. Long sheets of old tin roofing cover the pile.

Sometimes as I stack the wood in the stove I'll remember the particular tree it came from, say the wind-pushed hedgeapple along the path to the paved road. It had leaned almost to the ground, its root ball part of a widening mouth. I had to climb up its trunk with my chain saw to cut off many of the limbs.

After each cut a ring of milky sap formed just under the outer bark. The sap turned my gloves black.

I light the newspaper and close the stove door. The door has a glass front.

Jennifer gets out of bed and pees in a urinal I've made for her in a walk-in cedar closet close to the bathtub. I used a small stainless steel bar sink and built a barnwood toilet box around it, securing a toilet seat on top. The urinal drains under the house and connects to the pipe that carries away the kitchen sink water. Then she stands next to the stove in her pajamas, her hair undrawn like a curtain mostly covering a window. I open it further with both hands and kiss her warm, soft lips. I return to bed and read for an hour while Jennifer does yoga in front of the stove.

If it is a bread morning, Jennifer mixes the flour we'd ground the night before into a sourdough starter. I put a pot of porridge on the stove. Since the stove won't be burning all day, I also put something on for supper. If it is lasagna (I do like lasagna, as you might have noticed, and have refined the art of baking it in a variety of ways), I layer the ingredients in our cast-iron pan, place a lid on it, and set it on a trivet on the stove. The elevated cast-iron pan will act like an oven. The third item on the stove is a large pot, to be filled with water. I pump some into a five-gallon bucket. After two or three strokes of spurting air, the pump sputters. Water flows out. I love water. I am thankful, too, for my body leaning into a pump handle; for the sixty strokes to fill the bucket; for the body-like weight of rain caught out of the sky and contained.

I carry the bucket to the stove and pour it into the pot. We eat breakfast and fold the bread dough. The fire has died down by now, and we place a folded towel on the water pot, which keeps the water hot all day.

We always go on a morning walk with Shadow. By the time we return to the house, if it is still clear, the sun sends out its first shadow-making rays and colors our south windows with the solid yellow-orange of its rise.

SLOWSPOKE

Even with the frozen temperatures, the sun will keep us warm the rest of the day, and we will eat bread and lasagna.

～

I continued to inch up the mountain, attending only to the miniature goals I set for myself. I thought of a principle for *A Unicyclist's Guide to America*: when all other methods for progress fail, attempt myopia. Being at a unique angle at the side of the mountain, but concentrating only on the nearest shrub that could help me, I may have missed some inimitable views of creation, which could have ushered in epiphanies. But reaching the summit was not glorious in this way. At the top a blast of cold wind hit me, and I retreated to a ledge just below the crest. Keeping my foot against a small tree, I sat down and stared at the ragged beauty, the steepness of the slope I'd crawled up. I felt dizzied spatially but also temporally: in the sense of looking back at something that suddenly seems impossibly far away, like high school graduation. I put on my orange hat, and the brashness of its color steadied me. Two mountain goats, I noted with amazement, browsed close to the slope that had so paralyzed me. I unwrapped Salina's cheese and ate half of the wedge.

Before heading back to the crest, I pulled the rain jacket hood over my orange hat and tied it under my chin. I re-entered the wind. The mountaintop, I saw, curved like a horseshoe. Rather than immediately descending the mountain on the other side, I clung to the top, following it as it gradually curved around to the direction I wanted. I hunched myself into the wind. In twenty minutes or so, I stumbled into a small signpost supported by a mound of rocks. Faded, the letters were nonetheless legible: Santo Domingo Campground. This campground was close to Senales. I saw the trail—it headed downhill—and I stepped onto it, my body convulsing in shivers. As the trail descended, the wind that came at me had less bulk. It became warmer, and I began to breathe more deeply.

The trail curved back and forth, around boulders and low plant growth, descending. Going this way, the trail lasted about an hour. Then it straightened out and passed through aspen groves. My feet rustled through piles of golden leaves. On its way to the ground, a leaf, from time to time, would strike me. I heard a river.

Exhausted, I left the trail to set up camp next to aspen and an old downed tree. I would sleep parallel to the tree, which seemed like a live body, the holes in its trunk granting it expression. Still with a hard shell, the fallen tree's inside had softened, turned black. I stuck my hand in the tree's humus and brought some of it to my nose. It smelled rich and clean.

That night I dreamed I clung to a leaf in the sky as it sailed to the ground. That the leaf had a texture like pottery gave me hope that it would hold my weight but also the worry that I would reach ground too abruptly. I looked down and saw the wilderness I'd trekked across. A hundred feet or so from the ground, I saw my body, immobile, at the side of the mountain— and then I slipped off the leaf and began falling toward myself. As I fell I felt the edges of my body becoming harder and sharper. By the time I reached the ground, I'd become Peter Aiken's arrowhead, falling from my unicycle pouch.

On opening my eyes in the morning, I saw a layer of golden leaves had covered me during the night. Being safe and close to a trail, I felt now a certain reluctance to return to the civilization I'd longed to reach during my wilderness trek. Another piece of advice in *A Unicyclist's Guide to America*, I thought, would be that adventure begins only from a feeling of security. Thus I lingered a while in my leafy bed before rising.

∽

Our indoor hand pump, made as I've mentioned out of part of a red oak trunk, rests on a base of small flat rocks from Long Branch. I had not made the stand high enough for easy pumping and had to elevate it. The fastest way to have done this would have been with dimensional lumber or bricks.

But Jennifer and I felt that a relationship had been made with the stand as it was, between the movement of water and the trunk of a tree. Creek rock, we decided, would be the best way to preserve this relationship.

$$\backsim$$

A poodle trotting around a bend in the trail signaled undisputedly that I'd left the wilderness. A couple of men in appropriate walking clothes and shoes followed the poodle. They thought it was "cool" that I was able to ride a unicycle.

I ate breakfast at the Santo Domingo Campground. Before leaving for Senales, I put the Leavens' Bible in a recycling bin. In Senales that morning a couple of drunks asked me as I pedaled past them if I wanted some women. Someone outside of town yelled, "Hi, Mark," out a car window and stopped to talk. Apparently, another Mark in the area rode a unicycle. A couple of miles later, a car with a bumper sticker that said "I brake for whales," slowed down and almost stopped before accelerating past me. Would the car have stopped completely had I been a whale? Yet another car slowed down, and I thought I was going to have company, but instead a beer bottle flew out of the window, missing me by a yard. I kept going, a little shaky. Why did I anger some people?

In Las Trampas I called the Leavens' neighbors to let them know I made it through the wilderness. I ate a burrito in a diner. Aware of a young couple at a table next to me who shared a plastic fork so they wouldn't have to throw away two, I perhaps didn't taste my food as much as I ordinarily did. Outside Las Trampas the road dipped, and I began pedaling down a long, steep hill. I gradually made out someone with a camera waiting for me at the bottom. "I didn't want any harm to come to you," said a middle-aged, padded man, "but if you were to come down that hill at a hundred miles per hour, I wanted a picture of it."

Shortly after this encounter I left the road to camp in the Carson National Forest. In the morning I had a gradual, ten-mile descent into a red-soiled, juniper-studded, ruggedly hilly valley, passing on the way a motel and restaurant in Truchas, appealing places to stop—small, adobe—but I had plans instead on getting a motel in Española; anyway, I felt brave passing by. In Chimayo, a bigger town at the bottom, the traffic picked up and forced me off my unicycle to the sandy side of the road, where I had to step around broken liquor bottles. Every once in a while I would sneak back onto the road and make the cars go around me until I lost my nerve. In this way, going from timidity to brief acts of daring, I made it by early afternoon to Española, a disappointingly ugly town because of the major road that split it and the fast food restaurant chains, the first I'd seen in New Mexico. But, motels! I treated myself to one slightly more luxurious than the cheapest I could have rented.

I dropped my gear on the carpeted floor and stared at myself in the body-length mirror. I had greasy, unruly hair; a dry, wind-burned face; a sweat-stained shirt with one collar flap up and the other down, due to the way I carried my canteen. I had a long scratch across my upper nose. I hadn't looked at myself in days.

That evening, with newly bought groceries scattered about me on the bed, I watched Bill Clinton, Ross Perot, and George Bush debate on television. The candidates, with their particular ways of annoying me, caused me to want to respond to them. Instead I ate, turning a potentially contentious evening peaceful, with me falling asleep.

I woke disoriented. Out of bed, I angled out the blinds, solidifying a parking lot. Though I would be generally heading northwest toward the Navajo Nation I wasn't sure at the moment whether to head toward Sulfur Springs or Abiquiu. I decided on Abiquiu. I closed down the parking lot and stood again in the rectangle of my room.

The country I pedaled into was not high enough for pine, but juniper survived there, gripping sandy ground. The road, delightfully untraveled, wound around mesas and across washes, some of which had burst with cottonwood turned golden. Near one of these eruptions of color, I'd luxuriate in moving only inches forward at a time, lingering with yellow gold. The road went on for miles like this. Then I came to Abiquiu, where the Abiquiu Inn was hosting an art exhibit. No rooms for rent. The exhibit was upstairs. I could leave my backpack and unicycle in the downstairs lobby.

Entitled "Southwest Women Painters after Georgia O'Keeffe," the exhibit honored O'Keeffe, who had lived in Abiquiu. Though mostly abstract, the paintings all used colors I recognized from the landscape I'd just traveled. Going back downstairs, I felt my brain rolling over into another position. Though it was late afternoon, I didn't worry about finding a camp. In the lobby I opened a book for sale of O'Keeffe's paintings. I sat down and looked at it. I saw red rocks, mesas, washes, and crooked trees—not for what they were exactly, but for what they were, perhaps, after being with them for a day, after closing the eyes. In one painting a ladder hung at an angle in a blue sky, not quite reaching the moon. Her paintings let me approach a juniper or a moon or a red rock or a flower—often from a different angle or mindset—yet they never assumed arrival.

Outside, the setting sun spilled oranges and yellows and reds over distant hills, and I pedaled, lightheaded, into this swirl of color. The effect of the fading light on the landscape wasn't something I could completely see or understand or describe. Yet, I thought, I could be like the painter, take one imperfect angle of it all—say, a last beam of light on a boulder—and keep with that angle until I sensed a background being formed. Then I could venture as deeply into such a background as I desired.

At dusk I turned off onto a driveway, intending to ask for a place to camp. At that moment a car stopped. A woman stepped out and asked if I needed help. I told her what I was doing and without hesitation she invited me to Ghost Ranch. Ghost Ranch, she told me, was a Presbyterian retreat center on a thousand acres of land. It had trails, rooms, a dining hall, an organic garden, a wetlands for purifying wastewater, an anthropology museum, and a library.

At the moment, she said, a peace exhibit run by two young women was set up in the dining hall. She was the wife of the Ghost Ranch director. Her name was Saleena. I looked more closely at her in the dusky light. A crescent moon almost touched her head. Although wary, I said yes, putting the finishing stroke on what was perhaps my most aesthetically perfect day.

∽

I stayed at Ghost Ranch for three nights and two days, in part because Saleena had given me free lodging and meal passes, and in part because I was attracted to the women running the peace exhibit. They had cut a hundred thousand faces out of magazines and pasted them on display panels, which occupied much of the dining hall. The faces represented the number of Iraqis killed during the Persian Gulf War.

The peace exhibit women seemed smart and idealistic. They were pretty. One of them was more gregarious than the other. I desperately wanted them to know that I was traveling on a unicycle. I'd missed my first opportunity, when I went up to their table, to tell them that, instead asking some question about the exhibit. Now it seemed awkward to return to their table, just to tell them about my unicycle.

Instead, I spent a lot of time in the library, hoping to meet them there. They read a lot, especially the shyer one. I would keep my unicycle in the library lobby. Yet she didn't arrive.

On the third morning, I left Ghost Ranch in frustration. I'd decided to head to the Monastery of Christ in the Desert, a much-talked-about attraction at Ghost Ranch. The severity of my change of plans—from a quest for female companionship to a trip to a community of cloistered men—pleased me.

Chapter Thirty-Three

I'M REMEMBERING AGAIN that Springfield walk when Jennifer and I, years ago, left the convent grounds for the first time. After passing under a locust tree laden with blossoms, we stepped off the road for a soft bank sloping to a red metal gate. We climbed over the gate. A field rose to our left and to our right. We kept, however, inside its fold, entering a wet-weather streambed. Rocks jutted out in all shapes, angles. We stepped on the most horizontal of them, clapping, at times, one against the other. The roots of certain sycamores bulged from the banks and looped back into soil.

Our words seemed interchangeable, a collection of things, much like the rocks, in no special order. We commented on what we saw—the mottled white trunks of the sycamores, a patch of spring beauties, the incredible dart of a chipmunk from a log into a hole in the bank.

A large pool of water appeared at our feet. We climbed, then, from the streambed into a field of soft grass. As we began moving across the field toward a fence-line of trees, Jennifer told me about a hundred thousand faces she and a friend had cut out of magazines and glued to display panels, exhibiting them across the country as a protest against the Persian Gulf War.

I knew then that I had met her before. Wild cherry and locust expanded into view, as did my experience, five years ago, at Ghost Ranch. I felt both reeling with motion and stopped in my tracks.

Another man could have entered at this precise moment. In limbo, I'd watch as he would attempt to woo Jennifer. He'd be a bicyclist, or worse, a SUV driver, and would easily outpace the unicyclist in the courting game.

We had stepped under the drip line of a large wild cherry. "I wrote about you in my 1992 journal," I said.

⌒

Joel talked with Mr. Gregory. They didn't discuss figures, by intention; Joel wanted to keep the conversation general and friendly. They agreed to talk again next week.

⌒

"I was traveling on a unicycle," I continued, "and I visited your exhibit at Ghost Ranch in New Mexico. You were there, weren't you?"

"Yes," she said, and she proceeded with other words that I don't remember now—but I had the impression she was happily surprised.

The fence—a barbed wire—stopped us. Four strands stretched across the hillside, sometimes U-nailed to trees, sometimes to locust posts.

Would we cross it, I wondered, and continue on as we had before, on the other side, or would we turn around?

Wild grapevines often grow under native hardwood cherries. Indeed, a large grapevine wrapped around this cherry's trunk, climbing to the upper branches before fingering out into the canopy. The large, broad leaves of the wild grape swam through the roof of the tree, overshadowing the narrow, single-toothed cherry leaves.

I sensed that she was impressed by my unicycle journey, and I devoured that thought.

If I were Tim, who had proposed to Trina after only seeing her three times, I would have sent those same words out to Jennifer at that moment. Instead, I stared at the dark, scaly bark of the cherry. A honey-sweetened decoction of this bark and that of slippery elm is supposedly healing for the throat.

"The unicyclist is failing to propose," I thought to myself, as if taking notes. The scene, only an instant in length, unrolled for miles. A segment of the view: I'm a child in a central Kentucky field, chased by cows. I'm running toward a barbed wire fence that I'd crossed many times before. But now I fumble the crossing and scrape myself getting to the other side. The fence stops the cows. Yet I run with wobbly knees deep into this safer field, toward my house.

Jennifer guessed that we should turn back, yet she didn't move. She didn't know that with her words I'd begun (mentally) crossing that fence, yet going the other direction: from the safe field, slipping my body through the twisted and sharp wire, into the field with the cows. She didn't know that I was a child making myself as big as I could and as loud, attempting to scare the cows.

Thus she wouldn't have guessed that my response—"You think we should"—was a shout—a shout because I was already lifting my arm to put around her back. The words were only there so there could be words.

She came to me and both my arms then went around her, like wild vines.

⸺

A couple of miles from Ghost Ranch, happy for more wide-ranging movement, I noticed again that the high desert surrounded me, and that the sun rose behind me, red, like a loose boulder.

Large ruts and rocks compromised the unpaved monastery road, which generally hugged the Rio Chama on one side and cliffs on the other. It took me four hours to arrive.

Once there, I stood in front of a bell with a sign under it that read "Please Ring for a Monk." I read the sign several times and experienced in this period of inaction a loaded silence that perhaps prepared me for other aspects of the monastery, like the austere beauty of the church, and the long, silent, wooden tables of the dining hall.

SLOWSPOKE

What happened if I didn't ring the bell? Standing there in inaction, I found out. A young German traveler named Nicola came around a bend and found the sight of me standing by the silent bell with a unicycle at my feet intriguing enough to grant me a short burst of laughter. She asked me questions and invited me to the bookstore, where she had afternoon work duty. There, she made me a cup of tea and sat down with me on a couch. She spread a road map over our laps and asked me to show her the route I'd taken. I remember my finger straying into blank sections of the state, clumsily approximating my route, our hands briefly touching somewhere in New Mexico. This was not exactly what I had expected.

Coming so soon after my disappointment with the "hundred thousand faces" travelers, I was happily surprised by the turn of events. Suddenly the monastery seemed brimmed with meaning and beauty. The tall, angular chapel, I noticed, mimicked the cliff behind it, and the windows inside allowed the church to be set in the context of a landscape. Exposed log poles supported the chapel's arched ceiling, which dropped off at the sides to the lower ceilings of four open, adjoining rooms, each with a wood stove and a ceiling that replicated the central, high ceiling.

I would decide that I liked the chanting and intonations at some of the church services. The silent meals, which I'd imagined would be restrictive, ushered me in to their remarkably boundless range. I was grateful for the small table in the room I was given, with its arrangement of three rocks and a vase of dried grasses.

I liked what I found out about Nicola over the next two days: she wrote children's stories and was planning to work with children and the rainforest in Costa Rica; she had lived in the utopian community of Findhorn in Scotland; she rode horses.

I liked, too, her enthusiasm, and her insistence—on finding out I didn't sing—that she would teach me a song and that we would sing it together. My lessons took place in the chapel when no one was there, and finally I was able to sing nicely with her (or at least not discordantly) these lyrics:

> *When two or three are gathered*
> *In my name, then there I am*
> *Forever*
> *Amongst you.*

"See, you can sing," she said. "Now promise me, you must always believe in yourself that you can sing."

I liked her German accent, her imperfect English. I liked her strong, pretty features, her light brown hair.

I walked up to my room that first night in pure darkness after supper, bumping into the unfamiliar railing. Dizzy, I felt my way to the door, opened it, and groped for the matches on the mantle. I lit the kerosene lamp, creating the room's geography. The bed, the wood stove, the table. My backpack and unicycle lay on the floor, curiously inert. Exhaustion hit me, but I sat at the round table with the vase of dried grasses and the arrangement of stones that I was careful not to disturb and wrote in my journal. Then I fell fast asleep on a lumpy, single bed.

In the morning I stepped out on the balcony my room opened to and saw Nicola sitting in a small courtyard below, a band of early sunlight hitting her. I had the urge to greet her, but I couldn't remember her name. "Nakora" ricocheted erroneously in my head.

On the walk to breakfast, another guest reminded me of her name. "Nicola." Of course, I thought. Nicola.

Later that day, after I joined in some of the church services and helped the wood-splitting-and-hauling crew in the afternoon, Nicola invited me on a walk to the Rio Chama. Arriving there, the sunset swept in place by the current, we sat down on the bank close to each other. Nicola read me a fable she had written about a bear, a fox, a rabbit, a wise man, and an oak tree. By the time she finished, the sun had set. It was chilly. I mentally prepared myself to take her hand.

But the church bell rang out sharply through the crisp air, signaling supper. We got up and walked slowly to the dining hall. Nicola invited me to come to her room after supper so we could exchange addresses. We were both leaving the next day.

I knocked on her door that evening, my heart pounding. It opened right away, and Nicola ushered me in, smiling. We sat on the edge of her bed. First I showed her a packet of photos from home. She expressed delight in seeing my family's cabin and my parents and sisters. She told me she'd never seen a solar cooker.

I gave her my pocket notebook and watched as she wrote her name and temporary address in Santa Fe. Her handwriting had lots of curves in it. When I wrote my address, I focused on legibility.

Leaving, I told her I would see her in the morning, and I stepped out into the dark. Seconds later, though, she came running out. I had left my long-sleeved shirt. The light from the door outlined her body. "It's chilly," she said. The movement of my hand then was spontaneous, as if I were on my unicycle reaching into air for balance—in that process of inching closer to something, a movement that perhaps I thought wouldn't go anywhere or have any effect, heading as it seemed to be toward something that had been only a concept in my mind, only a dot on the horizon. So when I felt my fingers touching the hair by her face, I was electrified by their quick arrival. And by how Nicola responded, stepping close. My hand slid down her back, and our bodies drew together. We went back into her room, holding hands. Inside, though, I couldn't clear the dizziness from my brain, the feeling of being on a precipice. In the awkwardness that ensued, I wished her good night and went back to my room with a splitting headache.

We both left the next day. Rather than being upset with me, as I'd feared, Nicola was happy to see me in the morning. Her demeanor brightened my mood, and I was suddenly glad I'd been timid.

SLOWSPOKE

I packed my backpack and took it and my unicycle out to the dirt road. Soon I was alone again on the monastery road, pedaling around the large ruts. If I could now write another entry for *A Unicyclist's Guide to America,* I would muse on the connections among unicyclists, delayed desires, and cloistered religious communities.

I practiced Nicola's song, singing the words "forever amongst you" as loudly as I could, to the cliffs, the river, to a rut on the road, my voice sometimes on key, sometimes off.

Chapter Thirty-Four

THAT SONG PLAYS IN MY HEAD even now, as I look out this window and see a chickadee. In the summer and fall this bird will decapitate insects, eat their bodies, and tuck their heads under tree bark to store for the winter. How different (a couple of minor distinctions aside) could this preparation be from our summer storage, say, of potatoes in a root cellar? In the winter we can look for these potatoes we stored months ago and find them still firm and good. We boil them, mash them on our plates with forks, add butter, salt, and freshly ground pepper.

I can imagine, too, the kinds of bark the chickadee will find useful—the shag of the hickory, the scab of the oak and wild cherry, the corridors of the black walnut and slippery elm, and sassafras. We, too, utilize some of these barks for making syrups and teas.

I sense that two or three are gathered—the man, the bird, the forest—and that we are "forever amongst you." I want to linger here, but my feeling of gratefulness and awe often turns to anxiety. I worry about how our wood thrush are faring in their winter home in Mexico. I worry generally about humans changing the face of the planet, turning it warmer, altering migration routes.

I want winter to be a time for dormancy. I want the species that live here now to continue to live here and not have to migrate north. I want spring to come in gloriously, on time. I want the constancy of spring turning to summer turning to fall turning to winter.

I don't want you to be damaged.

༄

A day after returning to Ghost Ranch and being brought by a departing guest to my start point, I was pedaling toward La Jara, intent on a restaurant. Almost there, I looked up to see a solidly built, Native American-looking woman at the side of the road, motioning for me to stop. I dismounted and walked to her. She asked me if I wanted lunch, as if she knew I had been thinking about a restaurant. The few teeth she had were rotten. I accepted her offer.

"I knew you were my type as soon as I saw you," she said.

I wondered what that meant.

"Do you ride a unicycle?" I asked.

"Yes—I'm a hermit," she said, and laughed.

That threw me.

Her place, a tiny, rusted trailer, was set back but still visible from the road. We walked by a fenced lot and a horse. A dog on a rope lay near the trailer. As we got closer, I noticed a corral behind the trailer—the sheep lot, she told me later.

She opened the trailer door, motioning me in. The bed started where the kitchen counters and cabinets ended. Boxes of stuff filled up the corners. A cat that I almost stepped on ate out of a frying pan. With just one step into the place, I arrived at its end. She came in after me, her wide body precisely fitting between the kitchen counter and cabinet. For me to leave, she would have to leave first. I sat down on her bed to give her room to maneuver in the kitchen. She put water on for rice.

I told her that I lived in a small place too, without electricity. She looked at me. She had green eyes. "When," she asked, "was the last time you visited a place like mine?"

Of course I had never visited a place quite like hers, but I told her about the wilderness family and about heading to the Navajo Reservation.

"What's with you and sheep?" she asked.

I hadn't realized I had any particular connection with sheep.

"The wilderness family had sheep, I've got sheep, and the Navajos, if they are Navajos, will have sheep. You've been chasing sheep. Are you a shepherd?"

So this was how her mind worked.

"Yes. I ride a unicycle."

Her laugh rumbled in the small trailer, building, it seemed, on its own momentum.

We were getting along. Backed against one end of her trailer, I was glad of that. I watched her put onions in the rice and then olive oil, which she said cleansed the liver of anger. When the rice cooked, she sprinkled it with brewer's yeast and garlic powder and divided it onto two plates, adding tahini sauce last. She asked me if I wanted to camp that night. I opened my mouth to tell her I was going to keep traveling, but I heard myself, to my utter surprise, telling her, "yes."

When we went back out, she motioned around us.

"The people around here," she said, "don't understand me, and they don't like me. I call them bullies."

"What do they do?"

"They bother me."

She didn't say anything else.

"I'll show you the hogan I'm building."

I followed her as she went past the sheep lot.

"Stay on the path, please. I can hear plants scream."

I inwardly jumped. How had she known I had stepped off the path?

The hogan looked almost done to me. We walked inside. I could see her current project—leveling the floor. I offered to help, and she seemed delighted—not so much by the fact that just anybody was going to level her floor, but that a unicyclist was going to.

"You're just the man I needed for this job," she said, laughing. She left to do other chores, and I worked for a couple of hours with a grubbing hoe and a shovel before she returned.

"That's enough," she said.

I followed her out. She always seemed to be laughing or on the verge of laughing.

"Do you know how many right answers there are?" she asked. I didn't.

"As many as there are beings." She laughed.

We passed a pile of leaves close to her trailer and she asked me if I liked her cottonwood tree. I looked around but didn't see it.

"Oh, I'm starting with the leaves. The tree will come next."

We walked past her trailer and the corral and came to a shack that reminded me of a fort my sisters and I had made when we were kids. We had called it the Scrap Fort.

"This is my winter house," she said. "It has a wood stove. I built it for fifty dollars."

Before we entered, she remembered the sheep. "I have to get them in. Do you want to come along?"

Sure, since I was a shepherd.

All of a sudden she howled like a coyote. Again, I nearly jumped.

"The bullies do that," she said. "I know that they are bullies and not coyotes when their howls don't reach a crescendo. Then what I do is howl back at them, and they stop."

I followed her around a hill. The sheep weren't on the other side as she expected. We kept going. The sandy path became harder to see. We stumbled when we didn't see the dips it took. She turned around and looked at me.

"Do you know about the Power Gait? Don Juan's Power Gait?"

"Nope."

"Look at me. It's a way to get a good pace without tripping."

I watched as she hunched over and began to move quickly, lifting her legs almost up to her chest, a tiptoe blown out of proportion.

She motioned for me to follow. I did what I thought was most polite, she being a host and me a guest. Soon two of us galumphed in the dark, looking for lost sheep.

Breathless, she turned around and pointed out that we didn't even know each other's names. We laughed. I told her my name, but she didn't offer hers.

Rounding a bend, we practically stumbled into the sheep. They began heading back right away. We could walk normally.

Soon, after we corralled and fed the sheep, we ducked into her winter shack. She lit a lamp, and the ten-by-ten-foot room shrank. A thin metal stove took up much of the middle space. Making the same move I had made in the trailer, I sat down at the edge of her bed to give her room. She lit the stove and put water in a teakettle.

"You see this lid?" she asked, holding it up for me. "It doesn't fit right on the kettle. It used to. The bullies came in and hit it once with a hammer to make it out of round."

The room quickly became warm; anywhere you chose to sit you'd be, at most, three feet from the stove.

"That shelf behind you, too. I can't imagine putting it up crooked like that. You know, I think of them as demons, and they're easier for me to deal with."

When the tea was ready, she poured it in two enamel cups, adding sugar. The whole room smelled like cinnamon.

"Do you keep a journal about what happens here?" I asked.

"I don't write about the present anymore."

She handed me my cup.

"I'm concentrating on the future. I think it's best to start with utopia and then work backward."

We could hear the wind picking up outside.

"What part are you on now?" I asked.

She laughed. "I haven't started writing yet."

She finished her tea and told me that she was going to sleep in the trailer and that I could sleep wherever I wanted, where I was or in the hogan or outside.

I stayed inside for a few minutes, writing in my journal, but I quickly developed an urge to leave. When I blew out the lamp, utter blackness disoriented me. I had to feel my way to the door. Outside, I could at least see the forms of things. A chilly wind blew. I walked slowly down the path where we had started out looking for the sheep. Shortly, I veered off from that path, going up the hill instead of around it. Entering a stand of juniper, I lost my vision again. Keeping one hand in front of me, I made my way up the hill. On the first piece of ground that seemed flat, I rolled out my sleeping bag and bivy sack and got in bed. Closing my eyes, I would see her wild smile. An hour or two passed before I could fall asleep. It rained overnight and I woke up inside a damp sleeping bag. Walking through mud, I lugged everything to her winter shack. I shivered.

She wasn't inside. I draped my sleeping bag on one side of her bed. I thought about lighting a fire, but I didn't see much wood. The teakettle with its ill-fitting lid rested on the stove.

I sat down. The rain beat harder against the tin roof. I looked around for leaks but didn't see any. The Scrap Fort always had a leak. The shelf over her bed truly was very crooked. It would have been hard to do that intentionally. She had three books on the shelf. When I saw *The Magic of Findhorn*, I felt a bit of electricity run through my body. Findhorn. Where Nicola lived! I took down the book and read from the introduction: "A short distance from the Arctic Circle lies a still remote community where people talk to plants with amazing results: on previously barren soil, vegetable and flower gardens proliferate."

The rain pinged now against the roof. I looked up and saw bits of ice dropping into the room. How could sleet pass through a roof that had blocked rain?

At that moment she came into the room and asked me why the fire wasn't going. "I didn't think you were here," she said. "You see what the bullies did last night?"

She held up her right foot and pointed to a slit in her shoe.

"Why didn't they just steal it?" I asked.

"That's how these bullies are. They won't destroy me. They just want to torment me."

She put paper and kindling in the stove and lit it.

"They wouldn't break a window. They would take it out and put it in crooked. I've been to a psychiatrist before because I hear voices. That was a joke. He couldn't hear them, so he told me they didn't exist."

She put a pot of water on the stove and filled the teakettle.

"I'm glad you're here."

Was she expecting me to stay?

"Do people from the community ask about you?"

"Actually, I rephrase questions so people don't need answers. I don't know who the bullies are around here. I can tell you things because you are an outsider."

She had fed the fire with wood that seemed slightly damp, and it wasn't doing well. The sleet had stopped, but the wind batted against the shack. I felt cooped up and anxious to leave, even with the blustery weather.

"Do you know if I'm going to run into snow or anything today?" I asked.

"If you leave right now, I know what you're going to run into."

She told me she would listen to the weather in her trailer and let me know.

"I was in the open once with my sheep, and a big, black cloud was coming toward us. I waved a blanket at it, and it went away."

"Would a sleeping bag work?" I asked her.

She looked at me. "That would work. But if you did that, you would be insane."

I wondered why she didn't put dry wood in the fire.

"This Findhorn place sounds interesting," I said, holding up the book.

She looked up. "Yeah, but I haven't figured out if that place exists or not. I read it, and I think I'm dreaming. Have you read Castaneda?"

"No."

"I'll give you a copy of one of his books. It's a good day to read."

"Actually, I think I'm about ready to head out. My sleeping bag is getting dry."

"You have to eat my cereal first."

She put a piece of dry wood in the fire, and in a few minutes the stove roared. When the water boiled, she poured in blue cornmeal. It turned to mush, and we ate it with honey and cinnamon tea. She went out after eating, telling me she would check on the weather.

I waited for maybe an hour. How long did it take to listen to a radio? I went out, stepping through mud to her trailer and found her taking hay to her sheep.

"The weather's just like this," she said.

She threw the hay in the corral.

"Come here, I want to show you something."

I followed her to the trailer where she handed me a small tape player with earphones.

"This is my Dhyani tape. Listen to it before you leave."

Back at the winter shack a woman's calm, deep voice came into my head, telling me to imagine double helixes of light coming into me from the sky and the earth and meeting in my spine. The tape ended with the ha ha chant. Laughter, the woman said, could change anger to compassion.

With that I packed up and met her again by the trailer. I asked her to write down her address. She did that and included, after hesitating, her name—Lightning Elk. I told her it was good to know her name.

"It's hard to choose sometimes."

As I was walking to the road, she told me to say hello to the Navajos for her. "'D bay ash had a te' means 'how are the sheep?'"

"Okay."

"Remember," she said as I was just about at the road and she almost didn't have anyone to talk to, "freedom is just another word for nothing left to lose."

❧

Jennifer began to borrow a car from the convent to visit me once a week. She would spend the night in Toad Room, the guest space attached to Toad Hall. On chilly evenings, after a fire- or sun-cooked supper with my family, I would light the soapstone wood stove in Toad Room, and Jennifer and I would sit on the couch and by candlelight look at my family's photo albums. Small, Toad Room nonetheless had two levels. The couch, close to a window with a good view of oak and hickory, was on the lower, carpeted level. A step up from this level, a soapstone wood stove sat on a wood plank floor. One door on this level led to Toad Hall, the other outside, onto the path to the Duck. An alcove of windows around a chair, a small desk, and a manual typewriter adjoined the upper level.

Eventually one of us would blow the candle out. Limbs and trunks and leaves would slip in through the window by our couch. Toad Room would be a raft cast off from the cabin, and I would feel the thrill of the separation. I would feel, too, the danger and the loneliness. I would always be aware of my family, just down the slope from Toad Room, in the cabin.

Before wishing her good night, I would help Jennifer make the couch into a bed, make sure she had hot water and a tub in case she wanted to bathe, a flashlight for going to the compost toilet, and matches for lighting the candle. I'd walk down to the cabin, where everyone would be sleeping, and quietly step in and reach for the tree ladder to orient myself. Right foot first made the climb easy, we'd discovered. My hands would plant branch rungs in the dark as I climbed to my loft.

❧

I waved goodbye to Lightning Elk and pedaled away, continuing toward La Jara. A gust of wind hit me, and I stepped off my unicycle to keep from falling. Juniper and pine swayed. The whole landscape appeared unresolved. Still somewhat in a daze after leaving Nicola, I felt that my attention had softened somehow, allowing what came before me to sink inside me. I verged on understanding Lightning Elk.

What about this weather? I asked myself. Just approach one thing at a time, I responded. The first thing to do was to get to La Jara. The wind whacked at me from different angles, as if it were playing with me. I kept mounting and dismounting my unicycle.

La Jara didn't have a restaurant, but I bought a bag of ginger snaps in a small grocery. I left town in gusty winds, heading toward a low-hanging black cloud. The sky darkened as I pedaled. A plastic package of saltines appeared on the road shoulder. I stopped and put it in my backpack. If I had found shelter, instead, I would have chosen the shelter. In a few more turns of the wheel, a heavy snow came down, practically blinding me. I left the road for three tall pine trees. Close enough together, they blocked some of the wind and snow. I sat down and put cracker after cracker into my mouth. I ate the whole package and started on the ginger snaps.

The snow abated, then ended, and I turned onto a bigger road with a wide, paved shoulder, traveling maybe six more miles in windy, cold weather before I turned aside to camp—on a hillside next to a bone-colored log and enough live juniper to break the wind. Still, it was very cold. With two shirts, a sweater, and a rain jacket on, I ate the rest of the ginger snaps, creating a little ginger fire in my stomach. I curled up in my sleeping bag.

There, I dreamed that my grandmother was cooking a big meal. I tried to move a table to help organize the plates and dishes, but I realized I had no clothes on. I went to the bathroom, which turned into a parked car slipping down a mountain. I had to be careful to miss a barbed wire fence. Finally, the car stopped at the bottom, and I wondered why I had never noticed that the hills around Frankfort were snow-capped mountains. I found the candles that my grandmother had packed for my trip. Someone I had known from college called my name, and I found out she had been jogging with Nicola. Both of them were working under the mountain. Nicola had just bought Mace.

I woke up under layers of frost. I must have slept, for I had dreamed. Yet how, in such cold? Dead wood was scattered about me. Juniper, too, surrounded me. They all appeared to be about my height or a little taller—short enough to give you the sense when you were standing that you were close to having an overlook, yet tall enough to keep you from noticing anything but them, the wood they'd scattered, the sand, the rocks, the short, silvery plants.

I pulled out my feet one at a time to put them in boots. Was Nicola still in Albuquerque or had she left for Costa Rica? What was she like in a city? Was she friendly with everybody? Would she have been friendly with any young man who had showed up at the monastery? I stood up and shook the bivy sack and sleeping bag. A frost storm rose up in my face.

It didn't warm up that day as I pedaled into the homeland of the Jicarilla Apache Nation. At a roadside rest stop, I ate breakfast, facing the morning sun without feeling it. Heatless, the sun was simply picturesque.

To stay warm I pedaled up long hills without stopping. At midday, finally, the water sloshed in my water bottles, a sign of thawing. I crossed the Continental Divide. The roadside marker, at first, seemed like any other, but it soon struck me that I should recognize this major geographical feature. I turned around, pedaled back to the Divide, and crossed over it slowly, back and forth, a process that could be likened to someone working on a mathematical equation. No cars passed. No one was at the marker. I continued on then.

Counselor was the next community up the road, but everything was closed, with not even a restaurant open. I dropped off a postcard in a rusted U.S. Mail box and began pedaling again, toward hogan-shaped buttes in the distance. Counselor hadn't given me much of a break, but I guessed in the cold it didn't make much sense to take long breaks. Keep moving, I told my-self. The town of Lybrook had an ugly natural gas processing plant and a restaurant. I walked over to the restaurant, pushing my unicycle. When I was only three steps away from the door, I saw the Open sign flip to Closed. I stared at Closed for a second. How heavy a word it seemed, with just a few more letters, compared to Open, which was airy. I turned around.

A food mart, however, was open. There, I found out that a community up the road, Nageezi, had an inn with rooms. Stimulated by the news (and still cold), I pedaled on more energetically, arriving there at four thirty. Nageezi sat high in the desert. It offered sweeping views of snow-capped mountains.

The woman at the inn told me there were no rooms left, but she said I could stay in a backyard hogan for free. Grateful, I brought my gear into the hogan, which was about twenty feet in diameter, made of logs and mud as was traditional. The base of the hogan consisted of vertical logs, but the roof logs were horizontal, interlocking with each other as they sloped to the top and met around a stovepipe. If the hogan were turned upside down, it would resemble a basket. The floor was dirt, and it looked level. What was it with me and hogans, anyway?

I lit a fire in a metal drum stove and placed the few pieces of furniture—the stump chairs, the wooden table, and the single bed without a mattress—around the stove, creating my space for the evening. I sat down, happy. I'd traveled forty miles, a distance that had turned my need for warmth cavernous. Now it was the most luxurious feeling to fill up with that radiant heat from a rusted drum stove. I became thoroughly warm and went to sleep.

Gaps in the hogan's mud chinking led dawn in gently, and bit by bit I could make out my place—my wheel by the east-facing doorway, the walls, the roof that spread above me like finger-clasped hands. I opened the door a crack and morning light sprayed my body.

I headed out later on a long, unpaved road to Chaco Canyon. The road was sandy with little washboard ridges that for a uni-

cycle had the effect of speed bumps. I didn't mind them at first—
if I hummed, the bumps put a nice rhythm to the sound. I called
it the Anasazi chant. Gradually, however, the bumps tired me.
Juniper trees dwindled, giving way to more sagebrush. Mesas
roughened the horizon. I saw what looked to be a river of smoke
in the distance. Every once in a while I passed poor square
homes, often with one or two permanently parked cars close by.

The wind batted me. Unweathered, touristy cars and mini-
vans heading for Chaco Canyon National Historical Park would
pass with their windows up to keep out blowing dust. After
miles of wondering about the river of smoke, I made it to a long
bridge and discovered that it wasn't smoke or steam but instead
wind-hurled sand rushing through dry arroyos. Kimbeto Wash,
the map told me. I crossed, squinting my eyes.

Up from Kimbeto Wash, I entered Chaco Canyon National
Historical Park. Cliffs and rock formations rose in front of me,
and the road narrowed to wind among them. The wind curved
also, whirling sand. Upon seeing little whirlwind storms coming,
I would get off my unicycle and duck. Still, I was blinded at times.

The road dipped. At the bottom of the incline a white Lincoln Continental slowed next to me. Its window rolled down
partway. I saw a camera. It clicked, and the car accelerated past
me, sealing itself.

Entering a rugged valley, I couldn't feel the wind as much.
Maybe that was why the Anasazi had chosen to settle here. In
Navajo "Anasazi" meant "someone's ancestors." To my left was a
rock village. Intent on a camp, I pushed on to the visitor center
and campground, a long four miles away. Arriving, I discovered
that all the trails leading to the rock villages were a few miles
from the park center. At this park they assumed you had arrived
in a car. There were no showers at the campground; fires were
allowed if you brought your own wood. I lingered awhile in the
visitor center. The weather report posted at the front desk said
it was going to turn colder with gusty winds and possible rain
or snow showers. At a water fountain, I aimed a looping stream

of water into my canteen. That was a good thing, I thought, to fill my canteen.

I slept at the far end of the campground. Although I'd been planning a good stay at Chaco Canyon, I woke up in the morning intent on leaving. The cold weather had made me anxious. It was November already.

I headed off on the only dirt road going south. In a mile or two the Anasazi Canyon sank from my vision. By midday I made it to Seven Lakes Trading Post, where the dirt road intersected a paved one. I ate a PayDay candy bar and an apple in a heated store. A blaring radio announced a coming snowstorm. I asked if there was a motel in Crownpoint. No. Someone reminded me it was Election Day.

I pedaled away from the store. The land was flat and shrubby with low-growing plants—not good shelter—and I moved as if pressed by shrinking habitat. By late afternoon I hadn't found cover and resigned myself to ask for help in Crownpoint. Five miles out of town, however, a dry wash opened to my left. Hardly thinking, I crossed the road, ducked under a low strand of barbed wire. I went down, the ground surface rising to my waist, shoulders, and finally over my head, until I was at the sandy bottom. Sand banks flanked me. I walked forward, maneuvering around boulders as water would flowing downstream. In a quarter mile or so, I looked up to see the ground surface now risen very high, with much of the bank solid sandstone. Then I spotted a niche in one of the sandstone faces. I climbed up to it. My body would fit!

If my body were like a hand, then the feeling of crawling into that sandstone cleft was like putting a cold hand into a pocket. Inside, there was no wind. I unrolled my sleeping bag, lay down. In a few minutes the sun landed in the center of that rock mitten and stopped, no longer falling through the sky. It lay next to me like another body, pressing against my skin, warming it. I unpeeled the socks from my feet and clipped my toenails. They were yellow, beginning to curl. I was warm.

Chapter Thirty-Five

ONE OF THE DELIGHTS OF GOING OUTSIDE in the cold is returning to a warm, often sun-lit house. In recent years we've had some disconcertingly warm stretches during the winter. In these times sunlight seems excessive rather than miraculous. It upsets my equilibrium.

This winter, however, has been solidly cold, and I'm happy to be working on frozen ground in February, gathering next winter's firewood—this year one trunk of a large split-trunked red oak that had fallen in a December ice storm, almost hitting the garden fence. The tree had supported an old hunter's platform, which had spanned the two trunks, but since the fall the platform now dangles from the half of the tree still standing.

We had been cleaning up from lunch the day after this storm, and we heard a muffled crash, which we both thought was ice sliding down our roof, or from our solar panels onto the roof. We continued with the dishes, the wiping of counters. So when we looked out the window to see a significantly altered landscape—a canopy of a large tree now perpendicular to our path—we were surprised.

We have, of course, more quotidian memories as well—stepping into its pool of shade on a summer afternoon, ducking to get under one of its low, rain-heavy branches.

Just down the trunk from where I'm sawing is a row of small, orderly holes made by the yellow-bellied sapsucker. Recently, I witnessed—through binoculars—the making of these holes across the trunk of a different tree, a small maple. The woodpecker worked quickly, it seemed to me, probably making its holes faster than could be done with a power drill—if the time taken to select a bit and secure it and decide how deep to drill is considered. With eight shallow holes pecked out, the sapsucker ceased its carpentry and began simply to insert its beak into each of the holes. I read later that the sapsucker does not suck sap but laps it with a long tongue. Occasionally, this bird will mew like a cat.

How different, I thought, my penetration into this wood, a two-cycle motor screaming, a toothed chain saw zipping so many revolutions per second around an oil-lubricated bar, wood bits and splats of oil spitting in the air.

A piece of firewood drops to the ground, and I move down the length of the stove to make the next cut.

It's cold, but my body is warm because I'm moving it, and I feel, for the moment, that everything is as it ought to be.

That, for example, we started onions from seed in soil blocks, and they've now sprouted and are absorbing the sun on our south window sills; that lately I've been standing in front of our fruit trees, deciding which branches to prune, which to keep; that spring, coming after this cold, will thankfully again be astonishing and beautiful; that we can notice leaf buds again on the entrance trees.

Another piece of wood drops, and I move down the trunk, my blade each time tearing into widening material.

As I did when I lived at my parents' cabin, I've been exploring. I've recently entered the woods to the south of Snuggery, going a little deeper inside with each hike. I've dubbed the area, though an aerial view clearly would show its modest demarcations, the "Greater Frankfort Wilderness."

My blade now completely disappears into the wood, its length equal to the trunk's diameter.

On a hike a couple of days ago, forging farther than I'd ever gone, I reached the end of the Greater Frankfort Wilderness. Shadow had walked with me, tongue out and smiling despite his sore shoulders. First, I'd hiked a mile down a cedar and hardwood slope and had come to the end of the ridge. I'd gone over its lip and followed a steeply descending hill—distinguished by a line of thick, tall red oak, bigger than the one I'm cutting—to a bottom with a confluence of two intermittent streams and a massive sycamore that I'd reached on a previous foray. I continued on, walking in the bed of the stream around bands of clear, flowing water and ice-covered pools, on and over rock. The stream curved and sometimes descended sharply, and I'd climb or slide down little frozen waterfalls. At one point, I looked up surprised to see how steeply the wooded hills now rose above the stream. Toward the end of the hike, the stream widened and undulated with piles of rocks, a visual print of the last rush of water.

Eventually, I could see an opening in the trees, a hundred yards away, and I walked toward it, realizing I could no longer pretend that my wilderness would expand forever.

In a fantasy book I've been reading, a boy wielding a magical knife has the ability to cut open a window from his world into another. Was this such an opening? I climbed the stream bank and peered out my window from behind a cedar tree. Across a larger streambed that mine emptied into was a narrow paved road, which I guessed was the county road going east, the one I would use on occasion, heading to a festival. Now Jennifer and I are thinking about building a wood-fired brick oven and making bread to sell at the Frankfort farmers' market, a way to replace festival income. I wouldn't have to flash a game trailer with posters of pop icons like Taylor Swift and Justin Bieber and Sponge-Bob and Lady Gaga, and novelties like inflatable vinyl Dora the Explorer dolls and rubbery yo-yos with jellyfish tentacles.

Three large trees had been cut down by the side of the road. A partially deflated helium balloon in the shape of a heart had become snagged in the branches of one of the downed trees. To my right I could see one side of a house trailer and a small doghouse, next to which lay a skinny brown-and-white dog on a short leash. Suddenly, this dog stood up and barked, inch-worming his leash. I turned around.

SLOWSPOKE

In my fantasy book, the boy with the knife could also close the openings between worlds, using his thumb and forefinger. Lacking this skill, I simply retraced my steps to the streambed and walked against the flow of rock and water, toward my home. Following the first bend in the stream, I let an icicled bank return me to my wilderness.

↬

In the morning I left my sandstone cave and made it to Crown-point just as the Bashas Grocery Store opened at eight o'clock. To hide my greasy hair, I kept my hat on in the store. At least I had newly clipped toenails, though that wasn't apparent. My head became hot as I picked out groceries. I would pedal to Window Rock where I would get a motel room, a day and a half of traveling away. For some reason, I averted my eyes from the newspaper stand, not wanting to know yet who had won the election.

Although in the morning I passed through uneven, arroyo-split country, which offered numerous possibilities for camping, the land flattened out by the afternoon and became more populated. I kept pedaling, hoping for a change. The sky turned dark though. I walked up to a trailer, and a man told me that I could camp in a parked, green car that looked like it had been there for years. He and other members of his family came out to talk to me.

"Do you believe that Jesus is coming, or something like that?" he asked.

I told him I wasn't an evangelist. A little girl brought out coffee and donuts for everyone. I held her on the seat of my unicycle and gave her a ride.

With the snack finished and the family gone, I put my pack and unicycle in the back seat and spread my sleeping bag out in the front. The driver's side window was stuck partially open. I filled the gap with my rain jacket. Getting into my sleeping bag,

I moved slowly to not raise dust. The seat creaked. Somehow, the night passed.

I opened my eyes in the morning and saw a steering wheel, and I wondered for a moment if I were speeding across the country in a car. My mind gradually cleared; the car slowed down, stopped, became junked, and it was appropriate for me to get out.

I covered quite a bit of ground by eight thirty, at which point I found myself pedaling up to a Thriftway store. There, I ate breakfast and, two days after the election, found out that Clinton had beaten Bush and Perot. I pedaled on to Window Rock, Arizona, and up to the only motel in town, the Navajo Inn. The lobby sparkled. Rooms, I found out, were forty-five dollars. I paid the price, the most I'd ever paid for a room. I had ten dollars left.

Once in the room, though, I was glad to be there. A mirror showed that my face had reddened with cold and wind, that my hair stuck out like stiff brush bristles. I peeled off my clothes and jumped on the bed. This would possibly be the last motel room of my journey, and I would derive what pleasure I could from it. Water washed off me brown in the shower. I couldn't remember my last shower. Afterward, I blew the rest of my money on groceries and was surprised when the blowing of my money didn't translate into more groceries. Nonetheless, I now had an avocado, chips, salsa, and granola bars. Back inside, I ate for a solid hour. The television said the temperatures would dip into the teens that night.

Moneyless, but clean and well-rested, I headed out toward Fort Defiance in the morning, pedaling, luckily, on a paved shoulder the entire way. Past Fort Defiance, however, the shoulder ended, and I soon found myself in heavy traffic, cars and trucks passing me continuously. I kept my eyes on the ground for rocks. The roar of big trucks barged over the sides of the road, and in an hour, perhaps due to this particular road, or perhaps due to the cumulative effect of all the roads I'd been on since North Carolina, I became scared, and I left the road and sat down a few steps away from it, my back to its traffic. I stared at red rock cliffs in the distance, my eyes watering with the cold. I heard a wheel hit gravel and saw that vehicle swerve back to asphalt.

After attempting traffic for another half an hour or so, I left the road intent on an early camp, stepping into a band of juniper. As I walked, the slope I was on broadened out, and I found the perfect place, a level spot with a view of an immense valley. Turning around, I could still see the red cliffs. I slid my backpack off my shoulders and set it on sandy red soil. The sand now coped with its weight. Relaxing tremendously, I virtually floated about my camp, gathering dead juniper branches. I soon had a pile for a campfire. I sat and watched the sun go down.

I put my hat on. A red glow and cold air had replaced the sun. This, perhaps, would be my last camp, and I resolved to remember its details. I crumpled loose-leaf paper from my notebook, placed it on the sandy ground. Some of the sheets opened back up, as if blooming. I arranged twigs and sticks over them and lit one paper corner on fire. A small flame climbed the paper. The flame expanded, then, an acrobat in a maze of twigs and branches. With the first wave of warmth, my body responded by shivering. I stuck my hands out to the flames.

The twigs, reddened and crumbly, sank, lowering the fire. I added bigger sticks. Flames danced, traded places with each other, appeared and disappeared. I noticed a shade of yellow— then the whole spectrum appeared in the fire, from the colors of water to the colors of the sunset.

Daylight not gone, the fire became my little world, consuming the wood I'd gathered, consuming my attention, my thoughts, fragments from my journey. I tossed it all to the fire.

I could see a unicycle and a semi truck. I could see Nicola in my arms and her leaving. One form easily changed into another. In one instant I could see arrowheads, and in another, nuclear weapons. Mountains, landfills. Rivers, asphalt highways. I could make out both the beginning of the world and the ending of the world. I put the last three sticks on. Abundance, scarcity.

The wood bedded itself to coals. I soaked in the remaining heat and quickly climbed into my sleeping bag, cupping my body to hold its warmth. I slept deeply.

Getting up in the morning with the fire out, I did jumping jacks to warm up. I took off pedaling as soon as I could. The road, thankfully, was lightly traveled. In an hour, a pickup filled with people stopped, and a man inside asked me if I was Mark and my mother was Laurie. I'd met the Begays.

In the sixties my mother worked as a Vista volunteer in Lukachukai, and Mr. and Mrs. Begay, in time, considered her a daughter.

"I'm Jay," the man was saying, "and that's my wife, Amanda." Amanda was sitting by the passenger door. An old couple was sitting between them. "And these," Jay said, "are my parents. Your grandparents."

My mother had taught me some words in Navajo. I knew that "shima" meant mother and "sezhe" father. I knew a Navajo chant. I had a dim memory of being in a dirt-floor hogan, playing with Navajo kids and sitting at a long wooden table where I learned, by watching the big people, how to dip frybread into mutton stew.

My mother was just in her twenties when she was a volunteer. A family photo shows her on a galloping horse somewhere on the reservation.

I knew, too, something of the Navajo creation story, about Insect People getting in trouble with the gods, having to spiral out of the worlds they found themselves, always upward, to new worlds, which were different and more varied. The creation story began with the First World and continued to the Fifth, the present world, where the story included us, where we were at the moment, even the mountains beyond the hood of the pickup, and all the colors and plants and sounds and animals.

"Shima," I said.

SLOWSPOKE

"They are your grandparents," Jay said. "So grandmother is 'shumasun' and grandfather is 'shu-chay.'"

Shu-chay, I found out, had recognized me from a sketch my mother had sent him of me riding a unicycle. He had told Jay to stop.

They invited me to ride with them to Gallup, but I told them I wanted to complete my journey to Lukachukai. If I arrived before they did, I would wait at the Thriftway store.

I pedaled another three hours, passing by the pine-encircled Wheatfields Lake and the little community of Tsaile. When the land began to descend north of Tsaile, leading me toward red rock cliffs and buttes, I became aware that this was my last stretch of unicycle travel.

I could make out the community of Lukachukai, and I pedaled toward it in partial disbelief. It seemed to be a perfect place to stop. But at the same time I wanted my trip to keep going. Exuberance and sadness made circles in me.

I pedaled within a quarter mile of the Thriftway store. I dismounted and walked a few steps. I wanted to be comfortable and rested for my last tiny stretch. Being deliberate, not rushing the end, was the only way I knew to make a ceremony out of arrival. I pedaled smoothly to the store, not falling, and stepped down to pavement. I looked around. No one was near me. If I had been in a race I had either won or come in dead last. I could have gone farther on my unicycle, to the ocean maybe, but there is where I got off.

Chapter Thirty-Six

I SAT ON THE CURB in front of the Thriftway store, the sun hitting me, wondering if I had been expecting more to happen at the end of my journey. A man came up and asked me where I was going. The question threw me. I actually was where I was going. "Right here," I said, after a pause. He walked off, maybe thinking I was sarcastic or impatient.

Soon I climbed in the back of the Begays' truck, and we headed west on a bumpy dirt road flanked by sagebrush. In a mile we turned into a cluster of buildings—I could make out two hogans, a square house, a few sheds, teepee-shaped piles of wood, some junk scattered about, and a couple of bony dogs. The high desert resumed where the buildings left off, and the whole area offered a breathtaking view of the Lukachukai Mountains.

Letters had arrived for me at the Begay homestead—two from home and one from Nicola. Shumasun and Shu-chay showed me where I could stay, in a hogan close to the house. Shumasun said she was going to start a stew for tomorrow, and I knew that that was their way of saying good night. I slept as soundly that night as I had slept at any time on my trip. As long, too—I woke quite a bit after sunrise. I walked over to the house. Shu-chay was stretched out on the couch listening to country music from a small transistor radio. Shumasun worked in the kitchen. I felt awkward because they didn't respond to what I said, which I thought was "good morning" in Navajo. Shumasun put me to work washing dishes. Working near me, she started making frybread. I watched her over my shoulder. To shape the bread, she took a small handful of dough, rolled it into a ball, flattened it, and pulled its edges. When she had stretched it to about the size of one of her hands, she turned it from hand to hand, flapping it back and forth. The dough grew.

An eighteen-year-old grandson, Dennis, emerged from a bedroom, introduced himself to me, and began shredding potatoes for hash browns. Shumasun placed the dough in a skillet of bubbling lard. It spat at her. The dough responded by swelling. In a half minute she flipped it, golden side up. When it was done, she forked it out, dripping, onto newspaper. I finished the dishes and asked her if I could try one. Yes. I made a ball, but in the process of stretching out the dough I created a hole big enough for the Fifth World to fall back down to the Fourth. Shumasun fixed it with two fingers and put it in the skillet, despite its small size. Dennis was frying eggs. Shumasun told me to set the table.

Though Dennis didn't speak much at all, I grew to like him during my stay there. He didn't know Navajo very well, and I noticed that he often seemed confused by what his grandfather wanted but was unwilling or unable to ask him questions. Shumasun knew a little English. After lunch one day, Shu-chay stood up, said something, and walked out the door. Dennis looked at his grandmother, who didn't translate. So Dennis walked out the door, too. I followed Dennis. Shu-chay was already in the pickup. We both climbed in the passenger side, and he drove to Lukachukai and started going up the mountain. Dennis told me that he'd finally figured out that we were going to the summer sheep camp. The road ascended steeply. From where we had been in sagebrush, the mountain hadn't looked so high. Pine trees replaced low-growing plants. We kept climbing. Aspen appeared. We must be past what could be seen from Lukachukai, I thought. Shu-chay's eyes looked closed, but he made the turns deftly.

We reached the top—a wide meadow dotted with fallen, dead trees and a small lake pooled in the middle—and came to a structure of wood poles, the Begay sheep camp. A cold wind hit us as we stepped out of the truck cab. Dennis and I copied what Shu-chay was doing—untying the wire that banded the poles together, loading the poles in the truck. Dennis said he had known of me through stories. I told him the same. Mostly, though, we worked without talking.

Shu-chay, at ninety, was a renowned medicine man. During my stay, he allowed me to witness three ceremonies performed for Dennis, two by him and one by another medicine man, Julius Johnson. Dennis was quiet, I gathered, because he was not feeling well. Waiting for the first ceremony to start one afternoon, Dennis and I chopped wood. I remembered the story of my father arriving at night in Lukachukai and chopping my mother's wood for the day. Although surprised, my mother knew who had done it. My axe sank at right and left angles into the wood. I felt calm.

I looked up to see Kathleen, Dennis's mother. She told us the fire was ready in the ceremonial hogan. Dennis and I stopped working. We entered the hogan and sat down next to Shumasun, Shu-chay, and Kathleen. Julius Johnson sat in front of a bed of coals.

"Tell them how you are, Dennis," Kathleen said.

Dennis didn't say anything, however, and Julius Johnson and Shu-chay began talking in Navajo. Switching to English, Julius Johnson told me he could see things in coals, which were somewhat like a crystal ball.

Shumasun blew her nose, and again Shu-chay looked as if he were sleeping.

The medicine man finally asked Dennis to say something.

Dennis eventually spoke. "I'm bored all the time, stuff like that," he said.

"Are you bored at home?" Julius asked.

"Yes. I just want to have fun all the time. I can't concentrate."

"Do you smoke? Not tobacco, the other stuff?"

"No."

A bit of silence.

"You're going through a stage. It's hard on you. You don't

know which direction you want to go. We're going to take it out of you."

He went over to Dennis and began touching different parts of his body. "These are pressure points," he said. "We're going to take out what's bad in you."

He bent over and placed his mouth on Dennis's neck and sucked until he got a mouthful of whatever it was that had been inside Dennis. He straightened up and walked over to his things, retrieving a white napkin. He spat in it, making an awful, phlegmy noise, getting it all out of his mouth.

Kathleen and Dennis went over to look at the napkin, but I chose to stay where I was, just as I had when I'd occasionally gone to mass with my Kentucky grandparents and everyone else lined up to accept the body and blood of Christ. Kathleen shuddered when she saw the napkin. "It's like a worm," she said. Neither of them stared at it very long.

Julius did the same thing with Dennis's forehead, and the shape in his saliva was again like a worm. He folded both of the napkins and put them in an empty coffee can.

He sat down and sprinkled juniper needles on the coals. With his hands he brought some of the smoke to his face and looked up toward the hogan ceiling; he motioned for us, even me, to do the same. Dennis was the last to take in the smoke. As he stood up by himself, he seemed a little self-conscious and must have stopped the ritual too soon, for Kathleen said, "A little more, Dennis, pretend like it's water, and you are washing yourself."

Afterward, Julius gave Dennis the coffee can and told him to go outside and burn the napkins, marking the end of the ceremony. They called this the Mountain Smoke Ceremony.

Back to the woodpile. Dennis and I chopped wood the rest of the afternoon under skies that changed continuously. Two little purple blisters formed on my left hand. Dennis told me he had expected something more to come of the ceremony, but he was not sure what. That evening the ceremony would resume.

We continued chopping. It turned colder. As we armloaded the wood to a shed, it began to snow.

Shu-chay left supper early to prepare the ceremonial hogan. An hour later, I went with Shumasun and Dennis. We found Shu-chay chanting, the fire going, a lamp in front of him. Sometimes he would shake a gourd, which rattled. We sat down. He continued with the chant, often needing to clear his throat. By the time he stood up, holding a shell containing some kind of liquid, the rhythm of his singing so filled the hogan that when he stopped briefly, he held us in suspense. He walked unsteadily toward Dennis, resuming the chant. Reminding me of a creature with a huge wingspan, he bent over Dennis and with his long arms dabbed the liquid on Dennis's feet, chest, shoulders, head, neck, and back. When he offered the shell to Dennis, Dennis tried to dip his hands, too. He had to be told to drink it. Meanwhile, Shu-chay used an eagle feather to touch Dennis in those same places with wood ash. They called this the Blackening Ceremony.

The Begays' son, Sylvester, who was training to be a medicine man, his wife Michelle, and their kids came into the hogan. Michelle sat down next to Dennis on the black plastic. Sylvester helped prepare sheep fat and added more ashes to the pile in front of them.

Shu-chay resumed chanting and kept it up for several minutes before he said something to Dennis and Michelle. They both took off their shirts. The medicine man took a bowl of blackish liquid and stood in front of Michelle and Dennis, towering over them. The veins in his neck bulged as he chanted. He touched their legs, chests, shoulders, and heads, joining them in the end with a single, horizontal motion of his hand. He asked them to drink from the bowl—a tea made from mountain herbs, I found out later—and then passed the bowl around for everyone. We drank from it and dipped our hands in it, touching different places on our bodies. I was surprised to feel how heavy the bowl was. As I brought it to my face, I noticed several arrowheads at the bottom. The drink had a strong, bitter flavor.

Michelle and Dennis used what was left over to wash their bodies. Then they rubbed ash over themselves. Shu-chay and Sylvester dabbed red paint, a mixture of sandstone dust and sheep fat, on their ashy bodies. Thus marked, Dennis and Michelle were given sticks and told to make four marks on the sticks with ash. Shu-chay stood over them with eagle feathers, making circles above their heads and stopping his chant occasionally to make a sound that put me in mind of rising smoke— "puah"—whereupon he waved the feathers to the east, toward the hogan door. Dennis and Michelle blew on their sticks. Everyone in the hogan made the same east-flowing hand motions.

Michelle and the kids left, but Dennis had one more ceremony. For this one, Sylvester told me, I would be holding an arrowhead while Shu-chay prayed for Dennis; furthermore, I would probably have a vision.

The stove burned red-hot. Shu-chay sat in front of a pile of coals and a smoldering corncob. He lit a pipe. Shumasun used her bare hands to push the coals in a pile. I flinched, but she was unaffected. Maybe I needed hands (or spirit) like that to make frybread, I thought. I worried that I wouldn't have a vision.

Shu-chay set some dried grass on the coals and motioned for Dennis to bathe himself with the smoke. Afterward, he gave Dennis the pipe and resumed singing. Dennis grimaced as he puffed. Kathleen came in and told him to bring that smoke all the way inside him and to keep puffing continuously. She encouraged him to vomit, saying that would clean his system. When Dennis finished the pipe, Shu-chay prepared an ash drink, touching him with the liquid and letting him drink some. He passed the bowl around, and we all touched our bodies with the liquid and sipped it. With what was left over, including the dregs, Dennis rubbed the skin of his chest, forehead, arms, and legs.

Shu-chay next passed around a pouch of corn pollen. We each took a pinch with our fingers, tasted a little, and scattered the rest to the east.

SLOWSPOKE

For the second half of the ceremony, I was asked to go to the other side of the hogan. I almost stepped between the lamp and the medicine man when Kathleen told me I should go around Shu-chay.

I sat down in a new place. Shu-chay arranged arrowheads on a blanket. Kathleen said they were like people. Shu-chay gave us each an arrowhead, the men holding it in their left hand, the women in their right. Kathleen told me not to drop it or bring it down.

On a signal, I blew out the lamp, and we held up our arrowheads. Kathleen told me I could pray any way I wanted—this was a time that Shu-chay could help me, she said. It was a time to drive away bad dreams or thoughts and to think about things that were good. I thought mostly about certain camps I'd had on my journey. No visions, other than those I willed forth, came to mind. Occasionally, Shu-chay would say "puah" and we would make an upward motion with our hands and breathe out like we were singing.

When we finished, someone instructed me to light the lamp. Dennis walked outside, making a circle clockwise, raising his arms, looking around him. Kathleen had told him to notice the stars. I wondered if he had had a vision. He came back inside and sat down. Shu-chay placed the arrowheads in a pouch. It had been a marathon session for him. He looked up to me and all of a sudden spoke the first English words I'd heard from him: "Go to sleep." I laughed, and Shu-chay rewarded me with a smile. He told me to dump the coffee-can ashes outside. Then Dennis could leave the hogan.

In bed that evening I closed my eyes and saw arrowheads, feathers, saliva, coals, a gourd, firewood, a shell, Shumasun's hands, a white napkin, juniper needles, smoke, a coffee can. I didn't understand all the religious symbolism, but I liked the focus on objects. I liked knowing that you could make something, even a prayer, out of the materials around you.

With two inches of fresh snow, the world appeared newly

created in the morning. Dennis walked in to breakfast, his face still ashy and painted. He had to keep the markings on for a week. Also, he couldn't cut meat for a week. He could eat meat, but it had to be cut for him.

I walked out to take pictures of the snow with a camera my family had sent me. Everything beamed, the snow multiplying the sun's brightness. I looked through the cheap, pink camera and snapped pictures, hoping to capture the way the mountains perched on the snow-draped sagebrush, the hogans in the middle of the big landscape, the sparkles.

Shu-chay had a sand painting that day. I followed Shumasun into the hogan in the afternoon. Shu-chay sang, but it was softer and less like a chant than during the other ceremonies. A mother sat next to him, a baby in her lap. In front of them and the medicine man was a place swept smooth on the hogan's dirt floor. An older woman sat next to a north wall of the hogan, watching. Shumasun and I sat next to her.

Shu-chay's fingers dipped into one of several pouches next to him, and his hand went out over the swept spot on the floor. I stared at it as if it existed separately from his body and his singing. When it began to glide, a red arc appeared on the floor, copying exactly the motion of the airy hand. A circle formed, and Shu-chay's hand dipped into another pouch. Though I knew how he was making the painting, I nonetheless watched with fascination.

A yellow sand was next. Inside the circle, Shu-chay made two triangles that may have represented eyes. Overlooking the painting, we could see the pattern. Two triangles came out of the circle, pointing southeast. Then brown and black lines turned the triangles into feathers. Finally, Shu-chay created a rectangular base and top to the circle, and he was done. He made the baby drink from a shell and let the mother wash the baby with the leftover liquid. Then he shoveled coals out of the fire. The old woman sitting next to Shumasun and me stood and took the shovel from him, dumping coals where he pointed on the floor. She used her hands to scoot the coals into a pile, as Shumasun had done the day before. She, too, probably knew how to make frybread. Shu-chay sprinkled juniper needles on the coals and motioned for the mother to bathe the baby in smoke, the ending of the ceremony.

Shu-chay let me carry his medicine bag to the house. Inside, he told Kathleen and Shumasun that I was getting ready to be a medicine man.

Shumasun made pancakes for breakfast the following morning. Kathleen joked about Dennis not being able to eat meat until Friday. "But Friday morning you can butcher a cow if you like," she said.

Dennis wouldn't be able to cut wood with me that day either.

Shu-chay must have eaten early because he was on the couch, a newspaper covering his face.

"My father," Kathleen said, "always buys the paper even though he can't read. He looks at the pictures and the letters."

Outside in the bright cold, I let my axe fall on snow-draped logs. I chopped for four hours. I'd take breaks, look off into the Lukachukai Mountains. After lunch, although I was sore, I continued chopping. I had a burst of energy midafternoon and chopped until the sun set, depositing a red glow in the west. I knelt then and placed wood into the crook of my left arm to take into a shed and stack. Dennis helped.

When we were done, Dennis ran off to play with the dogs. Kathleen had told me that he was more like himself since the ceremonies. I took off running too, up the hill toward the sunset. Jackrabbits leapt in the teetering light. At the top a newly risen moon balanced out a sky still red with the sunset. It was my last day on the reservation. I would leave in the morning with Shu-chay and Julius Johnson, who were going to Gallup on their way to a conference.

A surprising breakfast greeted me the next day: turkey, mashed potatoes, gravy, and frybread. Was this because I was leaving? Dennis hunched over his food, finally able to cut meat for himself. Shumasun and Shu-chay must have eaten earlier. Shu-chay stared up at the ceiling. Kathleen told me then that Shu-chay was happy that I had come all the way on a unicycle. As if he were responding to Kathleen, he took his gaze off the ceiling at that moment and spoke. Kathleen burst out laughing.

"He said that you should find a beautiful Navajo woman and stay here."

I worked in my hogan after breakfast, packing and cleaning. Kathleen and Dennis entered, and Kathleen said that they were returning to Chinle. As she turned to go, I realized that she was saying goodbye. Dennis left the same way.

Finished packing, I leaned my backpack and unicycle against the hogan. Shumasun came in, bringing juniper bark, which she put in the stove. She touched a matchstick to it and the flame leapt up. Juniper bark caught better than paper. I was suddenly embarrassed by the amount of paper I had used the first time I lit the stove. She added kindling. The fire popped. Although it wasn't cold anymore and I wouldn't be staying in the hogan, she nonetheless lit a fire. We left my hogan with a fire in it. Shu-chay carried my unicycle.

All four of us fit in the cab of the truck. Shumasun came with us so we could drop her off at her son Allen's. She didn't want to be alone at the house. The image I had of her walking away from the truck toward Allen's house—her thick purple skirt and vest, her turquoise jewelry, her hair in a bun, her shuffle, how she didn't look back at me—reminded me of a cornhusk doll.

The three of us continued on to Gallup, and we arrived at the bus station. Julius and I got out of the truck, and I saw with a stab of loss that Shu-chay was staying in the cab. I wanted to say something to him. I wanted to shake his hand or hug him.

Instead, I turned my back to him and walked with Julius into the white-tiled station. A woman with a Greyhound insignia pinned to her suit jacket took a brief look at my unicycle and told me Greyhound wouldn't carry a bike like that. It had to be in a box, and there would be a ten-dollar luggage fee. She gave me a box. The bus I needed left in twenty minutes.

A few people had lined up behind me. The unicycle would have to be disassembled to fit in the box. I left the line and leaned my backpack against a wall bench. Julius watched as I sat on the floor with my unicycle and pulled out from under the seat the bottle of tools Roger Fulton had packed for me—all that I would ever need, according to him, although I wasn't sure he had envisioned me taking apart the unicycle. The pedals would have to be removed from the wheel, the wheel from the seat. The unicycle tire, I noticed, had deposited part of a cottonwood leaf and some hogan floor dirt on one of the white tiles.

I shivered, as I had when starting my trip.

Epilogue

SHADOW WALKED WITH ME in a dream, though he was older, with a good limp. It had been raining all night, and roiling clay-colored water rushed in the creeks. Even small tributaries flowed rapidly, and I had to jump them. Shadow waded, the water up to his chest. We made several crossings, following a long bottomland valley. Rain still fell. Soon I couldn't make the jumps; my landing foot would slip off the bank into the water, and I'd have to scramble to the other side.

It had been a long time since I'd come this way, from the other side of Long Branch, and I forged ahead with the nervousness and energy of someone returning home after being away in a distant land.

The valley ended, as I knew it would, and I began climbing a forested hillside. Everything was as I remembered it until I reached the top of the hill. There I saw that the canopy of my forest had fallen. They'd taken the big trunks away and had left the tops where they'd hit the ground. The stumps stared at a widened sky.

I didn't know how to get my bearings. Though I'd stood on this very patch of ground many times before, I understood how much I had depended on trunks wider than myself to pattern the sky and to offer familiarity to the way ahead. How often I'd glanced up at those big trees!

Of course now I couldn't return, the water paths behind me too wide. So I entered the wreckage, in the direction of a slope that had been distinguished by tall white oak, fire pink, early spiderwort, and a blanket of emerald moss at the banks of Long Branch. The tops of those trees, lying on the floor, were huge.

When upright, they had fit so well into the forest, but—as with all things out of place or not stacked well—they now cluttered the area and made walking arduous.

I had to lift Shadow over the fallen wood. We found out later that one of Mr. Gregory's sons had been practicing on these trees, in preparation for widespread logging. Sometimes I'd slip on the ground. Yet I kept going, for a return now was impossible.

~

Mr. Gregory left a message for Joel to come over and give him our final offer. Our hopes surged. Joel was busy and waited a few days before contacting him.

Meanwhile, a Nature Preserves botanist went out to Mr. Gregory's property, looking for the federally protected buffalo clover. Here was another plant that could secure this agency's involvement in the purchase of the property.

In my normal state of being, one not so intent on conjuring up this clover out of the other flora along Long Branch, I would have had a bigger view of the landscape and certainly would have seen the black walnut before I did. As it was, I looked up and was face to face with its severed body, its trunk and branches fallen to the ground, its stump, inches away, set agape at the sky. I may have also seen the downed red oak, basswood, and chinquapin earlier than I did.

When a tree goes down in a windstorm, it often brings up its root ball, leaving an indentation in the earth. In the old section of woods, some of these indentations are quite large—it would take a good leap to cross them. In a few places, the indentations are massive—two or three leaps to cross—made not from a tree like those currently standing, but from truly ancient, pre-settlement trees, whose girth and height we can only imagine, looking at the prints they've left for us. In one of these hollows, maidenhair fern orbit twinleaf to the bottom and back out; and we at once understand spring turning to summer turning to fall turning to winter.

SLOWSPOKE

The opposite of what I feel sitting on the lip of one of these forest dimples is what I felt then by the logged trees, at a loss for answers: the stopping of motion, the discontinuity, the disunion.

The trees seemed to have been cut arbitrarily, there being no logging road yet. We found out later that one of Mr. Gregory's sons had been practicing on these trees, in preparation for widespread logging. Shaken, we sent out second notices to people who had already received letters from us. In the next few weeks, thankfully, no further action was taken in the woods—and a member of Jennifer's book club, who had been looking for land in the country, visited the land, liked it, and agreed to buy a third of it. With her contribution, our cash and my family's, and a bank loan, we were able to offer Mr. Gregory what he wanted. Two weeks before he flew to the Philippines, he accepted, and we closed on the land.

∽

After our signing, I bounded into the woods and ran as fast as I've ever run, somehow evading deadfall and branches, jumping at times, like those horses in the New Mexico wilderness. I charged over the ridge top and down to Long Branch, where I leapt the water to an island of rocks. There, I sat down, aware—my eyes damp—of trunks, bushes, leaves, sticks, rocks, sunlight, shadow; and then, when I could no longer see, the wind sifted through this material, a roar buffed into a hum, almost a whistle, safe.

∽

One of those trees that had been arbitrarily cut, a black walnut, is becoming our floor in the addition. We cut two-inch slices off the trunk and some of the branches. We hauled the rounds from the forest to our house, and we de-barked them and sanded them. The whole while, we marveled at the rich dark color of the wood, and our marveling of it became the eulogy for the tree.

303

SLOWSPOKE

Now, with winter again turning to spring, we place the walnut rounds on the addition sub-floor, about two or three inches apart. The gaps will be filled with mortar, and the entire floor, when finished, will be sealed with a natural resin.

We place a few and step back and look at the effect, often rearranging the pieces. Some of the rounds are from the lower trunk, some from the higher branches, some cut across the union of two branches, containing two sets of rings. Several pieces were cut from a branch torn in two by the fall and look like half moons with ragged diameters. We want the arrangement to turn the floor alive, with a cohesion that includes interruptions and pivots, with some pieces swirling away from a contour and some orbiting, some beginning a trail and some lopping it off, the way a life would go.

Sometimes I squint at it, and the effect is just as we want it, the ripple of the wood coaxing us always to the center, closest to the birth of the tree, where we are encircled by a topography of beauty.

We will stake our lives here, venturing out, at times, to explore, but always returning. We might even hike to beauty's very edge and peek out. Here, we would look into a precipice from another story, in which these woods were cut down. Not wanting to slip, we'd step back.

Acknowledgments

WHEN I FIRST ALLOWED MY unicycle journey idea to emerge into the open (after a long dormancy), it was quite fragile. It needed, of course, sunlight, rain, soil—but also something beyond: it needed not to be scoffed at. I am forever grateful to my family (Charlie and Laurie, my parents; Chris and Trina, my sisters; and later, Joel and Tim, their spouses) for not, when I presented this thing to them, scoffing. Instead, they cheered. They gave it a real life. And me one, too.

I want to especially thank Trina, who read each one of my multiple drafts starting with the first—a 660-page handwritten account of everything that happened on my journey, including what I ate—helping it, with such good humor and patience and optimism, achieve its final form. Anthony Vital made the crucial suggestion that I link the journey with my present homesteading, for which I'm grateful. Florence Jackson provided me, too, with a good, insightful critique, presented in her sweet manner. Thank you, Patricia Grace King, for your early support and for help with the title. Thank you, John Schimmoeller and Betty Schimmoeller, for your encouragement, and Jeri Parker, for your superb literary eye, coming at just the right time. To Ruth Mullen, thank you for diving into each page, going deeper than anyone.

Thanks to the Sisters of Loretto Motherhouse and to Jack and Maggie Jezreel for graciously sharing Jennifer with me in the spring and summer of 1997.

Thanks to the Begays in Lukachukai for taking me in as they would a grandson.

The written encouragement I received from Wendell Berry, Nikky Finney, Bill McKibben, and Colin Beavan thrilled me.

Any hint in the book of exuberant velocity could be traced to them.

Kudos to Duane Stapp for the cover and interior design, which make me happy and excited, and to Dan Vantreese for the original cover design concept. Also, many thanks to Laurie Schimmoeller and Andy McDonald for their contributions.

And I would like to send out a bulk thank you—and I really mean this—to all those rejections from agencies and publishers, well over two hundred, which have given me time to move this book, bit by bit, closer to its perfect form.

By that I do not mean to devalue the affirmation I received from New York. Each slip of encouragement was an oasis! Susan Raihofer was an early New York supporter, as were Rita Rosenkranz and Harriet Wasserman. Ryan Harbage honored me with his stamina and faith. But it was Alice Peck who not only helped shape the book into its final form with her uncanny editorial skills, but who gave me the "yes" I'd been waiting for years to receive, publishing this book as an Alice Peck Editorial title. Chelsea Green Publishing gave me my second "yes," for which I'm hugely grateful. I especially want to thank Michael Metivier, who has, in being so meticulously responsive, so tuned to words, so kind, helped me, from the beginning, feel at home with Chelsea Green.

And, finally, to Jennifer, my sweet Jennifer, my most intuitive reader, I am so grateful that even though you didn't notice me at our first encounter, you have ever since.

About the Author

SINCE GRADUATING IN 1989 with a BA in English from Transylvania University, Mark Schimmoeller has devoted himself to off-the-grid homesteading in Kentucky. He has also (other than journeying on a unicycle) completed a semester of an MFA program at Warren Wilson College; attended the Squaw Valley Poetry Workshop; and published poems in journals and magazines such as *Midwest Quarterly, Orion,* and *Northeast Corridor,* and essays in *Home Power, Orion,* and *The Christian Science Monitor.* He also has coordinated the Appalachia Science in the Public Interest (ASPI) program to promote solar cooking in Peru, Honduras, and Malawi and conducted sustainable living workshops in Kentucky and at the Midwest Renewable Energy Fair in Wisconsin.

About the Foreword Author

AWARD-WINNING WRITER, naturalist, and activist Janisse Ray is the author of several books, including *The Seed Underground, Pinhook,* and *Ecology of a Cracker Childhood,* a *New York Times* Notable Book. She attempts to live a sustainable life on a farm in southern Georgia with her husband, Raven Waters.

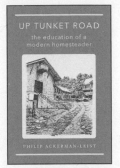
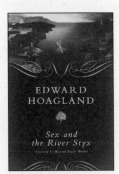

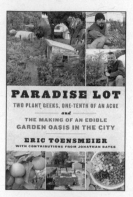
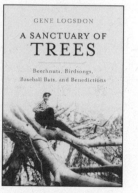